Dictionary of Movies and Films

Dictionary of Movies and Films

Prahlad Manjrekar

AUTHORSPRESS

Worldwide Circulation through Authorspress Global Network
First Published 2007
by
Authorspress
E-35/103, Jawahar Park
Laxmi Nagar, Delhi-110 092
e-mail: authorspress@yahoo.com

Dictionary of Movies and Films
ISBN 978-81-7273-394-0

Printed in India at Tarun Offset, Delhi.

Preface

Societies have particular collective realities and myths about themselves and performative traditions project them in ways depending upon the skill and motivations of the performers. Cinema, which brings forth movies and films, is one such projection of the self-image and desires of a collective unconscious, using machines to record images of life, combining still photographs to give images of continuing motion, presenting life itself, but also offering impossible realities approached only in dreams. One of the few arts that is both spatial and temporal, film-making or cinema blends in the rhythm of dance with the tone of music the shares and colours painting with the stories of the novel. No wonder then, that cinema today is one of the most respected art-forms, which has already i its short history spanning a 100 old years produced stalwarts like Ingmar Bergman, Akira Kurosawa, Orson Welles, Jean Renior and India's very own Satyajit Ray.

This book in the series of book designed for students pursuing their Masters in Education covers cinema, movies and films in an encylopeadic manner. Bringing under one roof a whole host of terminology which relate to cinema right from its earliest days in the silent era, the book delineates the efforts of cinema greats within the would of cinema technology, creations, movies, directors, technicians, writers and actors. The book also takes into account the current status of cinema worldwide, and brings within its purview current trends, developments and practices.

It is hoped that the insight and information of the book prove highly interesting to reader.

Prahlad Manjrekar

Preface

[illegible]

A

A wrap or "It's a wrap!": What to say when you are done shooting, either for the day, at that particular set, or on the entire film. Usually if it's not the final shoot you would say you are just going to "wrap for the day."

A&B rolls: The negative of an edited film, cut to correspond to picture, built into 2 rolls, A and B, to allow for invisible splices, instant changes of the timing lights and fades and dissolves without the need for opticals. The A roll will have all the odd numbered shots, with black leader in place of all the missing shots. The B roll will have all the even numbered shots, with black leader in place of all the shots on the A roll. The negative is printed in three passes through the contact printer, one for each roll and another for the soundtrack. Only after all the elements have been exposed onto the print stock is the print developed.

A.D.R.: Automated Dialogue Recording. This is just Dubbing, done in addition to or as a substitution for Location Sound. The term A.D.R., being something of a mysterious acronym, has a certain appeal, as it obscures the fact that dubbing was involved when it appears in the credits of your film. This might have something to do with the current prevalence of the term.

A.S.A.: This is the sensitivity to light of a particular type of film. It is the specific number used to measure Film Speed. It is the same as I.E. and I.S.O. A.S.A. stands for American Standards Association, the organization that standardized the scale of measurement of film speed.

A/B printing: Printing from original film stock which has been conformed into two rolls with alternating shots and black opaque leader. This methodology will eliminate any potential splice marks from showing up on prints and permits the incorporation of optical effects and titles.

A/B rolls: Two or more rolls of film having alternate scenes intercut with opaque leaders in such a way that the 'A' roll presents its picture at the same time that the 'B' roll presents opaque leader, and vice versa.

Abby singer: The second-to-last shot of the day. Named after production manager Abby Singer, who would frequently call "last shot of the day" or "this shot, and just one more," only to have the director ask for more takes.

Above the line: Usually refers to that part of a film's budget that covers the costs associated with major creative talent: the stars, the director, the producer(s) and the writer(s), although films with expensive special effects (and few stars) have more 'above the line' budget costs for technical aspects; the term's opposite is below the line.

Above the line budget: The amount of money allocated towards the major creative elements that constitute the film (ie producer, director, writer, major cast and rights for the script)

Above the line: Refers to the creative elements of a production such as the writer, producer, director and actors. Literally, these are the elements which appeared above a bold line which divided standard production budget sheets.

Above-the-line expenses: The major expenses committed to before production begins, including story/rights/continuity (writing); salaries for producers, director, and cast; travel and living; and production fees (if the project is bought from an earlier company). Everything else falls under below-the-line expenses.

Abstract (form): A type of film that rejects traditional narrative in favor of using poetic form (color, motion, sound, irrational images, etc.) to convey its meaning or feeling.

Absurd (absurdism): A stage, philosophical and literary term originally, adopted by film-makers, in which ordinary settings become bizarre, illogical, irrational, unrealistic, meaningless, and incoherent.

AC: Alternating Current. An electric current with periodically changing polarity (i.e. 60 times a second for 60Hz power).

Academy aperture: In 35mm this is the full frame exposed by the camera, with an aspect ratio of 1.33. When the film is projected there is a mask in the projector's gate to change the aspect ratio to 1.85 or 1.66, cropping the top and bottom of the image. Older films were not shot to be masked and should be projected without a mask. The Academy Aperture is sometimes called the Full Academy Aperture.

Academy awards: The name given to the prestigious film awards presented each year by AMPAS (the Academy of Motion Picture Arts and Sciences, or simply 'The Academy'), a professional honorary organization within the industry, since 1927. The annual awards show, in slang, is sometimes referred to as a kudo-cast.

Academy leader : This is standard countdown leader, counting down 8 to 3 and then with one frame of 2, at which point there is a single frame beep on the sound track. It is used at the beginning of a film for the lab to line up sound (using the beep) and later for the projectionist to know when to turn on the lamp and hopefully not miss the opening of the film. A common mistake is to count the footage from the 2, but actually frame zero is the one right before the first 8, a single frame with the words "Picture Start." Academy Leader is sometimes also known as S.M.P.T.E. leader.

Accent light: A light unit that emphasizes one subject. This might be a key light, a kicker, or a backlight.

Acetate base: The tranparent cellulose acetate plastic film which for years served as the backing for magnetic recording tape.

Acetone: An organic liquid chemical used in the manufacture of some types of film cement. Also used to clean film splicing equipment.

Acoustics: The science of the transmission of sound waves. Generally refers to the characteristics of auditoriums, theatres and studios with respect to their design.

Act: A main division within the plot of a film; a film is often divided by 'plot points' (places of dramatic change) rather than acts; long films are divided mid-way with an intermission.

Action cutting: The cutting of film from one shot to another in a way yielding the impression that action is continuous and uninterrupted.

Action: (1) Any movement or series of events (usually rehearsed) that take place before the camera and propel the story forward toward its conclusion; (2) the word called out (by a megaphone) at the start of the current take during filming to alert actors to begin performing; (3) also refers to the main component of action films - that often contain significant amounts of violence.

Actor placement: The placing of actors in relation to the camera, other actors, objects, landscape and so on within the three dimensional space of the set in order to achieve a specific relational effect upon the two dimensional space of the screen.

Actor: Refers either to a male performer, or to any male or female who plays a character role in an on-screen film; alternate gender-neutral terms: player, artist, or performer.

Actress: Refers to any female who portrays a role in a film.

Ad lib: A line of dialogue improvised by an actor during a performance; can be either unscripted or deliberate; improvisation consists of ad-libbed dialogue (and action) that is invented or created by the performer.

Adaptation: The presentation of one art form through another medium; a film based upon, derived from (or adapted from) a stage play (or from another medium such as a short story, book, article, history, novel, video game, comic strip/book, etc.) which basically preserves both the setting and dialogue of the original; can be in the form of a script (screenplay) or a proposal treatment.

ADC: Analog-to-Digital Converter. An electronic device used at the input of digital audio equipment to convert analog electrical signals to digital values whose numbers represent the level and frequency information contained in the original analog signal.

Address track: A control/timing track on the edge of videotape which contains control data for quick and accurate location of program material.

ADR: Automatic Dialog Replacement. Also known as "looping." A process of re-recording dialog in the studio in synchronization with the picture.

Advance: Of a composite print: the distance between a point on the soundtrack and the corresponding image. Of payment: an amount given before receipt of services.

Aerial shot: A camera shot filmed in an exterior location from far overhead (from a bird's eye view), as from a helicopter (most common), blimp, balloon, plane, or kite; a variation on the crane shot; if the aerial shot is at the opening of a film.

Agent: A person responsible for the professional business dealings of an actor, director, or other artist. An agent typically negotiates the contracts on behalf of the actor or director, and often has some part in selecting or recommending roles for their client.

Alan smithee film: The pseudonym used by directors who refuse to put their name on a film and want to disassociate themselves, usually when they believe their control or vision has been co-opted by the studio (i.e., the film could have been recut, mutilated and altered against their wishes).

Alan smithee: The sole pseudonym that the Directors Guild of America allowed directors to use when they wish to remove their name from a film. The name has reportedly been retired by the Directors Guild of America, after 1997's *An Alan Smithee Film: Burn Hollywood Burn* revealed the alias to the general public. It appears that project-specific pseudonyms are now used instead, selected on a case-by-case basis when the DGA agrees that a film has been taken away from a director and cut and/or altered to such an extreme extent that it completely deviates from that director's original vision.

A-level (or A-List): Usually refers to top-tier actors/actresses who are paid upwards of $20 million per feature film; can also refer to producers, directors and writers who can be guaranteed to have a film made and released.

Ali MacGraw's Disease: Movie illness in which only symptom is that the sufferer grows more beautiful as death approaches.

Aliasing: An undesirable distortion component that can arise in any digitally encoded information.

Allusion: A direct or indirect reference - through an image or through dialogue - to the Bible, a classic, a person, a place, an external and/or real-life event, another film, or a well-known cultural idea.

Alternate ending: The shooting (or re-shooting) of a film's ending for its theatrical release, usually enforced by the studio for any number of reasons.

Ambiance: The feeling or mood of a particular scene or setting.

Ambient light: The natural light (usually soft) or surrounding light around a subject in a scene.

Ambient noise: The total sound in a given are which is peculiar to that space (room tone).

American cinema editors: Honorary society of film editors founded in 1950 by Jack Ogilvie, Warren Low and others.

American federation of television and radio artists: An association with jurisdiction over some works that can be recorded by picture or by sound.

American society of cinematographers: An organization founded in 1919 and dedicated to advancing the art of cinematography through artistry and technological progress, to exchange ideas and to cement a closer relationship among cinematographers. Membership is international and by invitation based on an individual's body of narrative filmwork. Use of the abbreviation ASC, e.g. for on-screen credits, indicates membership in the society. The society publishes "American Cinemato-grapher" magazine.

Amplitude distortion: The nonlinear relation of input and output induced harmonics which is a function of voltage fluctuations or power consumption.

Amplitude: The strength of an electronic signal as measure by its waveform height.

Anachronism: An element or artifact in a film that belongs to another time or place; often anachronistic elements are called film flubs.

Analog recording: A means of recording audio or video whereby the recorded signal is a physical representation of the waveform of the original signal.

Analog: An electrical signal that continuously varies in strength as related to some form of input.

Anamorphic : A method of creating a wide screen image with standard film, using a special lens on the camera and projector that compresses the width of the image that is exposed on the film and then expands it when projected.

Anamorphic widescreen: DVD mastering process whereby a film source with an aspect ratio greater than 4:3 (usually also greater than or equal to 16:9) is transferred to the DVD video master in such a way that the picture is vertically stretched by a factor of about 1.33. The idea is to use as much resolution of the video master as possible so widescreen pictures use the 4:3 frame optimally, gaining another 33% of vertical resolution and looking markedly sharper. When playing a DVD with anamorphic widescreen the display has to vertically squeeze the picture by a factor of 0.75 so a circle is still a circle. If the display cannot do this the DVD player will do the squeezing and add black bars on the top and bottom of the picture. In that case the additional 33% resolution are not available.

Anamorphic: Related to different optical imaging effects; refers to a method of intentionally distorting and creating a wide screen image with standard film, using a conversion process or a special lens on the camera and projector to produce different magnifications in the vertical and horizontal dimensions of the picture; an anamorphic image usually appears "squished" horizontally, while retaining its full vertical resolution.

Ancillary markets: Any market outside of actual theatrical exhibition. That is, merchandising, production of a book, theatre play, soundtrack, a show about the 'Making of..' the movie, etc.

Ancillary rights: Contractual agreement in which a percentage of the profits are received and derived from the sale of action figures, posters, CDs, books, T-shirts, etc.

Angle of view: This is the size of the field covered by a lens, measured in degrees. However, because of the aperture masks in film, the angle of view for a given lens is generally described in terms of the height and width of a lens.

Angle, reverse angle: An editing technique whereby in successive cuts an action is first seen from one point of view, then from a point of view opposite the original angle. As with all editing techniques, the production must ensure that the footage is available to carry it out.

Animation: A form or process of filmmaking in which inanimate, static objects or individual drawings (hand-drawn or CGI) are filmed "frame by frame" or one frame at a time (opposed to being shot "live"), each one differing slightly from the previous frame, to create the illusion of motion in a sequence, as opposed to filming naturally-occurring action or live objects at a regular frame rate. Often used as a synonym for cartoons (or toons for short), although animation includes other media such as claymation, computer animation.

Anime: A distinctive style of animated film that has its roots in Japanese comic books (known as manga), yet covers a wide range of genres, such as romance, action/adventure, drama, gothic, historical, horror, mystery, erotica (hentai), children's stories, although most notably sci-fi and fantasy themes; originally called 'Japanimation' but this term is not used anymore; anime is found in a wide variety of storylines and settings, but usually recognizable and often characterized by heavily-stylized backgrounds, colorful images and graphics, highly exaggerated facial expressions with limited facial movement, simulation of motion through varying the background behind a static character or other foreground element, and frequently, big-headed characters with child-like, large eyes.

Answer print: This is the first corrected print made from the A&B Rolls, printed with the optical track. It is sometimes called a married print because it is the first time that picture and sound are wed together on the same piece of print stock. If you are not overly optimistic about the results of the timing, you can call this the First Answer Print. When there are further corrections in timing the next print is known as the Second Answer Print, followed by a Third Answer Print and so on.

Antagonist: The main character, person, group, society, nature, force, spirit world, bad guy, or villain of a film or script who is in adversarial conflict with the film's hero, lead character or protagonist; also sometimes termed the heavy.

Anthology film: A multi-part or multi-segmented film with a collection or series of various tales or short stories sometimes linked together by some theme or by a 'wrap-around' tale; often the stories are directed by different directors or scripted by various screenwriters, and are in the horror film genre; also known as an episode film or omnibus film; this term may also refer to a full-length, compilation-documentary film of excerpted segments or clips from other films (i.e., That's Entertainment (1974)).

Anthropomorphism: The tendency in animated films to give creatures or objects human qualities, abilities, and characteristics.

Anti-aliasing: Filtering of erroneous frequencies that are created during the analog to digital conversion process.

Anti-climax: Anything in a film, usually following the film's high point, zenith, apex, crescendo, or climax, in which there is an unsatisfying and disappointing let-down of emotion, or what is expected doesn't occur.

Anti-hero: The principal protagonist of a film who lacks the attributes or characteristics of a typical hero archetype, but with whom the audience identifies. The character is often confused or conflicted with ambiguous morals, or character defects and eccentricities, and lacks courage, honesty, or grace. The anti-hero can be tough yet sympathetic, or display vulnerable and weak traits. Specifically, the anti-hero often functions outside the mainstream and challenges it.

Antiheroine skin rule: In a Horny Teen-ager Movie, the "bad girl" who is the object of the hero's desire will always expose more flesh than the girl whom he ends up with at the end of the film, despite equal sexual activity. If the "good girl" is shown topless in a love scene, it must be accompanied by slow music. In a Dead Teenager Movie, the girl who exposes the least skin is inevitably the only survivor.

Aperture: (1) Lens aperture The variable opening within a camera lens which allows light to pass from the exterior towards the film plane. This opening is usually created by a circular frame formed by a series of movable, interleaved and inter linked, precision metallic elements; the whole unit is called an iris or an diaphragm. As in the human eye to which it is analogous, the more open the iris, the greater the amount of light to which the film is exposed. (2) Aperture plate A rectangular metallic frame, found in both cameras and projectors, which sits between the lenses and the film gate. As the shape of the metallic frame determines the area of the film which will be exposed to light through the camera, by that fact it establishes the exact aspect ratio of the image

Apple box : This is a wooden box, often helpful on the set to raise up equipment, for the cameraperson to stand on if the tripod is up very high etc. Often you will find them used as seats by the less involved participants. There are also half apples and quarter apples, which as you might expect, are half and one quarter as thick respectively.

Arc shot: A shot in which the subject(s) is photographed by an encircling or moving camera.

Arc: A lighting unit that generates illumination from an electrical arc between two carbon electrodes.

Archetype: A character, place, or thing, that is repeatedly presented in films with a particular style or characte-rization; an archetype usually applies to a specific genre or type classification.

Ark movie: Dependable genre in which a mixed bag of characters are trapped on a colorful mode of trans-portation.

Arm: A metal rod that is attached to a C-Stand which can extend off to the side.

Armorer: A person who is responsible for weapons on the set of a movie or television show. Duties include providing the correct weapons to suit the era and style of the film, advising the director on use of weapons, choosing the correct blanks, creating a safe set for the use of said weapons, teaching actors about handling and using weapons, making sure use of all weapons is properly licensed, and ensuring the safety of everyone on the set while weapons are in use.

Art department: The section of a production's crew concerned with visual artistry. Working under the supervision of the production designer and/or art director, the art department is responsible for arranging the overall "look" of the film (i.e. modern/high-tech, rustic, futuristic, etc.) as desired by the director. Individual positions within in this department include: production designer, production buyer, special effects supervisor, draftsman, art director, assistant art director, set decorator, set dresser, property master, leadman, swing gang, and property assistant.

Art director: Refers to the individual responsible for the design, look, and feel of a film's set, including the number and type of props, furniture, windows, floors, ceilings dressings, and all other set materials; a member of the film's art department (responsible for set construction, interior design, and prop placement).

Art-house film: Films, often low budget or 'art' films, that are acknowledged as having artistic merit or aesthetic pretensions, and are shown in an arthouse theatre; films shown usually include foreign-language films, independent films, non-mainstream (sometimes anti-Hollywood) films, shorts, documentaries, explicitly-erotic films, and other under-appreciated cinema of low mass appeal; began to appear in the 1950s and provided a distinct contrast to commercial films.

Arthouse: A motion picture theater that shows foreign or non-mainstream independent films, often considered high-brow or 'art' films.

Articulation artist: A person who takes an artist's designs and builds them in a computer, so that animators can manipulate the figures to tell the story of the film.

Artifact: A visual defect in an image caused by limitations or the malfunction of imaging equipment.

ASA: The exposure index or speed rating of a film which denotes the film's sensitivity.

Aside: Occurs when a character in a film breaks the 'fourth wall' and directly addresses the audience with a comment.

Aspect ratio: In general, a term for how the image appears on the screen based on how it was shot; refers to the ratio of width (horizontal or top) to height (vertical or side) of a film frame, image or screen; the most common or standard aspect ratio in early films to the 1950s was called Academy Aperture (or ratio), at a ratio of 1.33:1 (the same as 4:3 on a TV screen); normal 35mm films are shot at a ratio of 1.85:1; new widescreen formats and aspect ratios were introduced in the 1950s, from 1.65:1 and higher; CinemaScope (a trade name for a widescreen movie format used in the US from 1953 to 1967) and other anamorphic systems (such as Panavision) have a 2.35:1 AR, while 70mm formats have an AR of 2.2:1; Cinerama had a 2.77:1 aspect ratio; letterboxed videos for widescreen TV's are frequently in 16:9 (or 1.77:1) AR.

Asperity noise: (Hiss) Noise that is caused by minute imperfections in the surface of a recording medium.

Assemble: The work of organizing and joining the shots of a film in the sequence in which they will appear in the finished print.

Assembly: The first stage of editing, in which all the shots are arranged in script order.

Assistant camera: A member of the camera crew who assists the camera operator. This person is responsible for the maintenance and care of the camera, as well as preparing dope sheets. In smaller camera crews, they may also perform the duties of clapper-loader and/or a focus puller.

Assistant director: A First Assistant Director is responsible for the preparation of the shooting schedule and script breakdown used to plan the shooting of a film or television show. The AD works directly with the Director to manage of the minute to minute operations on the set during the process of filming, as well as co-ordinating the necessary communication of details of future operations as the filming progresses. Other duties include tracking the progress of filming versus the production schedule, observing all rules related to union crafts, labor contracts and location agreements, maintaining safety on the working set, and working with the Unit Manager to keep operational costs within the budgeted plan. A Second Assistant Director is responsible for information distribution and reporting, cast notification and preparations during the shooting process, recording of all data relative to the working hours of the crew and cast, management of the background cast (atmosphere or "extras"), preparation of call sheets, production reports,and other documentation. When needed, the Second Assistant Director can assume the duties of the First Assistant Director on a temporary basis.

Assistant film editor: Editing room crewmember responsible for providing any and all required logistical assistance to the editor(s). Duties vary, depending on whether the assistant is working with a picture or sound editor and whether the show is being edited on film or on a non-linear editing system. On a film-edited show, assistant picture editors will, during production: liase with the film lab and sound transfer facility regarding the processing of dailies; leader, sync and edgecode the dailies rolls; coordinate and take notes during dailies screenings; organize and maintain camera reports, sound reports, script notes, and lined script pages from the set, as well as lab reports and sound transfer reports; log all dailies footage; and reorganize footage for editing, if necessary. Ongoing, and during post-production, they will: reconstitute trims; locate and pull trims requested by the editor; check sync, clean, measure, re-splice, and add change-over marks to cut reels; coordinate screenings of cut work; take notes during screenings. Once the sound department begins work, the assistants produce change sheets detailing each day's changes to the workprint and production track and send them, along with any necessary duplicate trims, to the sound department. Assistants may be permitted by the editor to do some creative work, such as commenting on the editor's work; cutting temporary ("temp") sound effects and music into the track; and sometimes even editing scenes. After picture lock, the assistant: oversees the creation of optical effects such as fades, dissolves, etc. and cuts them into the workprint; continues to work with the sound department as necessary; and in some cases oversees the final stages of post-production, all the way through sound mix, negative conforming, and the production of final prints. The assistant editor chain of command consists of the First Assistant Editor(s), who bears the most responsibility for the smooth performance of the assistant team; the Second Assistant Editor(s); and the Apprentice Editor(s).

Assistant production manager: An assistant to the production coordinator.

Associate producer: An individual who performs a limited number of producing functions delegated to her/him by a producer, under the direct supervision and control of that producer. The term may also refer to a person who would qualify as an executive producer of a project, but for the fact that (s)he acts on behalf of a production company which is subordinate to another one on that project.

Association internationale du film d'animation: ASIFA was founded in 1960 in France, chartered under UNESCO, as a membership organization devoted to the encouragement and dissemination of film animation as an art and communication form.

Association of film commissioners international: A non-profit educational organization founded in 1975 to serve the needs of on-location film, television and commercial production.

Association of independent video and filmmakers: A membership organization serving local and international film and videomakers—from documentarians and experimental artists to makers of narrative features

Association of motion picture sound: A UK-based organization whose aims are to promote and encourage the science, technology and creative application of all aspects of motion picture sound recording and reproduction, and to promote and enhance the status and recognition of the contribution of those therein engaged.

Associational editing: The juxtaposition of shots in order to present contrast, comparisons or ideas.

Asynchronous sound: Refers to audio-track sounds that are mismatched or out of conjunction or unison with the images in the visual frame (or screen); sometimes accidental, but sometimes intentional.

Atmosphere: Extras who are staged and photographed to portray normal human traffic needed to add detail in various script situations.

Attenuate: To reduce a signal's strength.

Audible spectrum: When wave motion in the atmosphere has a frequency that lies between 20 and 15,000 Hz it produces a sound which is apparent to the average human.

Audience expectation: A concept which describes the a priori suppositions which an audience will have upon encountering a film text. For example, an audience which goes to see a Western will have a set of expectations as to what comprises the genre. They will expect, among other things, to see people riding horses, and the elaboration of a thoroughly familiar mythology about the American West. Though "mixed genres" are becoming more and more prevalent, an audience will not generally expect the Western to concern itself primarily with space travel, nor, to pick another example, an action- adventure film to have a conflicted love triangle as its principal narrative device. Audience expectation is to a large—but not exclusive— degree culture-specific: a contemporary American audience will have a different set of expecations when encountering a Western than, say, an Iranian audience, or an American audience in 1935. Nevertheless, it is fair to say that an audience of 14 year old boys will be indulging the imperatives of their testosterone rush when watching an action-adventure film irrespective of which cultural optic they watch the material through.

Audience: Refers to spectators, viewers, participants - those who serve as a measure of a film's success; although usually audiences are viewed in universal terms, they can also be segmented or categorized.

Audio bridge: Refers to an outgoing sound in one scene that continues over into a new image or shot - in this case, the soundtrack, not a visual image, connects the two shots or scenes.

Audition: The process whereby an actor-performer seeks a role by presenting to a director or casting director a prepared reading or by 'reading cold' from the film script, or performing a choreographed dance; after the initial audition, a performer may be called back for additional readings or run-throughs.

Australian screen directors association: The Australian Screen Directors Association (ASDA) is an industry association representing the interests of film and television directors, documentary filmmakers, animators and independent producers throughout Australia.

Australian screen editors: A cultural, professional and educational organisation, dedicated to the pursuit and recognition of excellence in the arts, sciences and technology of motion picture film and televisual post-production. It aims to promote, improve and protect the role of editor as an essential and significant contributor to all screen productions.

Auteur theory: Literally the French word for "author"; in film criticism, used in the terms auteurism or auteur theory, denoting a critical theory (originally known as la politique des auteurs or "the policy of authors") popular in France in the 1950s that was introduced by Francois Truffaut and the editors of the celebrated French film journal Cahiers du Cinéma and subsequently enlarged upon in the 1960s by American critic Andrew Sarris, among others; the theory ascribed overall responsibility for the creation of a film and its personal vision, identifiable style, thematic aspects and techniques to its film-maker or director, rather than to the collaborative efforts of all involved; the theory posited that directors should be considered the 'true' authors of film (rather than the screenwriters) because they exercise a great deal of control over all facets of film making and impart a distinctive, personal style to their films; simply stated, an auteur can refer to a director with a recognizable or signature style.

Auteur: A filmmaker, generally a director, who creates a body of work with a unified sensibility that reveals, through the interplay of themes and styles, a personal worldview. The term originated with François Truffaut, whose 1954 essay "Une certaine tendence du cinéma français" put forth the idea that the most interesting films were those that functioned as a medium of personal expression—and therefore bore the distinctive imprint of their "author." American critic Andrew Sarris later translated and expanded this idea into an "auteur theory," which proposed an evaluation of films based on their context within the filmmaker's oeuvre, rather than for their technical proficiency or greater historical significance. The term "auteur" later came to refer to any filmmaker who performed or was intimately involved in all aspects of the moviemaking process (writing, directing, producing, editing, etc.).

Auteurism: A critical theory, popular in France in the 1950s and 60s, that ascribed overall responsibility for the creation of a film to its director and thereby provoked renewed critical analysis of much previously neglected Hollywood work. The *"politique des auteurs"* (auteur policy) was first stated by Francois Truffaut in the January 1954 issue of *Cahiers du Cinema;* the main exponent of the auteur "theory" in America was the critic Andrew Sarris.

Auto audio rule: The sound a vehicle makes in a movie chase scene will in no way correspond to any sound made by same vehicle in real life (i.e., tires squealing on dirt or around corners at low speed, etc.).

Automated dialogue replacement editing: The process of editing sound during Automatic Dialogue Replacement.

Automated dialogue replacement editor: The person who performs ADR Editing.

Automated dialogue replacement mixer: The person who mixes the sound during Automated Dialogue Replacement.

Automated dialogue replacement: The re-recording of dialogue by actors in a sound studio during post-production, usually performed to playback of edited picture in order to match lip movements on screen. ADR is frequently used to replace production track of poor quality (e.g., due to high levels of background noise) or to change the delivery or inflection of a line. ADR can also be used to insert new lines of dialogue which are conceived during editing, although such lines can only be placed against picture in which the face of the actor speaking is not visible.

Automatic slating: A camera attachment which records the film shot and take numbers and a visible sync mark which corresponds to a tone fed to an audio recorder.

Automatically arriving automobiles: Whenever cars in a chase go through a four-way junction, unrelated cars must appear from each direction and skid into the center. These cars may either stop unharmed or crash into each other in the center, upon which all the drivers will get out and shake fists at each other. No cars actually involved in the chase are ever involved in the crash.

Avant-garde: Refers to an experimental, abstract, or highly independent, non-independent film that is often the forerunner of a new artistic genre or art form; avant-garde films self-consciously emphasize technique over substance; also loosely applies to a group of French and German filmmakers in the early 20th century and to some modern American experimental filmmakers (e.g., Andy Warhol), and their film movement that challenged conventional film-making.

AVID: Manufacturer of a popular non-linear editing system. Often used to refer to the system itself, as "AVID editor". Competitors include Lightworks.

A-wind and B-wind : This is the emulsion position of the film. There are two possibilities, just as there are two sides to a piece of film. Camera original is B-Wind. A print struck from it will be A-Wind. This is because film is printed emulsion against emulsion.

A-wind: An indication of the emulsion position on a roll of film. An 'A' wind is a roll with the emulsion facing the center of the roll.

Axis of action: In the continuity editing system, the "Axis of Action" is an imaginary line that passes through the two main actors of a scene, defining the spatial relations of all the elements of the scene as being to the right or left. The camera is not supposed to cross the axis at a cut and thus reverse those spatial relations. Also called the "180° line."

B

Baby legs: A short tripod.

Baby plate: A steel plate with a baby pin (5/8 inch pin) welded on to it. These plates are used for mounting lights or grip heads on a wall, box, or other surface.

Baby: Usually a reference to a 1K light unit. It is also used to describe any light unit which is smaller than a standard size unit of comparable intensity. For grips, it refers to anything with a 5/8 inch stud (i.e. baby plate).

Back lighting: Lighting directed at the camera from behind subject, which is therefore silhouetted.

Back lot: An area, on studio property, in an open-air, outdoor space away from the studio stages, where real-life situations with backgrounds are filmed; contrasted to on-location shoots that are more expensive; various studios in the Los Angeles area offer back lot tours.

Back projection: A photographic technique whereby live action is filmed in front of a transparent screen onto which background action is projected. Back projection was often used to provide the special effect of motion in vehicles during dialogue scenes, but has become outmoded and replaced by bluescreen processing and traveling mattes; also known as rear projection or process photography (or shot); contrast to matte shot.

Back seat inviso-syndrome: Film characters are invariably unable to see a person crouched in the back seat of a car (even a convertible) when, in the real world, it is an impossible place for a person to hide.

Backdrop: Refers to a large photographic backing or painting for the background of a scene (e.g., a view seen outside a window, a landscape scene, mountains, etc.), usually painted on flats (composed of plywood or cloth); a large curved backdrop (often representing the sky) is known as a cyclorama; backdrops were more commonly used before the current trend toward on-location shooting and the use of bluescreens.

Background artist: A person responsible for designing or constructing the art placed at the rear of a set.

Background: This is a term with a broad range of meanings, depending upon the context. In production, it has the same connotation as 'atmosphere', meaning extras who are staged to supply detail in the form of normal human traffic in a scene. In sound, it can mean the same as 'ambience' or it may refer to relative volume.

Backing track: Prerecorded accompaniment for a singer or voiceover actor who then listens through headphones to a replay as he/she performs. Generally, the two signals are ultimately mixed to produce the final recording.

Backlight: A light which is generally mounted behind a subject to light the subject's hair and shoulders without illuminating a subject's front. (Lighting)

Backlighting: This phenomenon occurs when the lighting for the shot is directed at the camera from behind the subject(s), causing the figure(s) in the foreground to appear in semi-darkness or as silhouettes, or highlighted; with backlighting, the subject is separated from the background.

Backlot: A large, undeveloped area on studio property used for constructing large open-air sets or for filming wilderness scenes.

Backwind: Rewinding film in the camera to shoot a Double Exposure.

Bad smoker rule: In any cop movie made since the mid-'70s, the bad guys smoke, while the good guy is trying to quit.

Baked potato people: The nice, good, sweet little people who form a chorus in the hero's background, especially during any movie set in a mental home. The lesson is always the same:

It's the real world that's crazy, and the crazy people who speak real truth. (Inspired by a sign seen on a baked potato in a steak house: "I've been tubbed, I've been rubbed, I've been scrubbed. I'm lovable, huggable, and eatable!")

Balance stripe: On magnetic-striped film, a narrow band of magnetic coating applied to the edge opposite the magnetic sound track which serves to make the film lie flat when it goes over magnetic sound heads.

Balanced: An audio circuit with 3 wires, two which carry signal, and a third which is contected to a ground (grounded).

Balloon rule: Good movies rarely contain a hot-air balloon. Most egregious recent use of a hot-air balloon: MEN DON'T LEAVE, where the heroine is cured of clinical depression by a ride in one. (Readers keep writing in with exceptions to this rule, including WITNESS, but the general principle still applies.)

Bankable star: A well-renowned actor/actress whose presence in a film is enough to guarantee finance and improve its gross takings.

Banned: Many countries have either government or official movie classification boards who are responsible for determining the suitability of a movie for release in their country or region. These boards occasionally block the release of a movie either in theaters or on video. Often, a banned movie will find its way around a ban by means of bootleg distribution.

Bar sheets (Lead sheets): A chart showing words of dialogue which have been recorded, and the number of motion picture frames of duration for each syllable.

Barndoors: Handy blinders on the sides of lights that can be used to keep light from going everywhere. They can also be used to clip on a lighting gel. They get very hot when a light is on, so it is best to wear work gloves when adjusting them.

Barney: A quilted cozy that fits around a camera to reduce camera noise. Generally it is only effective on a camera that is pretty quiet to begin with. The term comes from barney blanket, a kind of horse blanket.

Barroom bum slide: Most bar fights in the movies end with the loser being pushed so hard he slides halfway down the bar. In real life, this is impossible.

Base: Film has two basic elements: The base is the clear, perforated strip, and the emulsion is the thin, light-sensitive layer that is glued onto it.

Based on a true story: Films that consist of a story line that has at least some basis in real historical events, and may actually contain only a few factual elements. These films, loosely based on various biographies, stories, or events, may/may not significantly alter the characters or situations for greater dramatic effect; inspired by a true story indicates the film is even looser with the factual basis of the events.

Base-to-Base Splice: A splice made with the base side of the end of one piece of film overlapping the base side of the piece to which it is being attached.

Bayonet: A type of lens mount commonly used with heavier lenses, such as zoom lenses. In contrast to screw-mount lenses, bayonet lenses are attached to the camera with a locking mechanism. Bayonet lenses can typically be changed much faster than screw-mount lenses.

Bazooka: Similar to a 2K stand, but without support legs. It has a junior hole at one end and a junior stud at the other, and it usually has a sliding riser.

Beat: Refers to an actor's term for how long to wait before doing an action; a beat is usually about one second.

Beaver board: A 2K pigeon on an apple box.

Because They Are There: The top ten lines you can always count on in a mountain-climbing movie:

Bed: Background music used underneath a narrator or foreground dialog. Primarily applied to commercial radio or television spots.

Beef: The output of a light.

Beefy baby: A heavy duty 2K stand without wheels.

Beep: A short duration sound track tone aligned to a point on the film for precise reference in synchronization in the editing and printing processes.

Beginning, The: Word used in the titles of sequels to movies in which everyone was killed at the end of the original movie, making an ordinary sequel impossible. Explains to knowledgeable filmgoers that the movie will concern, for example, what happened in the AMITYVILLE house before the Lutzes moved in.

Behind the scenes: The off-camera events or circumstances during filmmaking.

Below the line budget: Any cast and crew budgeting costs not included in Above the Line Budgeting. Includes technical and construction elements needed to make the film.

Below the line: Refers to the technical elements of the production staff. Literally, these are the budget elements that appeared below a bold line on a standard production budget form.

Below-the-line expenses: All physical production costs not included in the above-the-line expenses, including material costs, music rights, publicity, trailer, etc.

Best boy: The chief assistant, usually of the gaffer or key grip. In charge of the men and equipment, scheduling the required quantities for each day's work. The term originates from promoting the crew's 'best boy' to supervising, allowing the gaffer and key grip to stay on set and carry out the cameraman's lighting needs. The origin of the term is from "pre-union" filming days when the line between Grip and Electric departments was less rigid. When the head of either department needed another body temporarily, he'd go to the head of the other department and ask him to "lend me your BEST boy". By default the 2nd in charge of either department came to be known as best-boy. This term may also have been borrowed from early sailing and whaling crews, as sailors were often employed to set up and work rigging in theatres. There are no "best girls" per se; female chief assistants are also called "Best Boys".

Best light: Similar to a One Light, but by implication, the timer has gone through the film more thoroughly in selecting a timing light that will agree with the majority of the footage.

Best play of the game rule: Every bad sports movie ends with the hero making an extraordinary catch/play/hit in slow motion to win the game at the final gun/bell/buzzer.

Beta: 1/2 inch videotape that was originally called Betamax.

B-Film (or B-Movie, B-Picture): An off-beat, low-budget, second-tier film, usually from an independent producer, shot quickly with little-known, second rate actors; often the second film (or the 'lower half') of a double-feature shown in a grindhouse; B-films are often characterized by sensational and catchy titles, campy acting, cheesy special effects, and gratuitous violence and sexuality; contrast to an A-pictures (first-class, big-budget films with high-level production values and star-power); not to be confused with cult films, although some B-films attain cult status.

Big lie, The: Refers to all scenes where bad guy paints a beautiful picture and then adds version of, "One more thing, Benny. I lied."

Big nod, The: Comes after the Last Word. After a character is fatally wounded, first he lies motionless and recites an incredibly meaningful statement. Then his head nods to one side.

Billing: A great deal of importance is placed on the relative sizes, positions, and order of names and the movie's title in printed publicity material as well as the opening credits. Generally, higher positions designate higher importance. Additionally, there is significant given to names which appear before or above the actual title of the movie. The person whose name is shown first in the credits or whose name is at the top of an advertisement is said to have received "top billing". If more than one name appears at the same time or at the same height, they are said to have "equal billing", with the importance of the people concerned decreasing from left to right. In some movies with a large number of stars, the publicity department must go to great lengths to satisfy the demands of various parties. "Diagonal billing" is where a different name appears first, depending on whether the material is read from top to bottom, or from left to right. In some extreme cases, multiple stars in the same movie have each demanded top billing, in which case an equal number of differently-billed advertisement have been created.

Bin: A reference to a storage container lined with a cloth bag, into which cut film or sound stock may be arranged and hung. In digital audio and video terms, this can be related to a film and/or directory from which stored shots or sound segments are selected for use.

Bio-pic (or biographic): A biographical film of the life of a famous personality or historical figure, particularly popularized by Warner Bros. in the 1930s; a sub-genre of drama and epic films.

Bit part (or bit player): A small acting role (usually only one scene, such as a waiter) with very few lines or acting; contrast to a cameo, extra, or walk-on role.

Bit: A minor acting role in which an actor may only speak a few lines.

Biz: In shorthand, refers to the "business", or "show business".

Black and white: Simply means without color; before the invention of color film stock, all films were black and white; monochrome (literally meaning "one color") usually refers to a film shot in black and white, although it can refer to a film shot in shades of one color; grainy B&W is often used to convey authenticity; abbreviated as BW, B/W, and B&W; contrast to color.

Black comedy: A comedy in which the humour is derived from subjects which are typically considered "serious", or for which humour is usually considered as unsuitable. Common examples are death, war, suffering, and murder.

Black leader or **Black emulsion leader:** Black leader is black, opaque film, often specifially called black emulsion leader. It is what the negative cutter uses when preparing A&B rolls. It is very important that it be emulsion leader rather than plastic leader when used for A&B rolls, since plastic leader cannot be cement spliced. It also must be very opaque, not any black piece of film will do.

Black wrap: Black Aluminum foil which is used for wrapping lights, to control light spill, and for making small flags.

Black/dark comedy: A type of comedy film, first popular during the late 1950s and early 1960s in which normally serious subjects, such as war, death, dismemberment, misery, suffering, or murder, are treated with macabre humor and satire through iconography, dialogue, and the characters; settings may include cemeteries, war rooms, funerals.

Blackface: The make up technique of making an actor, usually white, to resemble an African American or at least a caricature thereof such as in the final scene of The Jazz Singer (1927). There were also equivalents for Asians (Yellowface) and Native Americans (Redface). It was a standard practice in the early 20th century for the casting of actors in non-white roles and abandoned when it was recognized to be an insult to minorities which also cheated them of casting opportunies.

Blacklisting (and blacklist): Refers to late 40s and early 50s McCarthyism and the HUAC's (House UnAmerican Activities Committee) formal and informal discrimination and 'blacklisting' (effectively banning from employment) of various actors, artists and film-makers based upon their personal, political, social, or religious beliefs (i.e., "Communist sympathizers"); the blacklist was a roster of illegal artists who were not to be hired during the years 1947-1951.

Blaxploitation: A combination of the terms "black" and "exploitation"; refers mainly to sensational, low-budget films in the 1970's featuring mostly African-American casts (and directors), that broke the mold of black characterization in feature films; usually emphasized fads of the time in hairstyles, music and costuming, and also brutality, sleazy sex, street-life, racist and militant attitudes, etc.

Blighty: Used to refer to Britain.

Blimp: The housing a noisy movie camera is put in to prevent the sound equipment from picking up extra sounds.

Blimped camera or Self-blimped camera: The term is used not to mean a camera in a blimp, but a camera that is designed with internal soundproofing without the need for an external blimp. For instance, with an Arri BL the "BL" stands for "blimped."

Blip tone: A sync pop. This is usually done by placing a piece of 'toned' tape on a particular frame of film to establish a 'synch' point.

Blockbuster: Originally referred to a large bomb that would destroy an entire city block during World War II; now in common usage, an impactful movie that is a huge financial success - usually with box-office of more than $200 million (the new benchmark by the early 2000s, after the original mark was $100 million) upon release in North America; ticket lines for blockbusters literally go around the 'block'; also known as box-office hit; the term may also refer to a costly film that must be exceptionally popular in order to recoup its expenses and make a profit; the opposite of a blockbuster is a bomb, flop, or turkey.

Blocking a shot (or scene): The process of figuring out where the camera goes, how the lights will be arranged, and what the actors' positions and movements - moment by moment - are for each shot or take; often, the specific staging of a film's movements are worked out by the director, often with stand-ins and the lighting crew before actual shooting

Blocking: A process during which the director and actors determine where on the set the actors will move and stand, so that lighting and camera placements may be set.

Blonde: An open face 2K lighting unit, also known as a 'mighty'.

Bloop: The sound produced in an energized amplifier and speaker system when a film splice passes the photo cell to which the amplifier is connected.

Blooper: An actual error or mistake (misplaced action, or mis-spoken dialogue by a performer), usually embarrassing or humorous, made by a performer during filming; also known as a goof, flaw or flub.

Blooping tape: Tape used to cover unwanted portions of sound tracks.

Blooping: Any method of silencing unwanted noise produced by the passage of a splice through a sound reproducer. Traditionally, a small opaque tape is fixed over a splice.

Blow down: The actual term for the opposite of a blow up is a Reduction Print, but this term has been coined by Colorlab in Rockville, Maryland, for a reduction print made from super 16mm to regular 16mm, as an alternative to the much more expensive process of blowing up super 16mm to 35mm.

Blow-up: An optical enlargement of a film from one gauge to another, such as 16mm up to 35mm. The opposite of a blow up is a Reduction Print.

Blue sky: The potential for the movie to make a greater profit than that which is guaranteed by distribution and pre-sale agreements.

Blue-screen: A special-effects process whereby actors work in front of an evenly-lit, monochromatic (usually blue or green) background or screen. The background is then replaced (or matted) in post-production by chroma-keying or optical printer, allowing other footage or computer-generated images to form the image; since 1992, most films use a green-screen.

Blurb: Another name for a commercial or advertisement (usually for TV).

B-movie: A low-budget, second tier movie, frequently the 2nd movie in a double-feature billing. B-films were cheaper for studios because they did not involve the most highly paid actors or costly sets, and were popular with theater owners because they were less expensive to bring into their theaters while still able to draw revenue.

Bobbinet: Black mesh cloth which is used for grip scrims. It also is available in rolls for darkening windows.

Body double: For some shots, a director may consider that a particular actor's body may not be suitable for the impression desired. In these situations, the actor is "doubled" (replaced) by a person whose body is more suitible. Typically, body doubles are used for shots requiring nudity or depictions of physical fitness. Contrast with stunt double and stand-in.

Body makeup: Makeup applied below the neck or above the wrists.

Body switch movie: The brain of one character somehow finds itself in the body of another. Requires actors to confront an actor's nightmare, i.e., acting as if they were another actor.

Bolex: One of the more widely used 16mm non-sync cameras, it is made in Switzerland by the Paillard Company. There are many varieties, non-reflex, reflex, springwound and electric motor driven. But when someone says "Bolex," typically they mean a reflex, springwound model, such as the Rex-4.

Bollywood: Refers to the burgeoning film industry of India, the world's biggest film industry, centered in Bombay (now

Mumbai); the etymology of the word: from Bo(mbay) + (Ho)llywood; unlike Hollywood, however, Bollywood is a non-existent place.

Bomb: A movie which is a financial disaster. Exception: in the United Kingdom, when used with "down" (e.g. "went down a bomb"), the term means a rousing success.

Boom microphone: A long pole with a microphone on the end. The boom is extended out near the actors. Ideally, the microphone at the end should be placed in the camera's safe area.

Boom operator: A member of the sound crew who operates the boom microphone.

Boom shot: A continuous single shot made from a moving boom, assembled like a montage, and incorporating any number of camera levels and angles.

Boom: A traveling or moveable counter-balanced pole (also called fishpole or fishing rod), arm, or telescoped extension device upon which a microphone, light or camera can be suspended overhead above a scene and outside the frame during filming (by a boom operator or boom man).

Bootleg: An unofficial and illegally copied or distributed version of a movie, often of a substandard quality. Bootleg videos are often available for movies that have yet to be released in a particular country, or have been banned.

Bottom chop: A flag or cutter which is used to keep light off of the floor or the lower part of a scene.

Bounce board: A large white card made of foam or posterboard used to reflect soft light and for the soft key and fill.

Bounce card: A white or silver card used for soft indirect lighting of the subject by bouncing light off the card. Can also be used to provide a gentle brightening of shadow areas. Especially out-of-doors as it does not require power.

Box office gross/Gross takings: The total amount of money paid by the public for cinema tickets to the movie.

Box rental: A fee or allowance paid to a crewmember for providing his/her own equipment or other specialized apparatus for use in a production.

Box rule: Beware movies advertised with a row of little boxes across the bottom, each one showing the face of a different international star and the name of a character (i.e., "Curt Jurgens as the Commandant"). Example: Most films made from Agatha Christie novels.

Box-office: The measure of the total amount of money or box-office receipts paid by movie-goers to view a movie; also referred to as B. O. or gross; films with great box-office results or a strong and outstanding performance are often termed 'boff', 'boffo', 'boffola', 'whammo', 'hotsy', or 'socko'.

Bracketing: The filming of several takes of the same shot at different f-stops to achieve the desired result. Usually this technique is applied to shooting titles much more than anything else. (It is a good idea to film a few frames of black in-between, since it is sometimes difficult to tell where the camera was stopped.)

Branch holder: A pipe-like unit with a locking nut which is used to hold branches, wooden poles, or other items.

Breakdown script: A detailed list of all items, people, props, equipment, etc required for a shoot on a day-by-day basis. Recording such lists aids in continuity and allows optimization of the time of actors and the crew.

Breakdown sheet : Part of the Shooting Schedule, the Breakdown Sheet contains all the important information about each scene (except for those determined by the director). Displays length, description, cast, makeup and other special requirements to keep everyone informed.

Breakdown: The separation of a roll of camera original negative (or in some cases a workprint) into its individual takes or scenes. (Film Editing) Also a very common term which refers to a preproduction function where discrete elements of a script are isolated and noted.

Breast line: A guide line attached to anything being hauled up on a crane or by a pulley.

Bridging shot: A transitional type of shot used to cover or 'bridge' a jump in time or place or other discontinuity.

British Film Commission: The British Film Commission (BFC) is a government-funded organisation established in 1991, as an initial point of contact to assist in the making of international and domestic film and television throughout every stage of production in England, Northern Ireland, Scotland and Wales

British Film Institute: The BFI exists to promote greater understanding and appreciation of, and access to, film and moving image culture in the UK.

Broad: A rectangular open-faced light which is used for general fill or for cyc illumination.

Brotman's law: "If nothing has happened by the end of the first reel, nothing is going to happen."

Brute: A brute arc light, usually 225 amps DC powered.

Buddy film: A subgenre of film (comedies, westerns, dramas, action films, road films, etc.) in which two mismatched persons (usually males) are forced to work together, often a pair of police cops; situations are often contrived to present the pair with challenges or strains that both strengthen their bond and weaken it; buddy films are often action/comedy films with witty dialogue between the two characters and sometimes the inclusion of a love triangle; has been extended to include female buddies; compare to fish-out-of-water tale.

Buddy-brother road film: Three-way combo of buddy movie, road movie, and brothers who learn to love each other.

Building a scene: Using dramatic devices such as increased tempo, volume, and emphasis to bring a scene to a climax.

Bulk eraser: A device which magnetically aligns all of the iron oxide molecules on a magnetic tape or film, thus eliminating any 'sound' on them.

Bullitt shift: Cars in high-speed chases can shift through more gears than they have.

Bumper: Usually refers to the pre-film segment of pre-made film that contains studio trademark and logo or title identification; also refers to a period of positive financial growth (i.e., it was a 'bumper year' for films).

Burn-in time code: A videotape in which a "window" displaying the time code count on the tape is superimposed over part of lhe picture.

Bus: A mixing network that combines the output of two or more channels.

Butt splice: A film splice in which the film ends come together without overlapping.

Butterflies: Gauze-like fabrics of varying thicknesses and patterns which may be mounted in front of a lighting instrument so as to diffuse or "soften" the quality of the light.

Butterfly (Butterfly kit): Assorted nets, silks, solids, and grifflons which are used for light control; usually 5' x 5', or 6' x 6' frame size. Commonly a 12' x 12' or 20' x 20' is called a butterfly kit, however, it they should be called an overhead kit.

Butthead: A producer who thinks he knows more about a film technicians job than the tech himself knows. (Film) Someone who changes lanes without looking.

Butt-weld splice: A film splice made by joining the two pieces of film, without an overlapping portion, usually by applying both heat and pressure.

Buzz track: A soundtrack of natural, atmospheric, on-location background noise that is added to the re-recorded (or looped) track of actors' dialogue and other sound effects recordings to create a more realistic sound.

Buzz: Slang for the sense of excitement, expectancy, and hype that surrounds a film, an actor, or a director.

B-wind: An indication of the emulsion position on a roll of film. A 'B' Wind indicates that the emulsion is facing out, or away, from the center or core of the film roll.

C

C Stand: A general purpose grip stand.

C.R.: Abbreviation for Camera Roll.

C.T.B.: C.T.B. stands for Color Temperature Blue. This is an abbreviation for the color correction gels used in lighting to convert the color temperature from tungsten to daylight. They come in gradients: Quarter Blue, Half Blue, Full Blue.

C.T.O.: C.T.O. stands for Color Temperature Orange. This is an abbreviation for the color correction gels used in lighting to convert the color temperature from daylight to tungsten. They come in gradients: Quarter Orange, Half Orange, Full Orange.

C-47: Ordinary wooden clothespins which are used to secure gels to barndoors. They are also known as a #1 wood clamp.

Cable Sync: A somewhat archaic method of sync sound shooting, where a cable runs from a Pilottone generator in the camera to the tape recorder.

California scrim set: A scrim set with two doubles.

Call sheet: A sheet which notes which scenes will be shot the next day, and the basic cast, crew and special requirements for each scene, as well as scene times and call times.

Camel, Slow-moving: All camels in Middle Eastern thrillers are crossing the road for the sole purpose of slowing down a pursuit vehicle.

Cameo: Originally meaning "a small piece of artwork," refers to a bit part (usually a brief, non-speaking or walk-on role that is uncredited or unbilled) or special screen appearance by a famous actor, director, or prominent person who would ordinarily not take such a small part; contrast to a bit part; also refers to a type of camera shot in which the subject is filmed against a black or neutral background.

Camera angle: The angle of vision taken by a camera upon its subject. Distance of subject to camera in all three dimensions, lens used and the direction in which the camera points at the subject are determinant of angle. Angle may determine point of view; specific angles contribute significantly to the construction of the film text.

Camera blocking: The process of notating the changing position of the camera, lens size, and focus during a particular scene.

Camera car: A vehicle, either purpose-built or improvised, used to provide as stable a platform as possible when the camera is following action either at speed or across large distances.

Camera core: A 2 inch Core.

Camera crew: The group of crewmembers directly involved with operation of the camera. Individual job titles include: clapper-loader, camera operator, assistant cameraman, director of photography, focus puller, grip, key grip, dolly grip, additional camera.

Camera distance: The optical distance from the camera to a person, group, or object; the distance perceived on the screen by the viewer to an object or person.

Camera head: A device to which the camera is attached when being mounted. It acts as the movable interface between the camera and a tripod or other camera platform. An essential function of the camera head is to ensure smooth movement of the camera in executing pans or tilts. For smaller cameras this is achieved through the use of devices, friction or hydraulic, which place a resistance against the direction of movement. For larger studio cameras, movement is controlled by a gearing mechanism, hence the expression "gear-head" to refer to film technicians enamored of their technology.

Camera lenses: Camera lenses are the optical devices which "capture" light and focus it upon the desired area of film.

They are classified according to their ability to render more or less wide angles of vision, and more or less greater degrees of amplification of the image. Because a film image is a two-dimensional rendering of three-dimensional space, all lenses, of whatever type and usage, create spatial relationships which are defined by the viewer's perception of perspective. It is important to keep in mind that in addition to its other characteristics (described below), the type of lens used in a given shot will have a significant effect on the way in which perspective is rendered in the image. As with any technological system, compromises are necessary between clarity of image across the whole field of vision (not focus, which signifies clarity in depth), rendering of perspective (as mentioned), the accurate reproduction of movement, lighting conditions, and so on. No one lens is perfect for any given camera angle or shot distance. It is usually up to the Director of Photography to suggest a lens to the director which will render the shot as the director wants it. The focal lengths given below apply to 35mm film. These will differ for different film gauges, though their optical characteristics will remain the same in terms of the image rendered.

Camera loader: The person who operates the clapboard at the beginning of a shot, also responsible for loading film stock into film magazines. The action of slapping the clapper was invented as a way of synchronizing the visual and audio components of a shot. Recent innovations in audio-visual synchronization have made this unnecessary, but it still occurs extensively.

Camera log: A record sheet giving details of the scenes or shots photographed on a particular roll of negative.

Camera movement: The use of the camera to obtain various camera angles and perspectives.

Camera movements—compound: A movement executed by the camera, either on a dolly, crane, or hand-held, which combines any two or more simple movements. Thus a camera may be tracking back while panning right, or craning up while tilting down, etc.

Camera movements—simple: Any movement effected by the camera along a single plane or axis of movement and no other.

Camera noise: The sound of the camera running. Even supposedly quiet cameras will make some noise.

Camera operator: The person who operates the camera to the specifications dictated by the director of photography. A director or a director of photography sometimes assumes this role.

Camera original: A slightly more adamant way of saying Original.

Camera reports: A form of paperwork used to log shots and takes and put down any notes either to the lab or for future organization in the editing stage. There is generally one camera report per camera roll. Camera reports can be used to communicate specific timing requests to the lab (for instance, if a shot if lit with unusual color gels, this can be noted to let the timer know not to correct the color). Camera reports are extremely helpful to analyze any problem with the footage, since they provides a written record of the coverage (the least of which is that if the slate has the wrong information written on it, which happens now and then, a note can be made in the camera reports to keep the assistant editor from getting confused about which take is which).

Camera roll: Each roll that you shoot becomes a camera roll. It is often helpful to label them with a number in the order that they were shot. The usual way is with the abbreviation C.R. followed by a number. The lab will then assemble and print them in that order. This makes things less confusing when you first get back your footage.

Camera speed: The speed at which film passes through the camera (usually about 24-25 frames/second). Also a call issued by the First Assistant Director to check that the camera is rolling and up to speed.

Camera stock: This is film. It is also called camera stock to distinguish it from Print Stock.

Camera tape: Cloth tape specifically for use on film shoots, much like gaffer's tape. Camera tape is typically 1 inch wide and white so that it can be used together with a sharpie for labeling magazines with the emulsion type and camera roll number. It is valid to use the terms gaffer's tape and camera tape interchangeably (they are both really the same type of tape) depending on how the tape is being used. It is designed not to leave a sticky residue behind on the camera.

Camera wedges: Small wooden wedges, usually 4 inches long by 1/2 wide at the thickest end.

Camera: The basic machine involved in film-making, from a hand-held version to portables, to heavy studio cameras; some of the parts of a camera include the aperture, lens, film magazine (for storage), viewfinder, etc; the positioning of the camera is known as the setup.

Cam-lok: A feeder cable connector which is similar to a Tweco, but with a more positive locking mechanism which is easier to disconnect.

Camp: A form of comedic parody where the clichéd conventions of a dramatic form like adventure are deliberately exaggerated to the point of ridiculousness. Often unfairly used to describe superhero films and shows as Batman is a prime example of this form of comedy.

Can ("in the can"): Refers to the round metal/plastic container that holds or stores film (reels) for transport or for long-term storage; a film that has been completed is known colloquially as "in the can"; canned means pre-recorded.

Canadian society of cinematographers: Use of the abbreviation after a name indicates that the person is a member of the CSC.

Candela: A unit of light intensity, a standard candle. (Lighting)

Candlelight (lighting): Refers to lighting that is provided by candlelight, to provide a warm hue or tone, and connote intimacy, romance, and harmony.

Canted frame: Often described as a 'Dutch Angle' or 'Dutching'. This is a device or process whereby the camera is angled so that the horizontal frame line is not parallel to the horizon.

Capacitance: An electrical component's ability to store electrical charges.

Capsule review : A short movie review.

Caption: The descriptive, printed line(s) of text that occasionally appears on the screen, usually at the bottom of the frame, to describe the time/place, or to translate a foreign word/phrase; different from closed-captioning (closed captions are all white uppercase (capital) letters encased in a black box that require a decoder or television with a decoder chip to be viewed) for deaf or hard-of-hearing viewers.

Caricature: A character appearing ridiculously out of proportion because of one physical, psychological or moral trait that has been grossly or broadly exaggerated; a caricature often portrays a character in an unrealistic, stereotypical fashion

Caring blanket tuck-in: Effective in conveying the soft heart of an otherwise unappealing character. Also used in scenes involving the hero, usually as a set-up for a scene in which tucked-in child suddenly finds himself/herself in great danger.

Cartoon: An animated film that is usually not of feature length.

Cash cow: In movie terms, a definitely guaranteed, 'can't-miss' blockbuster film that promises to generate disproportionately tremendous profits due to its lucrative franchise.

Cast against type: An actor playing a role distinctly different from roles previously played.

Cast of thousands: An advertising claim, often used in big-screen historical epics of the 1930s-60s, when literally 1,000s of extras were hired for crowd scenes, battle scenes, etc.

Cast: A collective term for all of the actors/performers (or talent) appearing in a particular film: usually broken down into two parts: the leads with speaking roles, and the seconds or supporting characters, background players or extras, and bit players.

Casting couch: During the so-called "Golden Age" of Hollwood, it was not uncommon for would-be-stars to grant sexual favours to directors and/or producers in return for a role in films. These favours were usually rumoured to be on a couch in the filmmaker's office. The phrase "Casting Couch" has been popularized, and although the practise has diminished, the term remains in use.

Casting director: The person who auditions and helps to select all of the speaking role actors in film, television shows or plays. The CD must possess a vast knowledge of the actor pool and be able to match a variety of actors with just the right role. Directors and producers rely on the Casting Director to assist them with assembling the perfect cast for their production. Casting Directors are also responsible for serving as the liason between the director, and the actors and their agents. CDs negotiate the deals with agents once the actors have been cast and are also responsible for the contracts and SAG of each actor.

Casting society of america: The Casting Society of America is a professional organization of Casting Directors working in theatre, film, and television. The C.S.A. is not a union or a guild, therefore every Casting Director working in these mediums is not necessarily a member of this organization.

Casting: The process of selecting and hiring actors to play the roles and characters in a film production, and be brought under contract; the lead roles are typically cast or selected by the director or a producer, and the minor or supporting roles and bit parts by a casting director; type-casting refers to an actor playing only roles similar to those he/she has played before.

Catchphrase (film): Short phrases, expressions, or words that have become favored and/or popularized due to repeated use, often by film critics.

Caterer: A person or company who provides the main meals for cast and crew either on set or on location.

Catharsis: During a film's climax, the audience may experience a purging or cleansing of emotional tension, providing relief or therapeutic restoration.

Cautionary tale: A literary term, referring to a narrative with a moral message warning of the consequences of certain actions, ideologies, character flaws, technologies or institutions, often with a downbeat ending; many slasher horror films are semi-cautionary tales about one of the consequences of sex or experimenting with the occult — death.

CC Filters: Color compensating filters made in precise density values of the primary and secondary colcrs.

CD (Compact Disc): A digitally encoded disc capable of containing more than one hour of music at a sampling frequency of 44.1 khz. The data is read by a laser beam.

Cel (or celluloid, animation cel): Refers to each of the thousands of hand-drawn sheets (of clear, transparent material, either celluloid or Mylar) representing a single animation frame to allow several layers of composition. Cels consist of character cels (containing only the foreground characters or objects - those things that move from frame to frame) and background cels, (static drawings of scenery that remain the same). The character cels are placed against the background cels and filmed or shot one frame (or picture) at a time to produce the effect of motion. Celluloid also refers to the thin strip of transparent plastic coating that forms the film's highly-flammable, light-sensitive base layer; also used as an adjective related to some aspect of cinema; the light-sensitive substance coating on one side of the film base is termed emulsion; celluloid is also a slang word for a movie.

Cel animation: A form of animation where hand drawn pictures are transposed on to plastic sheets, each with a different element such as characters and background, and layered on top of each other to create a complete scene. The composition is then photographed and incorporated in the finished film. It was the predominate of form of animation until the rise of computer generated animation in the mid 1990's.

Celo: A type of cookie which is made from wire mesh coated with plastic.

Cement splice: A type of splice used primarily by negative cutters. In a cement splice the two pieces of film overlap each other and are fused together with film cement.

Censorship: The process of determining what can or can not be viewed by the public or depicted by the motion picture industry; also refers to changes required of a movie by some person or body.

Center track: A standard position for the placement of the audio signal on magnetic film. The placement is in a narrow band centered between the two edges of the film.

Centre international du film pour l'Enfance et la jeunesse: A 40-year-old international non-governmental organization whose goal is to promote quality films, television programmes and videos for children and young people around the world.

Century stand (C-Stand): A multipurpose grip stand.

Certificates: Various countries or regions have film classification boards for reviewing movies and rating their content in terms of its suitability for particular audiences. For many countries, movies are required to be advertised as having a particular "certificate" or "rating", forewarning audiences of possible "objectionable content". The nature of this "objectionable content" is determined mainly by contemporary national, social, religious, and political standards. The usual criteria which determine a film's certificate are violence and sexuality, with "mature" (adult) situations and especially blasphemy and political issues often being considered more important outside the Western world. This is by no means a hard and fast rule; see the Hays Production Code for an example. In some cases, a film classification board exhibits censorship by demanding changes be made to a movie in order to receive a certain rating. As many movies are targetted at a particular age group, studios must balance the content of their films against the demands of the classification board. Negotiations are common; studios agree to make certain changes to films in order to receive the required rating. The IMDb uses the term "Certificate" as opposed to "Rating" to avoid confusion with "ratings" meaning the opinions of critics.

CGI or Computer-Generated Imagery: A term referring to the use of 3D computer graphics and technology (digital computers and specialized software) in film-making to create filmed images, special effects and the illusion of motion.

Chain vise grip: A vise grip with a chain that is used for its clamping capability.

Change pages: When a script is being edited during production, changes are distributed to actors and the filmmakers on "change pages", which are usually a different color to the pages of the script.

Change-over cue: The small dot, oval or mark on the top-right corner of a film frame that signaled to the projectionist to change over from one projector (or film reel) to another (about every 15-20 minutes); nowadays, most film theatres have only one projector - the reels are spliced together into one giant roll and fed into a single projector from a horizontal revolving turntable called a platter.

Change-over marks: Most completed movies consist of more than one reel, and thus for an uninterrupted screening, at least two projectors must be used. Towards the end of a reel, one or more frames may include a small circle in one of the corners. These are signals to the projectionist that the current reel is approaching the end, and he or she should be ready to start the next projector, which should have the next reel prepared for projection. Also, many theaters have switched to a platter system which allows the entire film to be spliced together and put on a large platter. The film is fed through the center of the reel (unwinding from the inside out), then into the projector, and then back onto another platter. This process allows the film to be show back-to-back without having to rewind it.

Changing bag: A double chambered black bag with a zipper on one end and two elasticized arm holes on the other side, used for loading film into magazines.

Chapman crane: The trade name for a versatile, purpose-made flat-bed truck which carries a built-in camera boom and associated equipment. The truck moves from location to location by road using its own conventional engine. Once there it may be anchored down as a stable platform, but it can also "track" over smooth surfaces using electric motors which individually drive the wheels. It comes in various configurations, principally with regard to the length of the boom.

Character actor: An actor who specializes in playing well-defined, stereotypical, archetypal, off-beat, humorous, or highly-recognizable, fictional roles of a particular physical, emotional, or behavioral type, in a supporting role.

Character color coding: Refers to identifying a film's character or persona with a particular color; changes in color often represent transformations, shifts, merges, or changes in personal

Character study: A film that uses strong characterizations, interactions and the personalities of its characters to tell a story, with plot and narrative almost secondary to them

Chase-and-crash scenes: Replaces the third act or any other form of plot resolution in the modern thriller. After the hero has left dozens of burning cars and trucks behind him, we never see emergency vehicles responding to the carnage. Despite working under a Wrong-Headed Commanding Officer, q.v., the hero cop is never called on the carpet because yesterday he drove his squad car through the walls of several warehouses.

Cheat: When the camera is set up for a second shot at a different angle it is possible to move things around a little to improve the new composition, the difference in perspective and angle of the two shots hiding the fact that things are not exactly in the same place. Both actors and furniture on the set can be cheated. The term is often used as cheating something "into" a shot or "out of" a shot, as in telling an actor "We're going to cheat you in a little," and having them stand a little to one side so more of them is in the shot.

Cheater cut: The footage put into the beginning of a serial episode to show what happened at the end of the previous episode.

Check print: This is a print made from an internegative or an optical to verify the quality and success of an effect.

Checkerboard cutting: A technique of splicing A/B rolls in order to eliminate the image of the film splice from the duplicates or to allow for rapid readjustments of optical printer settings from shot to shot.

Chemistry (or screen chemistry): Referring to performances between actors who are uncommonly suited and perfectly complementary to each other; performances that lack screen chemistry can sometimes be disastrous for a film.

Chiaroscuro: Literally, the combination of the two Italian words for "clear/bright" and "dark"; refers to a notable, contrasting use of light and shade; often achieved by using a spotlight.

Chick flicks: Refers to films popular with women, but also used in a derogatory sense to marginalize films with heavy, sappy emotion and numerous female characters.

Child actor: Technically, any actor under the age of 18.

Children's film foundation: Training scheme in the UK to give schoolchildren experience of all aspects of film making. Now replaced by the Children's Film and Television Foundation

Chopsocky: Slang for a martial arts film.

Choreographer (and choreography): A person who plans, designs, organizes, sequences, and directs dancing, fighting, or other physical actions or movements in a film or stage production; a dancer is known as a hoofer.

Chromakeying: An electronic/computerized technique that allows for specific color elements (chroma) to be replaced with different picture elements.

Chute cowboys: Slang term for experienced parachutists that either perform or assist with stunts involving parachutes.

Chyron: Text graphics which appear at the bottom of a screen used to describe time, place, or name of person on screen; can also describe the technology used to add the text to the bottom of the screen.

Cinch marks: Not to be confused with sync marks. Cinch marks are small vertical scratches on a roll of film that are caused when the end of the film is pulled to tighten the roll, causing any dust on the film to make a small scratch. Too much drag on the supply while rewinding is one common way that cinching can occur.

Cineaste: Refers to a film/movie enthusiast or devotee; also used in the name of a leading film magazine.

Cinema audio society: A philanthropic, non-profit organization formed in 1964 for the purpose of sharing information with sound professionals in the motion picture and television industry. Use of the abbreviation after a name indicates that the person is a member of the CAS.

Cinema verité: A French word that literally means "true cinema" or "cinema truth"; a method or style of documentary movie-making with long takes, and little or no directorial or editing control exerted over the finished product; usually made without actors, and often with a minimum of film equipment, a small film crew (camera and sound), impromptu interview techniques, and a hand-held camera and portable sound equipment; sometimes used to loosely refer to a documentary-style film or minimalist cinema; popularized in the 1950s French New Wave movement; now widely used (often inappropriately) to refer to the popular, artsy trend of using hand-held camera techniques; also termed free cinema (UK) or direct cinema (US).

Cinema: A place where screenings occur. Cinemas can be hardtops or ozoners.

Cinemascope: The term commonly refers to widescreen processes or anamorphic techniques, that use different magnifications in the horizontal and the vertical to fill the screen; it is also the specific trademark name for 20th Century Fox's widescreen process, which uses an aspect ratio of 2.35:1.

Cinematic Business Pathology Syndrome (CBPS): Affliction that causes sociopathic or criminal behavior by officers of a corporation. Malady is characterized by several symptoms.

Cinematic: Relating to or suggestive of motion pictures; having the qualities of a film.

Cinematographer: Specifically refers to the art and technique of film photography, the capture of images, and lighting effects, or to the person expert in and responsible for capturing or recording-photographing images for a film, through the selection of visual recording devices, camera angles, film stock, lenses, framing, and arrangement of lighting; the chief cinematographer responsible for a movie is called the director of photography (or D.P.), or first cameraman; one of the earliest movie-picture machines, patented by the Lumiere brothers in 1895, was termed a Cinematographe.

Cinematography: The art and craft of photographing moving objects on lengths of continuous film; the devices, procedures and techniques used to achieve this. As is often said, cinematography is painting motion with light.

Cinerama: A wide-screen filming process that first used three cameras and three projectors to achieve an encompassing view of the subject matter, and was projected on a curved screen of about 160 degrees.

Cinex strip: A short test print in which each frame has been printed at a different exposure level.

Circle of confusion: A concept closely related to that of depth of field, the circle of confusion is an imaginary area on the screen which is defined by the relationship between the distance of the camera from the subject, the lighting conditions, the focal length of the lens used, and the aperture setting. All objects within this area will appear to a spectator to be in focus even though they may in reality be not located directly on the true focus plane.

Clamp light: A type of lighting fixture designed to hold a screw-in light bulb, with a not-so-dependable spring clamp for mounting on the side of an open door, etc. Often includes an aluminum reflector dish as well.

Clapboard: A small black or white board or slate with a hinged stick on top that displays identifying information for each shot in a movie, and is filmed at the beginning of a take. The board typically contains the working title of the movie, the names of the director, the editor, and the director of photography, the scene and take numbers, the date, and the time. On the top of the clapboard is a hinged wooden stick (called a clapstick or clapper) which is often clapped to provide audio/visual synchronization of the sound with the picture during editing; electronic clappers and synchronization are currently in use instead of the old-fashioned clapboard.

Clapper or Clapstick: The Slate, or just the two sticks that are struck together to mark a sync sound take.

Classic car rule: Whenever a beautiful classic car—usually the prized possession of an unsympathetic father—is introduced at the beginning of a film, that car will be wrecked by the end of it.

Classification and ratings administration: The division of the MPAA which is responsible for administering certificates.

Claymation: Refers to the animation of models constructed of clay, putty, plasticine, or other moldable materials, often through stop-motion.

Clean speech: A take in which all dialogue was performed without error.

Click track: A prerecorded track of electronic metronomic clicks used to ensure proper timing of music to be recorded. Essential in music scoring sessions.

Click: Slang denoting a 'hit' film.

Cliffhanger: A film characterized by scenes of great tension, danger, adventure, suspense, or high drama, often climaxing at the end of a film, or at the end of a multi-part serial episode, where the plot ending and the fate of the protagonist(s) are left unresolved; the name was derived from the movie serials of the 1930's where each week the hero (or heroine) was perilously left dangling from a cliff to increase interest for the next episode (sequel).

Climax: The highest point of anxiety or tension in a story or film in which the central character/protagonist faces, confronts, and deals with the consequence(s) of all his/her actions, or faces the antagonist in a climactic battle or final engagement; a crisis often leads to a climax; also called the film's high point, zenith, apex, or crescendo; a climax may be followed by an anti-climax or denouement.

Climbing villain: Villains being chased at the end of a movie inevitably disregard all common sense and begin climbing up something—a staircase, a church tower, a mountain—thereby trapping themselves at the top.

Clipping: The phenomenon where an input signal exceeds the capability of electronic or digital equipment to reproduce the signal. This results in an audible distortion (analog) or an incomprehensible noise (digital).

Close captioned: A system which displays the current dialog on screen for deaf or hard-of-hearing viewers. Contrast with subtitles, intertitles.

Close Shot (CS): The conventional definition of a close shot is one where an entire human face from chin or lower neck to top of head or equivalent part of the physiognomy or object fills the frame.

Close-up (CU): A shot taken from a close distance in which the scale of the object is magnified, appears relatively large and fills the entire frame to focus attention and emphasize its importance; i.e., a person's head from the shoulders or neck up is a commonly-filmed close-up; a tight shot makes the subject fill almost the entire frame; also extreme close-up (ECU or XCU) is a shot of a part of a character (e.g., face, head, hands) to emphasize detail; also known as detail shot or close on; contrast to long-shot (LS).

C-mount: A screw mount type of lens, commonly used on smaller 16mm cameras, like the Bolex.

Co-axial magazine: A type of magazine with two chambers side by side, with the supply and take up rolls rather like wheels mounted on either end of the same axle.

Code numbers: Inked-on edge numbers, usually added to a workprint and mag track after syncing, so that corresponding sound and picture can always be properly aligned during editing. They are also used for the general organization of the footage. Sometimes the term edge numbers are used, and although this is not incorrect, care should be taken that it is understood that you are talking about the inked-on numbers and not the Latent Edge Numbers.

Coded edge numbers: A system of marking films with a series of sequential numbers for the purpose of maintaining an established synchronous relationship.

Coin: A slang term for money or financing.

Cole rule, The: No movie made since 1977 containing a character with the first name "Cole" has been any good.

Color (film): A phenomenon of light or visual perception that enables one to differentiate otherwise identical objects caused by differing qualities of the light reflected or emitted; contrast to black and white.

Color consultant: A technical advisor with expertise in film stock and film developing, who provides advice for cinematographers and color timers.

Color temperature: Term that describes the color of light sources; literally, the temperature at which a blackbody emits enough radiant energy to evoke a color equivalent to that coming from a given light source. A high color temperature corresponds to bluer light, a low color temperature to yellow light. The color temperature of daylight is around 5500K.

Color timing: A process which adjusts the final print so that colors match from shot to shot, regardless of the film stock and camera used to shoot the scene. So named because one aspect is adjusting the exposure time of each shot. Performed by a color timer.

Colorist: An image artist who, during post-production of a movie or television show, utilizes computer-based alteration/ correction programs to go through the movie/show frame by frame to insure color and light continuity. The colorist may also tweak colors to stylistically heighten them.

Colorization: A film alteration process where an operator digitally alters a black and white image to include color. It is a controversial practice because many filmmakers and viewers believe it fundamentally alters an artistic creation. Early attempts at colorization in the 1980's were relatively crude in their shading range. Examples of this kind of alteration are versions of Casablanca and It's a Wonderful Life. Citizen Kane is notable in that Orson Welles was able to legally prevent its alteration.

Combo box: A six pocket stage box that can be converted from three-phase four-wire to single phase three-wire operation.

Combo stand: A heavy duty 2K stand without wheels. It is called a combo because it can be used for both reflectors and lights.

Comedian (comedienne): An actor who specializes in genre films that are designed to elicit laughter from audiences; also known as a comic.

Comedy (film): A film with elicits laughter or humor by celebrating or showing the eternal ironies of human existence; types include screwball, dark/black, farce, slapstick, dead-pan, parody, romantic comedy, etc.

Comic relief: A humorous or farcical interlude in a dramatic film, usually provided by a buffoonish character, intended to relieve the dramatic, built-up tension or heighten the emotional impact by means of contrast.

Coming-of-age (film): A film associated with difficult teen rites of passage (from adolescence to adulthood), the onset of puberty, the loss of naive innocence and childhood dreams, the experience of growing up, achieving sexual identity, etc.

Command performance: A great performance in a film by an actor, sometimes referring to the one before his or her death; it originally referred to a special performance that was requested by a sovereign, royal, head of state, or other important person.

Commentary: An objective opinion or description of characters or events occurring in the film, presented from an omniscient point of view by a commentator; the commentator's voice comes from off-camera, and is presented on the soundtrack as a voice-over; also refers to one of the added features on various DVDs in which a cast member, director, film critic, or film historian 'comments' on the film in some way.

Compander: Refers to a device that compresses an input signal and expands the output signal in order to reduce noise.

Compilation film: A film made up of shots, scenes, or sequences from other films.

Completion bond: An insurance guarantee that principal photography on a given film will be completed. It indemnifies a production against the unforeseen costs of any type, whether or not they result from problems which are covered by other types of insurance.

Complication: A plot event that complicates or tightens the tension of a film.

Composer: A musician whose music appears in a movie's score. Most movies have at least some original music written for the score, usually after the relevant parts of the movie have been filmed.

Composite print: In post-production, when a print of a film is struck from an edited negative and incorporates both the picture and the sound tracks, it is said to be a composite print. The creation of such a print usually marks the end of the editing process.

Composition: Refers to the arrangement of different elements (i.e., colors, shapes, figures, lines, movement, and lighting) within a frame and in a scene

Compression: The reduction of a span of amplitudes done for the purpose of limiting the reproduction of those amplitudes.

Concert film (rock or comedy): A film that records the live concert performance of musician(s), a band/group, or stand-up comic(s); concert films are often edited over the course of many performances and/or staged for the camera with multiple set-ups, and can be considered pseudo-documentaries; rock concerts are aka rockumentary.

Condenser microphone: The simplest type of microphone in which the capacitance (electrical charge) is varied by sound, causing movement in one plate (diaphragm) in relation to a fixed backplate.

Conductor: A person who directs the orchestra's performance of the score, often the composer.

Conformations: Progressive versions of a film in the editing stage are known as conformations, often identified by date. Conformations are only of any significance on a large production where different editing departments should be sure to be working with the latest conformation.

Conforming: The word to describe the negative cutter's matching of the original to the workprint.

Construction co-ordinator: Financial responsibilities include budgeting, tracking costs, generating reports, etc. Through drawings, a construction co-ordinator is directed artistically by the Production Designer and Art Director to produce their "vision" in three dimensions. Also responsible for the physical integrity of the structures built by the construction department.

Construction of meaning: The manner in, and devices by which, linguistic, filmic, or other texts generate meaning.

Contact printing: The method used by the lab to copy film. A contact print is made on a machine called (sensibly enough) a Contact Printer, in which the original film and unexposed print stock are sandwiched together, emulsion against emulsion, and are run at a constant speed past a light which shines through the original, exposing the print stock with the same image. All workprints, answer prints and release prints are contact prints. The only other type of printing is Optical Printing, which is usually done to add an effect or to blow up or make a reduction print.

Contingency: A designated amount of a budget which is added in anticipation of potential cost overruns.

Continuity: The system of editing that developed in the early 20th century to provide a continuous and clear movement of events/images in a film; refers to the final edited structure of a completed film, with the events or scenes/sequences arranged as if they had occurred continuously, when, in fact, they were shot out of sequence; continuity also refers to the degree to which a film is self-consistent without errors, jump cuts, or mis-matched shots and details; a continuity cut refers to a editing cut that takes the viewer seamlessly, unobtrusively, and logically from one sequence or scene to another, to propel the narrative along; a blooper or flub is a continuity error.

Continuity editing: The editing technique most favored by Hollywood and generally throughout the world, continuity editing seeks to create the illusion of seamless action, movement, and, ultimately, narrative. It does so by deploying a strategy consisting of procedures which, in direct contradiction to montage theory, hides (or at least minimizes) the shift from one cut to the next, in effect making the edit as "transparent" as possible.

Continuity report: A detailed list of the events that occured during the filming of a scene. Typically recorded are production and crew identification, camera settings, environmental conditions, the status of each take, and exact details of the action that occurs. By recording all possible sources of variation, the report helps cut down continuity error between shots or even during reshooting.

Continuity: The degree to which a movie is self-consistent. For example, a scene where an actor is wearing a hat when seen from one camera angle and not from another would lack continuity. A person is often employed to check that continuity is maintained since reshooting embarrassing lapses in continuity can be prohibitively expensive.

Continuous printing: A method of printing in which both the original and the raw stock move continuously past the point of exposure.

Contract player: An actor (both stars and bit players) who has a contractual commitment or agreement to a studio/producer/ company.

Control track: A recorded track used to adjust or manipulate a recording or playback device. Generally, these are used to maintain consistent playback speed of video and/or sound recorders consistent with the recorded speed.

Conventions: The expected elements in a type of film, without question, thought, or judgment.

Coocoloris: A fancier way of saying Gobo or Cookie.

Cookie: A flat board, like a flag, but full of irregular holes used for creating a pattern of shadows when put in front of a light.

Cooter rule, The: When the young good-looking hero goes back to his boyhood farmhouse, he'll inevitably have a fight at the dinner table with an older, less attractive brother. The fight is usually about abandoning the farm and "Spitting on Daddy's memory" or the hero's annoying use of correct grammar. The hero storms out of the house, and sits down on a fence in the backyard. He is followed by his sweet, long-suffering sister-in-law. She says, "Trap, you're gonna have to forgive Cooter/Hunter/Trip/Billy Bob. He loves you. He don't mean nothin'. It's just his way, is all."

Co-producer: A producer who performs a substantial portion of a creative producing function, or who is primarily responsible for one or more managerial producing functions. A co-producer has less responsibility than a producer for the completion of a project. Note that if a project has more than one producer, it doesn't mean that these individuals are "co-producers" in the technical sense of that term.

Copyright: The protection of a creative work by the law. Only the holder of the copyright can distribute, copy, broadcast and sell the work without express permission. Often bought by filmmakers as a property. After a certain period of time following the copyright owner's death, the work becomes public domain, and is free to all.

Core: A plastic hub used to hold film without a reel. There are 2 inch cores (small cores) and 3 inch cores (large cores). 2 inch cores can also be called camera cores.

Corrected print: Same as a Timed Print.

Corrections: Further changes in the timing of a print are known as corrections.

Costume (or wardrobe) and costume design: Refers to the garments or clothing worn by actors/performers in a film; a costume (or wardrobe) designer researches, designs, and selects the costumes to be appropriate to the film's time period, the characters, their location, and their occupations, whereas the costumer (or stylist) is responsible for acquiring, selecting, manufacturing, and/or handling the clothing and accessories; a costume drama is a film set in a particular historical time period, often with elaborate costuming.

Costume designer: A person who designs the costumes for a movie.

Costume supervisor: The person in charge of costumes, usually preparing them for use and making sure they are accurate and faithful to the designs. Other responsibilities include consulting with the designers and training, supervising, and scheduling the costume staff.

Costume: The clothes worn by actors when being filmed.

Costumer: A person responsible for handling the costumes worn by actors.

Costumes: The person or department responsible for obtaining wardrobe items specified by the costume designer. Most items are borrowed from the studio's costume stock or rented from outside companies; others may be created specifically for the production.

Counter: A device for measuring lengths of film by counting the number of frames.

Coupler: A chemical incorporated into the emulsion of color film stocks which produces a dye image associated with the developed silver image.

Courtroom drama: A drama and/or mystery story, in which the main protagonist is a lawyer, and a majority of the drama and dramatic action takes place in a courtroom setting; the plot revolves around the preparation of a trial and its result of guilt or innocence.

Cover set: A location which is kept in reserve to serve as an alternate shooting site in case the chosen shooting site is unusable. It is most commonly used in the context of shooting planned for an out of doors location.

Coverage: Coverage is used to describe the architecture of breaking down a script into the shots that will allow the scene to be cut together. Although coverage addresses the bare-bones question of getting shots that will cut together smoothly, it is important not to be too distracted from bigger aesthetic question of getting the right shots for the scene to work.

Cowboy shot: A shot framed from mid-thigh up. Got its name during the filming of many westerns, when this was a common framing used.

CP filters: Color printing filters made in precise density values for the colors; yellow, cyan, and magenta.

Crab dolly: A metallic camera dolly (usually aluminum) which has an incorporated though relatively short crane on which the camera is mounted. It moves on rubber-covered wheels and gets its name from the fact that its very tight turning radius and four articulated wheels enable it to virtually move sideways.

Craft service: The person (or people) available to assist the other crafts which include camera, sound, electricians, grips, props, art director, set decorator, hair and makeup, service the other crafts during the actual shooting of a motion picture, with tasks including providing snacks and cleaning the set.

Crane shot: A camera shot taken from a large camera dolly or electronic device, resembling a extendable mechanical arm (or boom), that can raise the camera up in the air above the ground 20 feet or more; the crane allows the camera to fluidly move in virtually any direction (with vertical and horizontal movement), providing shifts in levels and angles; crane shots usually provide some kind of overhead view of a scene.

Creative consultant: A multi-faceted individual that works primarily for the director of a feature, who helps with the creative process of a film in more than one field (e.g. script, special effects, photography sound design, music, etc.) In many cases, creative consultants go unaccredited, like ghost writers, for various reasons.

Creator: The writer or other primary creative force behind a movie, series, or group of characters.

Credits: In general, this term refers to the list of technical personnel, cast, and crew of a film; specifically, it refers to the list of names and functions of persons and corporations contributing and responsible for the artistic or intellectual content of a film, such as: "Story by...", "Screenplay by...", "Photography by...", etc.; sometimes distinguished from the cast (the performers in front of the camera).

Crew: Refers to those involved in the technical production of a film who are not actual performers.

Crewmembers: A collective term for anyone involved with the production of a movie who does not appear in the movie. This term is usually used to refer to the more subordinate members of a production team.

CRI: Color Reversal Intermediate. This is a duplicate color negative which is made by the reversal process.

Cribbing: Short pieces of lumber which are used for various grip purposes.

Crisis: The period of highest tension just before the climax of a film (there can be more than one); the point at which events reach their highest level of tension.

Critic: An individual who writes and/or publishes a review of a film from either an artistic or entertainment point of view. Film reviews often analyze and discuss a film's details, its content and characters, a critique of the performances, camera work, directing, editing, production, and script; film critics are usually more philosophical and theoretical than film reviewers or commentators; film criticism refers to the analysis of the narrative, historical and stylistic characteristics of film; 'critics' is sometimes abbreviated as crix.

Critical end!: What to label your film can when turning it in at the lab when the roll ran out during a very important shot and you want to make sure you get every last frame possible.

Cross cutting: Cutting back, giving the impression of parallel action and the two events happening simultaneously. Famous examples include the finale of D. W. Griffith's *Intolerance* (1916), where the chase to save the pardoned hero from execution in the modern story is cross cut with Christ's procession to Calgary; and the scene in *The Godfather* (1972), where the baptism of Michael Corleone's godson is cross cut with the violent elimination of Corleone's underworld rivals.

Cross modulation test: Sometimes called "cross mod" for short. This is a test the Mixing House will do in conjunction with the lab you plan to use to make sure the optical track is exposed and developed for optimal sound quality.

Cross processing: A technique used much more by still photographers. Cross processing is the use of color reversal film stock to be developed as a negative. A positive print struck from that negative will have strange and rich colors, intense contrast and on overall yellowish hue.

Crosscut: The technique of interweaving pieces of two or more scenes, usually in order to show simultaneous actions or illuminate themes.

Cross-cutting: The editing technique of alternating, interweaving, or interspersing one narrative action (scene, sequence, or event) with another - usually in different locations or places, thus combining the two; this editing method suggests parallel action (that takes place simultaneously); often used to dramatically build tension and suspense in chase scenes, or to compare two different scenes; also known as inter-cutting or parallel editing.

Crossfade: The gradual mix of sound sources accomplished by the simultaneous manipulation of two or more mix console faders.

Crossmodulation tests: Tests which are used to determine the correct negative and print densities for a variable area optical sound track.

Cross-over and cross-over appeal: A film or production that is made for one audience, but may easily 'cross-over' to another unexpected audience; also refers to a film, actor, or production that appeals to different demographic groups or age groups and can move between two or more distinct franchises.

Crossover: The frequency at which a signal is split in order to feed separate parts of a loudspeaker system.

Crosstalk: In stereo, this is the breakthrough between channels measured as separation (in decibels) between the wanted sounds of the desired channel and the unwanted sounds from the second channel.

Crowd shot: A shot or image of a large group of people (often extras) in a film.

Crystal sync: Specifically, a way of recording Sync Sound where the camera runs at correct speed with a quartz crystal-governed motor, and tape recorder records its pilottone using a built-in quartz crystal pilottone generator. The crystal is much like the kind used in a quartz watch. Unlike cable sync, the camera and tape recorder are not attached.

C-stand: A type of light stand with fixed legs that swing out, or together when not in use, usually equipped with an arm, and typically used to hold a flag.

Cucoloris: A perforate material used to break up light or create a shadow pattern. Also known as a cookie.

Cue cards: A device (cards, scrolling screen, teleprompter, or other mechanism) printed with dialogue provided to help an actor recite his/her lines; an electronic cue card is called a (tele)-prompter; derogatively called idiot cards or idiot sheets.

Cue patch: A piece of self adhesive magnetic or metallic material placed on the edge of film as a means of actuating a printer light change or an automatic stop on a projector.

Cue sheets: A road map, of sorts, for the mixer to find the sounds on your tracks during the mix. It is laid out as a grid with each track forming a column and time moving ahead in rows measured in 35mm footage (even if your film is 16mm you must convert the footage to 35mm).

Cue: A signal or sign for an actor to begin performing, from either another performer, from the director, or from within the script; a cue is often the last word of one character's line(s) of dialogue, when another performer is expected to 'pick up their cue' to speak.

Cueing: A term with a broad range of meanings depending on the particular context. For Voice-Over Narration or Dialogue Replacement: The marking of the cue point in a way which will permit a signal to be given to the 'talent' to begin each element of work at the appropriate time. In General: Any system used by a second person to signal 'talent' that recording should begin.

Cup blocks: Wooden blocks with a dish or indentation in the center which are used to keep the wheels of light stands from moving.

Cut: An abrupt or sudden change or jump in camera angle, location, placement, or time, from one shot to another; consists of a transition from one scene to another (a visual cut) or from one soundtrack to another (a sound cut); cutting refers to the selection, splicing and assembly by the film editor of the various shots or sequences for a reel of film, and the process of shortening a scene; also refers to the instructional word 'cut' said at the end of a take by the director to stop the action in front of the camera; cut to refers to the point at which one shot or scene is changed immediately to another; also refers to a complete edited version of a film (e.g., rough cut).

Cutaway shot: A brief shot that momentarily interrupts a continuously-filmed action, by briefly inserting another related action, object, or person (sometimes not part of the principal scene or main action), followed by a cutback to the original shot; often filmed from the POV of the character and used to break up a sequence and provide some visual relief, or to ease the transition from one shot to the next, or to provide additional information, or to hint at an impending change; reaction shots are usually cutaways; cross-cutting is a series of cutaways and cutbacks indicating concurrent action; a cutaway is different from an insert shot.

Cutaway: A shot, usually a closeup of some detail, or landscape, that is used break up a matching action sequence, and is often very helpful in editing to rescue you from an impossible break in continuity or coverage. A cutaway, as the name implies, is a shot that does not focus on some detail of the shot before or after it but cuts away from the action at hand, unlike an Insert Shot. However, the two terms are sometimes used vaguely or interchangeably, although this is not always a useful practice. The best cutaways are the ones that have some logic to them, that relate to the scene.

Cutting: The selection and assembly of the various shots or sequences for a reel of film.

Cyan: A blue-green color which is the complementary color to red.

Cyberpunk: A subgenre of science fiction that typically has elements which include a futuristic tone, massive urban areas in decay and poverty, partial environmental collapse, extremely powerful business corporations, random street gang violence with the overall presence of extremely powerful computer, robotic and information technology. Blade Runner is considered the definitive cyberpunk movie.

Cyc lights: Row lights for evenly illuminating a cyclorama or other background.

Cyclorama: Permanent background built in a studio which is nearly always coved or curved at the floor line to create a shadowless, unending backdrop.

D

Dailies: The immediately processed, rough cuts or first prints of a film (w/o special effects or edits) for the director (producer, or editor) to review, to see how the film came out after the day's (or previous day's) shooting; more commonly in the form of videotape dailies nowadays; aka rushes (referring to the haste taken to make them available); used to determine if continuity is correct, if props are missing or out of place, or if sound is poor, etc., to help decide whether to re-shoot.

Dance floor: A floor built of 3/4 inch plywood which is usually covered with masonite to provide a smooth surface for free-form dollying.

Dark horse: In film terms, a little-known, unlikely movie (often a sleeper, a low-budget film, indie, or a foreign film) that is, surprisingly, nominated for a major award (i.e., Academy Award or Golden Globe).

DAT (Digital Audio Tape): Two-channel digital audio has become increasingly common as a professional master reference and for use in field recording.

DAW (Digital Audio Workstation): A computer-based recording and editing machine used for manipulating sounds.

Day for night: The process of filming in the daytime a scene which in the action of the narrative occurs at night. The effect of nighttime is accomplished both by the pattern of lighting and by a special lens filter. Because this process was first used by American cinematographers, it became known in France as "La Nuit Americaine", or, the "American Night".

Day out of days: A form designating the workdays for various cast or crewmembers of a given production.

Day-for-night shot: A cinematographic technique for using shots filmed during the day to appear as moonlit night shots on the screen, by using different lenses, filters, special lighting and underexposure; very common during the 50s and in the 60s, but rarely used in present-day films.

Daylight balanced: The color temperature of daylight which is 5,400K on the color temperature scale (it does vary during the day, being higher at noon and lower in the earlier and later parts of the day). Color film for outdoor shooting is balanced for daylight, otherwise the image would appear blue in hue. If daylight balanced film is used indoors without a correction filter the image will have a orange hue.

Daylight spool: An aluminum spool holding 100 feet of film with solid, opaque sides, painted black, which will protect the film from becoming completely exposed when loading a camera in daylight. The name daylight spool comes from the fact that the film may be loaded without total darkness. There are also 400 foot daylight spools, but these are very rarely used as they do not always work very well in a magazine.

Dead spot: A place in which a sound waves are canceled by reflections arriving out of phase with the wanted signal thus creating an area of silence or poor audibility.

Dead sync: An editorial term meaning that sound and picture elements are perfectly aligned.

Dead teenager movie: Generic term for any movie primarily concerned with killing teen-agers, without regard for logic, plot, performance, humor, etc. Often imitated, never worse than in the FRIDAY THE 13TH sequels. Required complete loss of common sense on the part of the characters. Sample dialogue: "All of our friends have been found horribly mutilated. It is midnight and we are miles from help. Hey, let's take off our clothes, walk through the dark woods, and go skinny-dipping!"

Deadly change-of-heart: When the cold heart of a villain softens and he turns into a good guy, the plot will quickly require him to be killed, usually after maudlin final words.

Deadpan: A specific type of comedic device in which the performer assumes an expressionless (deadpan) quality to her/his face demonstrating absolutely no emotion or feeling.

Deal memo: A form which lists the pertinent details of salary, guaranteed conditions, and other essentials of a work agreement negotiated between a member of the cast or crew and a production company.

Decoder: The device which reads the enclosed signal or pulse and turns it into some form of usable information.

Decoupage: A French term referring to the design of a film - the arrangement of its shots.

Deep focus: A cinematographic technique which enables several planes of action, from the foreground to the deep background, to be seen simultaneously—and in focus—on the screen. Sincea number of actions can be seen in relation to one another without the need for intercutting, deep focus has significant implications for the manner in which cinematic narrative unfolds.

Deep-focus shot: A style or technique of cinematography and staging with great depth of field, preferred by realists, that uses lighting, relatively wide angle lenses and small lens apertures to simultaneously render in sharp focus both close and distant planes (including the three levels of foreground, middle-ground, and extreme background objects) in the same shot; contrast to shallow focus (in which only one plane is in sharp focus).

Degausser: A device used to erase recordings on magnetic tapes and films or to demagnetize magnetic recording heads.

Del close's rule: Never share a foxhole with a character who carries a photo of his sweetheart.

Deleted scene: Refers to a scene that was edited out of a film's final cut, for several possible reasons: the scene was poorly done, the scene was unnecessary, the film's running time needed truncation, the film was avoiding an R or NC-17 rating, the film's studio disapproved of it, etc. Deleted scenes are now commonly included on DVDs, either re-edited into a director's cut or as a separate feature.

Denouement: The point immediately following the climax when everything comes into place or is resolved; often the final scene in a motion picture.

Density: A factor which indicates the light-stopping power of a photographic image.

Depth of field: While a lens focuses on a single plane of depth, there is usually an additional area in focus behind and in front of that plane. This is depth of field. Depth of field increases as the iris is closed. There is more depth of field the wider the lens and less the longer the lens. There is a deeper area in focus the further away a lens is focused than there is when a lens is focused close. Depth of field does not spread out evenly; the entire area is about 1/3rd in front and 2/3rds behind the plane of focus. To factor together all these variables it is best to consult a depth of field table, such as the ones found in the American Cinematographer's Manual.

Designer: Someone who creates plans for visual aspects of a production (e.g. costume designer).

Detour rule: In any thriller, it is an absolute certainty that every road detour sign is a subterfuge to kidnap the occupants of a car.

Deuce: A 2K fresnel lighting unit.

Deus ex machina: Literally, the resolution of the plot by the device of a god ("deus") arriving onstage by means of a piece of equipment ("machina") and solving all the characters' problems; usually refers to an unlikely, improbable, contrived, illogical, or clumsy ending or suddenly-appearing plot device that alleviates a difficult situation or brings about a denouement - just in the nick of time; can sometimes refer to an unexpected, artificial, or improbable character.

Developing: The chemical process which converts a photographic exposure into a visible image.

DGA: Director's Guild of America. A union which represents directors, assistant directors, production managers, and various video personnel.

Dialect coach: A person who helps train an actor in diction and/or the use of accents to suit the character an actor is playing.

Dialogue coach: A person who helps train an actor in diction and/ or the use of inflections, so that his or her speech fits the character and situation.

Dialogue editor: A sound editor who specializes in editing dialogue.

Dialogue track: A sound track which carries lip sync speech.

Dialogue: Any spoken lines in a film by an actor/actress; may be considered overlapping if two or more characters speak simultaneously.

Diaphragm: A mechanical device, placed within the camera lens, whose function is to open and close according to the f-stop setting desired by the camera operator. The more open the diaphragm is, the more light which is allowed to pass and strike the film; the more closed, the less light. If this sounds familiar it is because the function of a diaphragm is almost exactly analogous to that of the iris in the human eye. Indeed, it is sometimes called the iris of a lens. In its construction, the diaphragm is made up of a series (usually five or six) of extremely thin and light metallic leaves which are mounted in a circular fashion. Being spring loaded, they may move closer towards the center of the circle around which they are mounted, or, of course, farther from it.

Diegesis: A term used in film criticism and theory, it designates the totality of the physical world experienced by the characters in a film. For example, if a character slams a door on screen and the sound of the door is heard on the sound track, the sound would be called a diegetic because we would have seen the justification for the sound on the screen as would a character in the film. On the other hand, a sudden upsurge of violins under a tender love-scene would be called a non-diegetic sound unless the love-birds were seen sitting by the fiddlers who were making the music. Diegesis is not, however, limited to sounds. The credits of a film, for instance, obviously not perceived by the characters but clearly so by the spectator, would be another example of non-diegetic material.

Diegetic: Simply means realistic or logically existing; refers to the narrative elements of a film (such as spoken dialogue, other sounds, action) that appear in, are shown, or naturally originate within the content of the film frame; the opposite is non-diegetic elements, such as sounds (e.g., background music, the musical score, a voice-over, or other sounds) w/o an origin within the film frame itself; in an objective shot, the most common camera shot, it simply presents what is before the camera in the diegesis of the narrative

Diegetic sound: A sound that is created by something or someone visible on the screen or whose source is implied to be present by the action of the film.

Differential rewind: A device designed to permit simultaneous winding of film on more than one reel at a time even though the diameters of the rolls are unequal.

Diffusion: The reduction or softening of the harshness or intensity of light achieved by using a diffuser or translucent sheet (lace or silk) in front of the light to cut down shadows; materials include screen, glass, filters, gauze, wire mesh, or smoke.

Digital compositing: A technique whereby separately filmed components are combined through digital editing. Contrast with optical printing.

Digital editing: Editing a portion of a movie by digitizing one or more frames and altering them electronically or combining them with other digitized images, and then printing the modified frame.

Digital imaging technician: A person who provides on-set quality control, image manipulation & color correction, production continuity, trouble shooting and consultation to assist in fullfilling the requirements and vision of the cinematographer in film-style digital production.

Digital recording: A method of recording in which samples of the original analog signal are encoded on tape or disk as binary information for storage or processing. The signal can then be copied repeatedly with no degradation.

Digital theatre systems: A company which has produced a digital soundtrack standard. Competitors include Dolby Digital and SDDS.

Digital versatile disc: Digital Versatile Discs resemble audio CDs in appearance, but have a much higher storage capacity. Hence, they can store rich digital media such as video in addition to audio and computer software. DVD was once called "Digital Video Disc" but the name change reflects its wider uses. As a video medium, DVD offers full length feature films to be stored with exceptional picture quality accompanied by high end digital sound, such as Dolby Digital and DTS.

Digital: A reference to a system whereby a continuously variable analog signal is reduced and encoded into discrete binary bits that establish a mathematical model of an original signal or other information.

Dimmer: A device for varying power to the lights.

Dingle: Branches which are placed in front of a light as a cookie would to cut the light and provide a shadow pattern.

Diopter: The diopter is part of the viewfinding system of a camera that can be adjusted to compensate for your own particular eyesight, allowing you to see the groundglass clearly.

Direct sound: The technique of recording sound simultaneously with the image.

Directing animator: The animator responsible for creating the key poses or key frames of an animation.

Directing the eye: In cinematographic terms, using light and dark to emphasize what is important (that which is kept lit) and what isn't important (that which is kept dark)

Directional characteristic: The variation in response or perception for different angles of sound incidence.

Director (and directing): The creative artist responsible for complete artistic control of all phases of a film's production (such as making day-to-day determinations about sound, lighting, action, casting, even editing), for translating/ interpreting a script into a film, for guiding the performances of the actors in a particular role and/or scene, and for supervising the cinematography and film crew. The director is usually the single person most responsible for the finished product, although he/she couldn't make a film without support from many other artists and technicians; often the director is called a helmer (at-the-helm); the assistant director is known as the a.d. ; the director of photography (or cinematographer) is known as the d.p.

Director of photography: More than simply the head of the camera crew, the director of photography is responsible for all aspects of cinematography during a production. This would include, primarily but by no means exclusively, lighting the scene, deciding on which film stock to use, at what f-stop to film the scene, how to deal with problems of focus, and so on. Working in the closest possible collaboration with the director, and having the crews of electricians and grips under his or her control, the DOP ensures that the deployment of the cinematographic apparatus for each shot will render exactly what the director desires. Any director, therefore, must have absolute faith in the director of photography.

Director: The principal creative artist on a movie set. A director is usually (but not always) the driving artistic source behind the filming process, and communicates to actors the way that he/she would like a particular scene played. A director's duties might also include casting, script editing, shot selection, shot composition, and editing. Typically, a director has complete artistic control over all aspects of the movie, but it is not uncommon for the director to be bound by agreements with either a producer or a studio. In some large productions, a director will delegate less important scenes to a second unit.

Director's cut: Contracts under the terms of the Hollywood Director's Guild usually allow 6 weeks for a director to assemble a cut of the movie without studio interference as he or she would like it to be seen. This *director's cut* is fully edited and has a synchronized soundtrack. This cut is usually not color corrected or density corrected and may not even have the final music and effects tracks. In more recent times the term *Director's Cut* has taken on a popular meaning that implies a polished final cut of the movie that the director has complete artistic control over.

Directors guild-producer training plan: The Director's Guild of America has various training programs whereby successful applicants are placed in various productions and can gain experience working in the film or television industry.

Dirt equals virtue: In technology movies, a small, dingy, cluttered little lab and eccentric personnel equal high principles; large, well-lighted facilities mask sinister motives.

Discovery shot: In a film scene, when the moving or panning camera unexpectedly comes upon or 'discovers' an object or person previously undisclosed to the viewer.

Disney-fication or Disney-fied: Refers to the making of an adapted, sanitized, 'family-friendly' version of a book or play, by removing objectionable elements and modifying plot elements to make the tale more acceptable, entertaining, predictable and popular for mass consumption by audiences, as first exercised by the Disney studios in the 50s; now used as a derogatory term for how popular culture has been homogenized and cultural diversity has been minimized.

Dissolve: A transitional editing technique between two sequences, shots or scenes, in which the visible image of one shot or scene is gradually replaced or blended with the image from another shot or scene; for an instant, one image is superimposed on or gradually blended with the other to soften the cut; often used to suggest the passage of time and to transform one scene to the next; lap dissolve is shorthand for 'over'lap dissolve; also known as a soft transition or dissolve to.

Distortion: A modification of the original signal appearing in the output of audio equipment which had not been present in the input.

Distribution: The rights to market and distribute the finished film to different exhibitors for a fee.

Distributor: The organization responsible for coordinating the distribution of the finished movie to exhibitors, as well as the sale of videos, laserdiscs, and other media versions of movies.

Docudrama: TV term for extended-length program which stars a disease or social problem and co-stars performers willing to give interviews on how they experienced personal growth through their dramatic contact with same.

Documentary: A non-fiction (factual), narrative film with real people (not performers or actors); typically, a documentary is a low-budget, journalistic record of an event, person, or place; a documentary film-maker should be an unobtrusive observer - like a fly-on-the-wall, capturing reality as it happens; aka doc or docu; also called direct cinema; one type is termed docudrama; contrast with cinema verite and mockumentary.

Dogme 95: A filmmaking movement launched in 1995 by Danish directors Lars von Trier and Thomas Vinterberg, among others. The Dogme 95 Manifesto renounces special effects and other forms of "gimmickry" in favor of stripped-down techniques. In order to qualify for Dogme status, filmmakers must abide by the following ten rules: 1. Shooting must be done on location. Props and sets must not be brought in (if a particular prop is necessary for the story, a location must be chosen where this prop is to be found). 2. The sound must never be produced apart from the images or vice versa.. 3. The camera must be hand-held. Any movement or immobility attainable in the hand is permitted. 4. The film must be in color. Special lighting is not acceptable. 5. Optical work and filters are forbidden. 6. The film must not contain superficial action. 7. Temporal and geographical alienation are forbidden. 8. Genre movies are not acceptable. 9. The film format must be Academy 35mm. 10. The director must not be credited.

Dolby digital: This is a 5.1 channel digital film format that if optically recorded on to a film release print in the blocks of space located between the film's sprocket holes.

Dolby noise reduction: Dolby Laboratories, Inc has produced a number of noise reduction and sound enhancement processes. Competitors include DTS and SDDS.

Dolby SR: Spectral Recording. An encoding/decoding noise reduction system developed by Dolby Laboratories and used increasingly in film sound.

Dolly (shot): Refers to a moving shot in which the perspective of the subject and background is changed; the shot is taken from a camera that is mounted on a hydraulically-powered wheeled camera platform (sometimes referred to as a truck or dolly), pushed on rails (special tracks) and moved smoothly and noiselessly during filming while the camera is running; a pull-back shot (or dolly out) is the moving back ('tracking back') of the camera from a scene to reveal a character or object that was previously out of the frame, dolly in is when the camera moves closer ('tracking in') towards the subject, and dollying along with (or 'tracking within') refers to the camera moving beside the subject; also known as tracking shot, trucking shot, follow shot, or traveling shot; contrast with zoom shots.

Dolly shot: A dolly shot is one where the camera is placed on a dolly and is moved while filmming. Also known as a tracking shot.

Dolly tracks: A set of tracks upon which a camera can be moved.

Dolly: A dolly is a small truck which rolls along dolly tracks carrying the camera,some of the camera crew and occasionally the director. "Dolly" is also the action of moving the camera towards (dolly up/in) or away from (dolly/pull back) the object that it is pointing at. The term often appears in screenplays. There is a subtle difference between the results of a zoom shot and a dolly shot. In a zoom, the relative positions and sizes of all objects in the frame remains the same, whereas in a dolly shot this will change as the camera moves. Alfred Hitchcock's much-imitated shot in Vertigo used a combination zoom-in and dolly back, resulting in a dramatic change in perspective.

Domestic box office: Total money spent on tickets by moviegoers in the United States and Canada.

Doors: Hinged metallic panes mounted on a device which permits them to be placed in front of a lighting instrument. Closing or opening them determines the height, width, narrowness or thickness of the stream of light.

Doorway Dolly: A plywood dolly with four soft tires which is narrow enough to fit through a doorway. It is used to carry a camera on a tripod or for transporting other heavy items.

Dope Sheet: A list of scenes from the script that have already been filmed, or a list of the contents of an exposed reel of film stock. An accurate dope sheet is the responsibility of the assistant cameraman.

Dots: Small nets and flags used to control light.

Double Bill: Two movies shown consecutively, typically for a discounted single admission price. Often the movies are sequels or are otherwise related (by genre, eg).

Double exposure: A double exposure occurs when (prior to development) an exposed piece of film is reshot with a second image on top of the first. Several exposures can be made, but it still valid to call it a "double" exposure rather than a "triple" or "quadruple" exposure. It is perfectly alright to say "five double exposures," as numerically incongruous as it may sound.

Double perf: 16mm film with a row of perforations running along both edges. On the film can this will be indicated by **2R** appearing on the label.

Double reel: In 35mm a double reel is 2 single reels joined together, the maximum size being 2,000 feet. Double reels are labeled 1 A/B, 2 A/B etc., to distinguish them from single reels.

Double system projector: A projector designed to project a workprint and play a mag track in sync.

Double system: The term double system refers to sound and picture as two separate elements, recorded, edited or projected in sync. 16mm and 35mm use the double system format. A camera photographs the picture and a tape recorder records the sound. In the end, the final print is Single System, combining sound and picture onto the same piece of print stock.

Double take: A comedic convention that refers to the way in which an actor first looks at an object (subject, event, scene, etc.), then looks away, and then snaps his head back to the situation for a second look - with surprise, disgust, sexual longing, etc.; a variation is termed a spit-take.

Double: An actor who stands in for another actor in certain scenes, some of which may involve dangerous circumstances or require special skills. Sometimes body doubles are used in scenes that call for nudity or intimacy. Contrast with stand-in.

Double-system sound: Sound and picture on separate transports. This refers to the normal methodology of recording the picture on a camera while recording sound of a separate magnetic tape recorder.

Down under rule: No film set in Australia is allowed to use the word Australia in its title where "Down Under" is an acceptable alternative.

Draftsman: A person who creates the plans for set construction.

Dresser: A wardrobe assistant who helps actors with their costumes.

Drift: Flutter which occurs at random rates.

Drive-in: An outdoor movie theatre in which the patrons viewed a film from their automobile; films projected were often B-films or low-budget films; reached their peak in terms of popularity and numbers in the 1970s; also called a passion pit, ozoner; contrast with a hard top (or indoor movie theatre).

Driver: A person who drives either equipment or passenger trucks, typically between location shootings, sets, and the studio. The chief driver is called the transportation captain.

Drop Frame: American system of time code generation that adjusts the generated data every minute to compensate for the spread of the NTSC television system running at 29.97 frames per second.

Drop Out: Loss of a portion of a signal, usually due to a loss of a tape's oxide coating or due to dirt or grease covering a portion of a tape.

Drop-In: The process of inserting recorded audio by playing up to a chosen point and switching from playback to record mode.

DTS: This is a film sound system which utilizes a CD-ROM disc which is sychronized to film by means of timecode which is optically encoded into the exhibition film print.

Dub (or dubbing): The act of putting a new soundtrack on a film or adding a soundtrack (of dialogue, sound effects, or music) after production, to match the action of already-filmed shots; also refers to adding translated dialogue to a foreign-language film; as opposed to direct sound - which is sound recorded when filming a scene; contrast to looping.

Dub stage: Term generally used in California but to refer to the room where the final audio mix is made for a program or film. It might also be known as a mix stage.

Dub: To make a taped copy of any progam source record, CD, tape. Also, the copy itself. Sometimes used to refer to the ADR process.

Dubber: A high quality sound reproducer which is mixed with outputs from other dubbers that are generally loaded with sprocketed magnetic film.

Dubbing: An actor's voice synchronization with lip movements which are not the originally recorded sound. This is used to replace unusable dialogue or recordings, and also used to prepare foreign films for new markets.

Dunning: The process or technique of combining shots filmed in a studio with background footage shot elsewhere.

Dupe: A dupe is a positive copy of a positive. A dupe can also be a negative copy of a negative. A dupe is a print made in the reversal process. It can sometimes be clearer to call something a dupe, because to simply say "positive print" you could just mean a positive copy of a negative, which would not be a dupe.

Dutch angle: This is the process where a camera is angled so that the horizontal frame line is not parallel to the horizon.

Dutch tilt: A composition with the camera viewing the scene at a diagonal. Same as a canted angle. Some nice examples can be seen in Carol Reed's "The Third Man."

Duvetyne: A heavy black cloth, treated with fire proofing material, which is used for blacking out windows, making teasers, hiding cables, and hundreds of other uses.

Dynamic distortion: Alteration of volume range of a sound when it is transmitted.

Dynamic frame: A photographic technique used to mask the projected image size and shape to any ratio that seems appropriate for the scene (e.g., the image narrows as an actor passes through a narrow passageway, and then widens as he emerges).

Dynamic range: The difference in decibels between the loudest and quietest portions of audio.

E

E.C.N.: E.C.N. stands for Eastman Color Negative. It is simply your developed negative.

E.D.L.: E.D.L. stands for Edit Decision List. It is used by the negative cutter when you have cut digitally, in order to conform the original without the usual workprint.

E.I.: Abbreviation for Exposure Index.

E.S.: Abbreviation for Editorial Sync.

Ear: To put a flag up on the side of a lighting unit to block light. Better known as a 'sider'.

EBU: European Broadcast Union. This generally identifies a 25 FPS time code standard.

Echo: A sound wave that has been reflected and returned with sufficient magnitude and delay to be perceived as a wave distinct from that which was initially transmitted.

Edge fog: Exposure along the edge of the film from raw light, in most cases from a lightleak, due to the camera door not being taped. Edge Fog can sometimes be visible in the frame or sometimes outside of the frame effecting the clarity of the latent edge numbers.

Edge numbers or **Latent edge numbers: 1.** The edge numbers are small numbers running along the edge of the film, in between the perf in 16mm, and just to the far side of them in 35mm. The are photographed onto the film in its manufacture, and are there to aid the negative cutter in lining up shots in the process of conforming the negative. They are sometimes called latent edge numbers to distinguish them from inked-on code numbers. **2.** Code Numbers are sometimes called edge numbers.

Edge track: A standard position for the placement of the audio on a single perforation magnetic film.

Edison plug: An ordinary household plug with two flat blades and a ground pin.

Edit Decision List (EDL): The list of SMPTE codes, in footage and frames, and including instructions for fades, dissolves and other special effects which corresponds to all the segments that the editor of a film or videotape production has decided to use in the final cut.

Edit master: Video industry term for the tape containing the finished (edited) program.

Edit points: Also known as "edit in" and "edit out." The beginning and end points of an edit when a video program or soundtrack is being assembled.

Edit: **1.** The cutting and arranging of shots. **2.** In the different stages, or at the completion of editing the edited film itself can be referred to as "the cut" or "the edit."

Editor: The process (performed by a film editor) of selecting, assembling, arranging, collating, trimming, structuring, and splicing-joining together many separate camera takes (includes sound also) of exposed footage (or daily rushes) into a complete, determined sequence or order of shots (or film) - that follows the script; digital editing refers to changing film frames by digitizing them and modifying them electronically; relational editing refers to editing shots to suggest a conceptual link between them; an editor works in a cutting room; the choice of shots has a tremendous influence upon the film's final appearance.

Editing bench: A workbench with rewinds attached, and sometimes a built-in light table in the center.

Editing: At the most basic level, this means simply joining individual pieces of film to make up scenes, sequences, groups of sequences, and finally the entire film. At its first stages the pieced together version is called an assembly. As this is further refined it is called a first cut, then, many refinements later, a final cut. The basic level, however, doesn't nearly tell the whole tale, for it is precisely the juxtaposition of shots, the one to the other throughout a film, which gives motion pictures their unique power, whether the shots are arranged according to the precepts of continuity editing or montage theory or some combination of the two. Editing, therefore, makes a fundamental contribution to the construction of meaning which the whole film text generates.

Editorial sync: A set of sync marks on picture and sound that line up at the same frame, as opposed to Printer's Sync, where the picture and sound are displaced. Sometimes it is usedful to label a sync mark E.S. to know that it is an Editorial Sync mark.

Effective output level: The microphone sensitivity rating defined as the ratio in dB of the power available relative to sound pressure.

Effects stock: Special film stock that is typically used by the second unit to generate computerized composites. Effects stock usually has finer film grain, and is usually rated several stops lower than standard stock.

Electrical department: The department in charge of all electrical matters (primarily lighting) for productions.

Electrician: The person or grip in charge of and familiar with the electrical equipment on the set.

Ellipsis: The shortening of the plot duration of a film achieved by deliberately omitting intervals or sections of the narrative story or action; an ellipsis is marked by an editing transition (a fade, dissolve, wipe, jump cut, or change of scene) to omit a period or gap of time from the film's narrative.

Emcee: Another term for master of ceremonies.

Emulsion batch: The emulsion batch is the series of numbers on the film can the come after the Emulsion Type. When the film is made, each batch is given a number so that you can shoot a single sequence with one particular batch. Just as a suit where the pants and jacket were cut from different bolts of fabric might be a little off, a sequence shot with different emulsion batches might also be a little off. From one sequence to the next, of course, this doesn't matter.

Emulsion leader: Unlike plastic leader, emulsion leader can be cement spliced.

Emulsion type: A film's emulsion type refers to the composition of its emulsion, whether it was manufactured to be fast, slow, grainy, fine-grained, colorful, pastel, black and white or color, daylight balanced, tungsten balanced, etc. The emulsion type is represented by a number. For Kodak it is a series of four numbers, such as 7248. The "72" always stands for 16mm camera stock, and the same emulsion type is found in 35mm as 5248, "52" being the designation of 35mm. Fuji uses a system where the film's emulsion type is a little more telling, such as 250D, which is daylight balanced film with an Exposure Index of 250. When picking out a stock to use the film speed, and in the case of color film, whether the film is daylight or tungsten, are the primary reasons for choosing a certain emulsion type. Allowances might also be made to achieve a certain look, as in using Kodak Vision, or Fuji film. Several different emulsion types are usually used on a project, fast for night scenes, slow for daylight scenes, etc. However, unless you are trying something novel, it is a good idea to shoot a single unbroken sequence with one emulsion type.

Emulsion: A gelatinous chemical suspension in which, most commonly, particles of silver halide are embedded. These particles have the property that when exposed to light they undergo a chemical reaction by which they group together into larger clumps. These units, the size of which represents the degree of density of light to which they were exposed, and which taken together comprise the latent image, are rendered visible by submitting the emulsion to another chemical process called development. For color film, additional layers of color sensitive dyes are added, also in the gelatinous suspension. These dyes react to the primary colors of blue, green, or red, and combine with the image-rendering qualities of the silver halide particles to form color images. Generally speaking, the smaller the number of the silver halide particles per given area (thus the larger the individual particle), the less able the film to render the image sharply. These types of film stocks are designated as coarse-grained. Conversely, the larger the number of particles (thus the smaller the individual particle), the better able the film to render sharp images. Such film stocks are designated as fine-grained.

Engine equalization law: Movie phenomenon which allows a 100hp Escort to outrun a 300hp Corvette, or vice versa, and allows large, lumbering Cadillac stretch limousines filled with bad guys to keep up with heroes in exotic sports cars.

Ensemble (film): A film with a large cast without any true leading roles, and usually with multiple plotlines regarding the characters; it also literally means 'the group of actors (and sometimes directors and designers) who are involved in a film'.

Envelope: The shape of the graph as amplitude is plotted against time. A sound's envelope includes its attack, decay, sustain and release (ADSR).

Environmental sound: General low level sound coming from the action of a film, which can either synchronous or nonsynchronous.

Epic: A costly film made on an unusually large scale or scope of dramatic production, that often portrays a spectacle with historic, ancient world, or biblical significance.

Epilogue: A short, concluding scene in a film in which characters (sometimes older) reflect on the preceding events.

Epiphany: A moment of sudden spiritual insight for the protagonist of a film, usually occurs just before or after the climax.

Episode: A self-contained segment or part of an anthology film or serial; a number of separate and complete episodes make up an episode film.

Equalization: The alteration of sound frequencies for a specific purpose, such as to remove 'noise' frequencies or to improve speech clarity.

Equity: A trade union for actors. In the UK, an actor must belong to Equity before being allowed to perform in any "legitimate" theater or film. Similar organisations exist in other countries but because other organisations often exist membership isn't as essential.

Equivalent noise: A microphone in a completely silent room still generates some residual noise. This noise can be measured and can be computed. That computation is the 'Equivalent Noise'.

Errors of continuity: Disruptions in the flow of a scene, such as a failure to match action or the placement of props across shots.

Establishing shot: Usually a long (wide-angle or full) shot at the beginning of a scene (or a sequence) that is intended to show things from a distance (often an aerial shot), and to inform the audience with an overview in order to help identify and orient the locale or time for the scene and action that follows; this kind of shot is usually followed by a more detailed shot that brings characters, objects, or other figures closer; a re-establishing shot repeats an establishing shot near the end of a sequence.

Estar base: a brand name for Polyester Base.

Exciter lamp: A special lamp in the projector used for the playback of Optical Sound. The projector reads the track by passing it between the exciter lamp a light-sensitive photo-electric cell.

Exec or exex: Abbreviations for 'executive' or 'executives'.

Executive producer: A producer who is not involved in any technical aspects of the filmmaking process, but who is still responsible for the overall production. Typically an executive producer handles business and legal issues.

Exhibition: The act of screening the feature film to the public. Also selling tickets.

Exhibitor: An organization which represents cinemas.

Experimental film: Refers to a film, usually a low-budget or indie film not oriented toward profit-making, that challenges conventional filmmaking by using camera techniques, imagery, sound, editing, and/or acting in unusual or never-before-seen ways; sometimes aka avante-garde, art films.

Exploitation film: A sensational, often trashy B-film aimed at a particular audience and designed to succeed commercially and profitably by appealing to specific psychological traits or needs in that audience without any fuller analysis or exposition; often refers to films with extremely violent or sexual scenes; not necessarily a derogatory term; various types include blaxploitation, sexploitation, splatter films.

Exposition: The conveyance (usually by dialogue or action) of important background information for the events of a story; or the set up of a film's story, including what's at stake for the characters, the initial problem, and other main problems.

Exposure index: This is the sensitivity to light of a particular type of film. It is the specific number used to measure Film Speed. Your film will list an E.I. number on the box or the film can as the film speed. It is the same as A.S.A. and I.S.O. on your light meter.

Exposure meter: A device used to measure the amount of light present upon a surface or area.

Exposure: The measure of the quantity of light to which film is exposed, a factor of lens aperture and shutter speed. when one image appears on the screen on top of another, one concrete, the other abstract; often used to suggest a thought, a feeling, dream, imagination; sometimes called Double exposure.

Expressionism (and expressionist): Refers to the distortion of reality through lighting, editing, and costumes, to reflect the inner feelings and emotions of the characters and/or the filmmaker; a cinematic style of fantasy film common in post-WWI Germany in the 1920s and 1930s, characterized by dramatic lighting, dark visual images and shadows, grotesque and fantastic shots, distorted sets and angles, heavy makeup, highly stylized acting, and symbolic mime-like action and characters; opposed to realism.

Extension tubes: These are a handy way to turn any long lens into a macro lens for ultra-close shooting. They are hollow metal tubes that are mounted between the camera and the lens. Typically they come in a set of different lengths which can be combined. It is a good idea to open up the lens a little when using an extension tube, as a little light is lost. It should be noted that they do not work when used with wide lenses.

Exterior: The designation of a scenic location as being out of doors. This does not mean, however, that the scene must be shot either on an actual location or even outside. Though the practice has faded somewhat, perfectly credible exteriors can be constructed inside a sound stage.

Extra(s): A person who appears in a movie in a non-specific, non-speaking, unnoticed, or unrecognized character role, such as part of a crowd or background, e.g., a patron in a restaurant, a soldier on a battlefield; usually without any screen credit; also termed atmosphere people; contrast with walk-on and non-speaking role, bit players, or principals.

Extreme close-up: A shot in which the subject is much larger than the frame. Provides more detail than a close-up. The abbreviation is often used in a slug line.

Eye line: Eye line is the direction an actor should look off-screen to match a reverse angle or a P.O.V. shot. It is best to give the actor an actual thing or spot to look at rather than a blank spot on an empty wall or an empty space in mid air.

Eyeline match: A technique used in visual effects to make sure an actor is looking at the "face" of the character/creature to be inserted later. One approach, used on Stuart Little (1999), is to sync a laser to the camera so that it is on only when the shutter is closed, and makes a dot where the creature's eyes would be. More commonly, a grip holds a target on a pole.

F

Fade: A transition from a shot to black where the image gradually becomes darker is a Fade Out; or from black where the image gradually becomes brighter is a Fade In. Fades are done at the lab in the printing phase, but prepared by the negative cutter, who cuts in an overlap of black into the A&B rolls. Labs will only do fades in fixed amounts, such as 24 frames, 48 frames, etc.

Fake shemp: Anyone appearing on screen whose face is not seen and who has no lines; can include stand-ins and extras. The term originated with Sam Raimi and his colleagues, who borrowed it from Hollywood lore about a stand-in used to finish Three Stooges films after Shemp Howard's death.

Fallacy of elaborate death techniques: Any method of attempting to kill someone in a movie that is more complicated than shooting, beating, strangling, etc. will inevitably fail.

Fallacy of the predictable tree: The logical error committed every time the good guy is able to predict exactly what the bad guy is going to do. For example, in FIRST BLOOD, law enforcement officials are searching the woods for John Rambo. A cop pauses under a tree. Rambo drops on him. Question: Out of all the trees in the forest, how did Rambo know which one the guy would pause under?

Fallacy of the talking killer: The villain wants to kill the hero. He has him cornered at gunpoint. All he has to do is pull the trigger. But he always talks first. He explains the hero's mistakes to him. Jeers. Laughs. And gives the hero time to think his way out of the situation, or be rescued by his buddy.

Falling villain, The: At the end of virtually every action-adventure movie, the villain must fall from a great height onto a hard surface. If possible, the villain should crash backward through a plateglass window and land on an automobile.

Fanboy effect: Certain films have a very loyal following, usually due to their source material. These people will flock to the film as soon as it opens, either over the opening weekend or, more likely, opening night. This inflates these numbers, reducing both the Internal Multiplier and the overall Multiplier.

Farce: Refers to a light-hearted, gleeful, often fast-paced, crudely humorous, contrived and 'over-the-top' comedy that broadly satirizes, pokes fun, exaggerates, or gleefully presents an unlikely or improbable stock situation (e.g., a tale of mistaken identity, cross-dressing, etc.) often characterized by slapstick, pratfalls, and other physical antics; types of farces include screwball comedy, bedroom/sex farce/comedy; contrast to parody and satire.

Far-off rattle movies: Movies in which the climactic scene is shot in a deserted warehouse, where far-off rattles punctuate the silence.

Fast motion (or accelerated motion): A camera device or effect to compress reality and highlight a scene or cause a dramatic effect, created by filming a scene with the film running at a rate less than the normal 24 frames per second and then projecting it back at standard speed, thereby creating the effect of moving faster than normal; generally used for comic effect; contrast to slow-motion or time-compression.

FAST: The camera assistant's motto. Everything he/she must do before each shot.

FAY: A 650 watt PAR light with daylight balance dichroic fliter.

Feather: Moving a 'flag' closer to or further away from a light source that it is in front of will feather (soften/harden) the shadow on the surface upon which the light falls.

Feature film: A "full-length" motion picture, one greater than 60 minutes in length - but usually about 90-120 minutes on one particular topic; also known as a theatrical; contrast to shorts.

Feature presentation: The main or advertised movie during a screening.

Featured background: A term used to describe the perfomers who are placed in prominent positions in the background of the major action of a scene.

Featurette: A term often used before the 1970s to refer to a 20 to 45 minute film (longer than a short subject but shorter than a feature film), usually a "making of" or "behind the scenes" mini-documentary, or an extended trailer, which was usually displayed by theater owners to "sell" a film for exhibition in their movie house — nowadays, featurettes are commonly run on premium cable stations, or offered as a 'bonus feature' as part of a DVD's extras.

Feed lines: Lines of dialogue which are read outside camera range for the benefit of an 'on camera' or 'on microphone' actor or voice over artist.

Feedback rule: Every time anyone uses a microphone in a movie, it feeds back.

Feel good film (or movie): Usually a light-hearted, upbeat comedy or romance that ends with an audience-pleasing conclusion; sometimes used derogatively; compare to tearjerker.

Femme fatale: Literally: "Deadly Lady"; a slang term used to describe a character in a movie.

Festival: An event at which films can often premiere. Festivals can be used as by studios to show their wares and sell rights to distributors, or to officially mark a movie's release so as to make it eligible for award ceremonies with hard deadlines that can't be met if they waited for a general release. Some festivals are competitive, giving awards from a jury or selected by the audiences.

Field of vision: In common with still photography and, to some degree, painting, cinematography renders three-dimensional reality in two dimensions. The width of the frame establishes the field of vision. Depth of field, on the other hand, is a perception of depth or perspective in the image.

Fifty-five gallon drum rule: Fifty-five-gallon drums are a culturally-rooted symbol of evil, because they usually contain a substance with a long name that we can't identify.

Fill leader: Film leader used to fill in the blanks in picture workprint.

Filler, Fill or Sound fill: Filler is scrap film, most often used to keep a sound track running the same length as the picture, even though there is just silence. When used this way in can also be called sound fill. Filler is usually a print with the emulsion scraped off the center all the way along, perhaps to prevent bootlegging, but also useful in that a mark can be seen on both sides through this wide scratch.

Film aesthetics: The examination or study of film as an art form.

Film artifact: Unwanted film damage that could be a defect or error - dust, hair, specks, emulsion scratches, splices, reel-change marks, a hiss, crackle or pop on the soundtrack, mottling of the image, scratches on the negative being printed positive, etc.; film preservation, restoration, and archival efforts help to keep older, decomposing, and endangered films from deteriorating and acquiring artifacts, through painstaking processes (often digital restoration).

Film base: The flexible, usually transparent support on which photographic emulsions and magnetic coatings are carried.

Film buyer: A person who arranges to purchase films from an distributor on behalf of an exhibitor.

Film cement: A liquid that is actually not a glue, but a chemical that melts and fuses two pieces of film together.

Film clip: A short section of film removed from a movie and often exhibited; a part of a film, and sometimes a complete scene or sequence, taken from a film; similar to an excerpt.

Film d'art: An early movement in French cinema to film more respectable stage productions.

Film developing: A process whereby images recorded on film stock are transfered to a negative print.

Film gate: An opening in the camera or projector past which the film passes intermittently.

Film gauge: The absolute measure, in millimeters, of the width of a piece of film. Super 8 millimeter, 16 mm, Super 16 mm, 35 mm, and 70 mm are the most commonly used gauges, though Super 8 is almost extinct, done in by camcorders. The prefix "super" refers to the size of the frame and the size and arrangement of the sprocket holes, not to the overall width of the film itself.

Film grain: The tiny particles of light-sensitive material on film stock that record images. Finer grains give higher image quality, but coarser grains allow a faster shutter speed. Graininess is an artifact which results from the use of coarse grains, and gives images a slight mosaic appearance.

Film magazines: A reel of film stock ready for use in a camera. The clapper-loader is responsible for inserting these into a camera.

Film noir: A French phrase literally meaning "black film" that developed in the early 40s; refers to a genre of mostly black/white films that blossomed in the post-war era in American cinema, with bleak subject matter and a somber, downbeat tone; the plot (often a quest), low-key lighting (chiaroscuro) often in night scenes, camera angles (often canted or high angle shots), the setting (the gloomy underworld of crime and corruption), iconography (guns, urban settings), characters (disillusioned, jaded), and other elements combined to present a dark atmosphere of pessimism, tension, cynicism, or oppression. Film noirs, often crime films, were usually set in grim and seedy cities, with characters including criminals, anti-heroes, private detectives, and duplicitous femme fatales.

Film notcher: A device used to punch out a small portion of the edge of a piece of film in order to permit electrical contacts on a printer to come together and thus activate light changes.

Film plane: The film plane is the plane of depth from the lens of the film, behind the gate, in the camera. It is also the point from where the distances on the focusing ring should be measured from, and is indicated on the outside of the camera with a little symbol that looks like the planet Saturn turned on its side.

Film printing: The process of transfering images from a negative print to a print.

Film review: An evaluative oral or written judgment about the quality of a movie, based upon various assumptions, facts, biases, etc; professional film reviewers are known as critics; a film review usually includes a brief synopsis (avoiding spoilers, usually), a balanced notation of both the film's plusses and minuses, quotablè wording, and some judgments; more extensive, in-depth film evaluations are called analytical essays.

Film speed: The sensitivity to light for proper exposure of a given film stock. This is primarily a result of the size of the silver halides in the emulsion, the larger the grain, the less light is needed for exposure. Film stocks are generally spoken of as being fast or slow, a fast film having large grains and needing less light, a slow film having smaller grain and needing more light.

Film stock: Film of whatever gauge labeled according to whether it is: a. monochrome or color b. fine or coarse grained c. negative, positive, or reversal. The labeling will also carry an indication of the range of tones which the film is capable of reproducing as well as an index of its sensitivity to light. This is a critical designation, and is usually refered to as or its exposure number. This number is set out either according to the American Standards Association exposure index (known as the ASA number), or according to the DIN index. Whichever index is used, however, the number represents the mid-point in a sensitivity range which the cinematographer must consider when designing a shoot, factoring in such variables as lighting conditions, type of action being filmed, and so on. Generally speaking, the more sensitive the film to light, the coarser the resolution of the image. Thus, film with an ASA number of 125 will in principle have a sharper image than film with an ASA number of 400. Recent advances in film technology, however, have allowed for films with higher and higher ASA numbers—in other words, with greater sensitivity to light—to have acceptably sharp resolution.

Film within a film: A particular story-telling approach, literally, to have one film within another; in some cases, the characters are aware of the 'film-within-a-film,' and break the fourth wall and enter into or interact with it; aka subset film or picture within a picture.

Film: (1) as a verb, to record a scene or make (or lense) a motion picture; (2) as a noun, refers to a motion picture, or (3) the thin strip of material on the film negative (with a base and light-sensitive coating of emulsion) that is used to create images - through light exposure.

Filmmakers: A collective term used to refer to people who have a significant degree of control over the creation of a movie: directors, producers, screenwriters, and editors.

Filmography: A comprehensive (often chronological by year) listing of films featuring the work of an actor/actress, director, or other crew member; may also be a list of films for a specific genre or topic; a filmographer is another term for a film-maker or a person who studies film See filmographies of many prominent actors and actresses, or director-filmographies.

Filter: A tinted glass or small tinted plastic sheet placed in front of the lens or behind the lens in a filter holder, used to change the color rendition of the entire shot. Filters are used to convert tungsten balanced film for use in daylight or vice versa. The can also be used for aesthetic reasons, such as a red filter to darken the sky when filming in black and white.

Final cut: The finished edit of a film, approved by the director and the producer. This is what the audience sees.

Fingers: Small flags used to control light.

First law of funny names: No names are funny unless used by W.C. Fields or Groucho Marx. Funny names, in general, are a sign of desperation at the screenplay level.

First rule of repetition of names: When the same names are repeated in a movie more than four times a minute for more than three minutes in a row, the audience breaks out into sarcastic laughter, and some of the ruder members are likely to start shouting "Kirsty!" and "Tiffany!" at the screen.

Fish-eye (clip: 884 K) from Brazil: So called because they resemble the globular construction of a stereotyped fish eye, round and bulging, these lens are extremely wide in their field of vision, but are also subject to considerable optical distortion. In 35 mm systems, lenses having focal lengths less than 12-14mm are generally called "fish-eye" lenses. Perspective relationships are greatly exaggerated by these lens, making a scene and the objects within it seem considerably "deeper" than in fact they are. As a consequence, objects filmed close to the camera with them appear to be grossly "fatter" or thicker, rounder, spherically distorted. Furthermore, the right and left edges of the frame will seem to curve inward towards the center. Any movement of the camera while filming with fish-eye lenses will exaggerate these distortions. It stands to reason, therefore, that fish-eye lenses are used principally when some kind of distortion effect is purposely sought.

Fish-eye lens: An extreme type of wide-angle lens with a very short focal point, that exaggerates and distorts the image, somewhat like looking through a mirrored glass ball with straight lines at the edges of the image appearing to curve around the center of the image; it has an angle of view exceeding 100° and sometimes in excess of 180°; with a nearly infinite depth-of-field.

Five minute class, the: No scene showing a class in session ever lasts more than five minutes. Even the most stimulating session is invariably interrupted by the bell.

Fixing: The removal of unexposed silver halides from the film during processing.

Flag: This has two meanings. **1.** It can be a large black cloth on a frame used on a shoot to keep light out of part of the composition. **2.** In the cutting room it is a small piece of tape attached to a shot in a roll and used exactly as you would use a bookmark. The flag sticks out the side of the roll, making it easy to find that shot again quickly.

Flare: This has two meanings: **1.** When using film on a daylight spool, the erratic pattern of raw light that washes out the beginning and end of the roll are known as "the flares." **2.** A flare of the other kind is a Lens Flare. It is caused when light strikes the lens and either causes the entire image to be fogged in appearance, or for a little row of polygons (the silhouette of the iris) to appear from the light hitting the surfaces of the many elements in the lens. It is solved by flagging the lens.

Flash frame: 1. A flash frame is a single frame that is completely clear between two shots. It occurs when the camera is stopped with the gate open, allowing for a very long exposure on that single frame. Rather than a problem, a flash frame can actually be a very helpful thing in the editing room, making it very easy to see where one shot ends and another begins. This type of flash frame usually does not occur with spring wound cameras, like the Bolex, except when the spring winds all the way down, but the second type is something with which to be more concerned. **2.** A flash frame is also used to describe the first few overexposed, brighter frames at the beginning or the end of a shot, due to the camera needing time to reach speed. These can often be hard to see while editing, but are much more noticeable in a final print.

Flash in the pan: Transitory, impermanent success or recognition; derived from panning for gold experience; see fifteen minutes of fame.

Flashback: A filmic technique that alters the natural order of the narrative; a flashback may often be the entire film; it takes the story order back chronologically in time to a previous or past event, scene, or sequence that took place prior to the present time frame of the film; the flashbacked story that provides background on action and events is often called the backstory; contrast to flash-forward

Flash-forward (or flash-ahead): A filmic technique, often preceded by a slow dissolve, that depicts a scene, event or shot taking place (or imagined) in a future time beyond the present time of the film, or it can be a flashforward from the past to the present; the opposite of flashback.

Flat: Usually an agreement to perform work or provide a service for a fixed fee or wage which will not be affected by overtime restrictions of unexpected costs. Also used in terms of sets and set construction elements which are generally used to create walls.

Flatbed: An editing machine resembling a desk with a screen in the middle. The film sits flat on plates which are threaded through the center section that has transports for picture and sound.

Flex-fill: A round cloth bounce card mounted on a flexible ring that can be folded up when not in use.

Flick: The flickering image in early films gave rise to the generic term flicks when referring to the movies; often used in a condescending way, such as stating that a film is a 'horror flick' or 'chick-flick'.

Flicker: Refers to the unsteady, stroboscopic, fluctuating effect perceived by the viewer, often produced by an improperly-photographed or projected film; similar to the old-time movie effect.

Float: Periodic vertical movement of the image which occurs as a result of mechanical faults in the camera, printer, or projector.

Floating luggage: In every scene where actors carry luggage, the luggage is obviously empty. They attempt, with pained expressions on their faces, to pretend the bags are heavy, and yet they can flick them around like feathers.

Flood: A lamp that provides general diffuse lighting on a studio set.

Flop: A film that is a failure at the box-office; also known as floppola, bomb, turkey.

Flop-over: An optical effect in which the picture is shown reversed from left to right.

Flutter: The rapid period variation of frequency caused by unsteadiness of the film or tape drive.

Flux: An amount of light which is present as measured in lumens.

Foam technician: A person responsible for creating foam latex prosthetic appliances from a sculpture created by a makeup artist.

Foamcore: Polystyrene which is sandwiched between paper. It is used to relectors, soft boxes, and other items because it is stable and easily cut.

Focal length: The distance, measured in millimeters, from the center of a lens to the film plane. This measurement, in conjunction with others such the width of the lens, defines certain significant characteristics of the lens such as amplification and depth of field.

Focus group: A group of approximately ten to twelve members of the public unrelated to a movie's production who attend a sneak preview. A single focus group is usually composed of a selection of people within the boundaries of a movie's intended audience. The group is extensively questioned by the filmmakers following the screening, and their opinions are incorporated into any further editing that may occur before the premiere.

Focus pull: The refocusing of a lens during a shot to keep a moving subject in focus or to change the person or object of attention.

Focus puller: A member of the camera crew who adjusts the focus of the camera during filming.

Focus: Refers to the degree of sharpness or distinctness of an image (or an element of an image such as a person, object, etc.); as a verb, it refers to the manipulation or adjustment of the lens to create a sharper image; terms related are deep focus, shallow focus (very common in close-ups), soft focus, and rack focusing.

Fog level: The minimum density of the unexposed area of processed film.

Fog: This is when stray raw light has found a chance to expose you film.

Foil: An acting role that is used for personality comparison or contrast, usually with the protagonist or main character, as a means to show and highlight a character trait.

Foley artist: In the post-production and editing stage of a film's production, the foley artist (named after pioneer Jack Foley) creates or adds sound effects/noises (e.g., footsteps, kisses, punches, storm noises, slamming doors, etc.) to the film as it is projected, often with props that mimick the action

Foley editor: Edits the sounds created by a foley artist.

Foley mixer: A sound mixer who works with a foley artist to record sound effects.

Foley: The art of recreating incidental sound effects (such as footsteps) in synchronization with the visual component of a movie. Named after early practitioner Jack Foley, foley artists sometimes use bizarre objects and methods to achieve sound effects, e.g. snapping celery to mimic bones being broken. The sounds are often exaggerated for extra effect - fight sequences are almost always accompanied by loud foley added thuds and slaps.

Follow (or following shot): A shot with framing that shifts to follow and keep a moving figure or subject onscreen; also known as a type of tracking shot.

Follow action: As the phrase suggests, the camera follows the action wherever it leads in the shot. Today, follow action shots are frequently done either by a hand-held camera or with a steady-cam. In large, sweeping, panoramic shots the camera would follow action either on a camera car or on a crane such as a Chapman Crane.

Follow focus: A shot where focus is changed while shooting to correspond with the moment of the subject (or the camera).

Follow-up: Refers to a cinematic work that comes after, regardless of whether it is a sequel or a prequel; contrast to a prequel, serial, series, sequel, spin-off or remake

Food fight: Dialogue which replaced "Westward ho!" as American movies ended the long frontier trek and began to look inward for sources of inspiration.

Foot candle: Measurement of light. One foot candle is the light of one candle, one foot away. Many light meters will use foot candles as a starting number, which then must be converted into an f-stop based on the sensitivity of the film you are using. (Because of the great variety of different film speeds it is sometimes ambiguous to talk too much about foot candles, since a given number of foot candles will not yield the same f-stop from one film speed to another.)

Footage: Any length, portion or sequence of film (either shot or to be shot) measured in feet; also refers to a particular sequence of events depicted in a motion picture.

For your consideration: A phrase often used in special trade advertisements (in publications such as Variety) that are paid for by studios to promote "Oscar-worthy" films (and their actors) and create Oscar buzz for Academy Award nominations, especially for borderline films and/or lesser known indie efforts and lesser-known performers that would probably be overlooked without the additional publicity.

Forced perspective: A technique used to create a sense of great distance or to make a space seem much bigger than it is, forced perspective is created by using objects that are vary in size, and placing them specific distances from one another, to create the effect of objects fading into the distance.

Foreground (abbreviated as f.g.): Objects or action closest to the camera; contrast to background

Foreign film: A feature-length motion picture produced outside the US with a predominantly non-English dialogue track.

Foreshadow-ing: To supply hints (in the form of symbols, images, motifs, repetition, or mood) within a film about the outcome, or about an upcoming action that will take place.

Format: The size or aspect ratio of a motion picture frame.

Fourth wall: Refers to the imaginary, illusory invisible plane through which the film viewer or audience is thought to look through toward the action; the fourth wall that separates the audience from the characters is 'broken through' when the barrier between the fictional world of the film's story and the "real world" of the audience is shattered - when an actor speaks directly to the viewers by making an aside.

Frame handles: Frame handles are extra frames at the beginning and the end of every shot, the exact number will vary from one application to the next, which are used primarily when preparing original material for optical printing, such as the Zero Cut method of blow up, or the creation of a superimposed title, etc. The purpose they serve, in the case of zero cut, is to make sure the registration pin of the printer is not grabbing a splice, which can cause the image to wobble. With opticals they are often used merely to avoid printed-in dirt, which is much more prevalent close to a splice where bits of film cement can flake off.

Frame line: The small sliver of space between frames. This is where two shots are cut apart and joined.

Frame rate: Movies are created by taking a rapid sequence of pictures (frames) of action. By displaying these frames at the same rate at which they were recorded, the illusion of motion can be created. "Frame Rate" is the number of frames captured or projected per second. The human optical system is only capable of capturing about 20 images per second; hence to give a realistic illusion of motion a frame rate greater than this is required. Most modern motion pictures are fiimed and displayed at 24 fps. Earlier films used lower frame rates, and hence when played back on modern equipment, fast motion occurs due to undercranking.

Frame: Refers to a single image, the smallest compositional unit of a film's structure, captured by the camera on a strip of motion picture film - similar to an individual slide in still photography; a series of frames juxtaposed and shown in rapid succession make up a motion (or moving) picture; also refers to the rectangular area within which the film image is composed by the film-maker - in other words, a frame is what we see (within the screen).

Framing (or framed shot): Refers to the way a shot is composed, and the manner in which subjects and objects are surrounded ('framed') by the boundaries or perimeter of the film image, or by the use of a rectangle or enclosing shape (such as a shadow, mirror, door or hallway) within the film image; also, camera angles such as low-angle and high-angle shots contribute to the framing; reframing refers to short panning or tilting movements of the camera to adjust to the character's movements and keep them onscreen, centered, and in the frame.

Free cinema: A documentary movement in England in the 1950s that was a springboard for the careers in film of directors such as Lindsay Anderson, Karel Reisz and Tony Richardson.

Freeze (or freeze-frame): An optical printing effect in which a single frame image is identically repeated, reprinted or replicated over several frames; when projected, a freeze frame gives the illusion of a still photograph in which the action has ceased; often used at the end of a film to indicate death or ambiguity, and to provide an iconic lasting image.

French flag: A small black metal flag attached to the camera with a positionable arm that is used to shade the lens from light in the case of a Flare.

French new wave: The name given to an extremely influential movement of young filmmakers in France between approximately 1957 and 1965. Though most of them began their film careers as critics (Truffaut, Godard, Rohmer, Rivette), others in the movement actually came up through the ranks of the conventional film industry (Malle, Resnais).

Frequency discrimination: Exaggeration or diminution of particular frequencies in relation to others.

Frequency response: This represents the sensitivity of a given sound, video, or other recording/playback system.

Frequency: The number of times a signal vibrates each second as expressed in cycles per second (cps) or Hertz (Hz).

Fresnel: A stepped convex lens. It is most commonly used to descripe tungsten-incandescent lamps.

Fruit cart : An expletive used by knowledgeable film buffs during any chase scene involving a foreign or ethnic locale, reflecting their certainty that a fruit cart will be overturned during the chase, and an angry peddler will run into the middle of the street to shake his fist at the hero's departing vehicle. (Of all the definitions in the glossary, this has become the most popular. It has been gratifying to be part of an audience where people unknown to me have cried out "Fruit cart!" at appropriate moments. The movie SKI PATROL even contained a "Siskel and Ebert Fruit Cart.")

F-stop: The scale used to measure the size of the opening of the iris on a lens. Opening the iris wider lets in more light, and closing it down, smaller, lets in less light. F-stops can be a little confusing, because the larger the number, the smaller the opening of the iris, and conversely the smaller the number, the larger the opening. The typical f-stop scale is 1.4: 2 - 2.8 - 4 - 5.6 - 8 - 11 - 16 - 22. When the reading is between stops, this should be accounted for it setting the lens, however, it is much more clear, even if it sounds grammatically incorrect to the mathematically inclined, to say "One third above 5.6" rather than "5.8" because it is very hard to judge the distance in decimals between numbers like 5.6 and 8, whereas 1/3rd above 5.6 is perfectly clear.

Fullcoat - Fullcoat is Mag Stock with a layer of oxide that completely covers one side, unlike Stripe. All 16mm mag is fullcoat. 35mm is available in both fullcoat and stripe. The difference in 35mm is that fullcoat can be used for recording several tracks, and it typically used for the Mix Master. Fullcoat is also more expensive than stripe.

Fullscreen: Fullscreen is a term used to describe the shape of the picture a movie is displayed in order for it to fill a regular (as of 1998) TV screen. At the time of writing, most TVs are squarer than the newer widescreen TVs on the market. With these older sets, for every 4 inches/cm of horizontal screen size there are 3 inches/cm of vertical size, hence a 4:3 aspect ratio. Widescreen TVs have 5 and 1/3 inches/cm horizontal size for each 3 of vertical. Rather than write that as 5.333:3, we use 16:9. So fullscreen=4:3, widescreen=16:9. When a movie is played in fullscreen format for a 4:3 TV, the movie is almost always adjusted to fit. You may be familiar with the phrase "this movie has been modified from its original version. It has been formatted to fit your TV." What that almost always means is that much of the original picture has been thrown away, i.e. the pan and scan procedure has been used to pick the most appropriate pieces of the picture to keep because the old TV screen is the wrong shape to show the whole picture. In terms of home cinema, fullscreen is inferior to widescreen and is often considered to be an unacceptable format. The 4:3 shape TV is expected to become obsolete over the next decade as TV moves to digital and HDTV formats, which are widescreen based. DVDs often offer both fullscreen and widescreen formats, however many are already only available in widescreen and anamorphic format, so as to cater for the growing audience of home cinema enthusiasts who have already abandoned fullscreen.

G

Gaffer: The head of the electrical department, responsible for the design and execution of the lighting plan for a production. Early films used mostly natural light, which stagehands controlled with large tent cloths using long poles called gaffs (stagehands were often beached sailors or longshoremen, and a gaff is a type of boom on a sailing ship). In 16th Century English, the term "gaffer" denoted a man who was the head of any organized group of laborers.

Gaffer's tape: Cloth tape specifically for use on film shoots, usually 2 inches wide in black or silver. The nice thing about gaffer's tape is that, unlike duct tape, it is designed not to leave a sticky residue behind.

Gag-based comedies: These are comedy films that are often non-sensical and literally filled with multiple gags, are designed to produce laughter in any way possible, and often with comic or spoofing references to other films.

Gain: The ratio of the signal level at the output of an audio device to the signal level at its input. Expressed in decibels (db).

Gamma: The degree of contrast in a negative or print.

Gang synchronizer: A synchronizing device having more than One sprocketted wheel which is used to set up synchronized relationships between film and sound tracks which have been recorded to magnetic film.

Gate: The opening on a camera or a projector just behind the lens, through which a single frame is exposed (in the camera) or projected (in the projector).

Gauge: A measurement of the film width. Usually 16mm or 35mm. Home camcorders are usually 8mm.

Gel: A large sheet of transparent tinted plastic used as a filter for a movie light, or to cover a window. There are two basic types: ones that will covert one color temperature to another (such as C.T.O. and C.T.B.), and others that come in a wide variety of colors.

Gender twist: A role traditionally played by a male or female that is switched and played by a member of the opposite sex.

Gender-bending role: Usually, a cross-dressing role in which a male or female plays a character of the opposite sex

General release: Refers to the widespread simultaneous exhibition of a film.

Generation squeeze: New Hollywood genre which tries to bridge the generation gap by creating movies which will appeal to teen-agers at the box office and to adults at the video rental counter. Typical plot device: An adult becomes a teen-ager, or vice versa. Also sometimes masquerades as a movie apparently about adults, but with young actors in the "adult" roles.

Generation: Usually refers to the number of times a videotape has been copied; third generation means three steps away from the original media master.

Generator: A mechanical engine which produces electricity from fuel (usually diesel). Frequently used for location shooting, either due to the unavailability or insufficient quantities of electricity locally available.

Genre: Originally a French word meaning "kind", "sort" or "type"; refers to a class or type of film that shares common, distinctive artistic and thematic elements or iconography, narrative content, plot, and subject matter, mood and milieu (or setting) or characters. Film genres are distinct from film styles (a recognizable group of conventions used by filmmakers to add visual appeal, meaning, or depth to their work) that can be applied to any genre.

German expressionism: A style of film common in Germany in the 1920s, typified by the dramatic lighting, distorted sets, symbolic action and characterisation.

Gigabyte (GH): A unit for measuring computer memory capacity, equivalent to 1,000 megabytes (MB).

Giraffe: A mechanically extendable and manipulated boom microphone.

Go motion: A form of animation similar to stop motion, but which incorporates motion blur. Ordinary stop motion cannot produce motion blur as motion only occurs between frames. Robotic models that are moved during the exposure of each frame produce motion blur, and thus are more realistic. Pioneered by Industrial Light and Magic for Dragonslayer.

Gobo: A grip head or "C" stand head used as a clamping device for holding other equipment.

Gothic: A literary or film style characterized by dark and dreary influences, such as ghouls, the supernatural, the grotesque, deathly forces, and the mysterious. Settings include old mansions, castles, and a threatened heroine. Often used in reference to horror films with these characteristics, to increase the film's prestige

Grading: The process of selecting the printing values for color and density fo successive scenes in a complete film to produce the desire visual effects.

Grand guignol: Literally meaning 'large puppet' in French; originally a reference to the famous classic shock Parisian theatre (during the 1900s) which specialized in gruesome melodramas with gory special effects; the term now refers to a play/film with sensational, macabre, horrifying, dramatic, and gothic content.

Greenlight or "greenlighting": A term denoting the 'go-ahead' for a film to be made; contrasted to being redlighted; shouldn't be confused with green-screening.

Greenscreen: A newer technique similar to bluescreen, however utilizing a key green background. Research showed that substantially better results could be gained by filming on green instead of blue, as effects stock was more sensitive to separating key green from other (foreground) colors.

Greensman: A member of the crew who procures, places, and maintains any vegetation on a set.

Grifflon (Griff): A durable material made of three ply high density rubber. The material is attached within a frame and used as either a soft reflector of sunlight or cut or soften direct sun. It generally comes in three sizes: 6' X 6', 12' x 12', and 20' x 20'.

Grindhouse film: A grindhouse originally signified a burlesque, strip-tease theatre (for "bumps and grinds") in a red-light district, or a blue-collar downtown cinema-house that featured racy films, chopsocky films, or other marginal fare; as a film, it first referred to a cheap, low-budget, non-mainstream, sleazy, hard-core film that played in an 'adults-only' venue, scruffy downtown area or drive-in in the 60s or 70s; early topics included nudist pictures, kung-fu flicks, and cheesy/sexy potboilers, but then branched out to refer to any genre of film with little plot, but with lots of action, sex and nudity, violence, taboo drug-use, lewdness, atrocities, Hong Kong martial arts content, or just plain weirdness.

Grindhouse: A term used to describe movie theaters common in the U.S. from the 1950s onward, that specialized in showing, or "grinding out" as many B movies as they could fit into their schedules. The term is also used to describe the type of B movies — commonly violent, exploitative, or just plain racy — that were shown in such theaters.

Grip tape: This is Duct tape style tape, also known as gaffer's tape or cloth tape.

Grip: The crew member responsible for setting up dolly tracks and camera cranes, erecting scaffolding, moving props or scenery, or the adjustment or maintenance of any other production equipment on the set; the key grip is the head grip who coordinates all of the other grips in the crew, and receives direction from the gaffer or head lighting technician; the key grip's right-hand assistant is known as the best boy grip.

Gross: Refers to the box-office take - the total amount of money taken in during theatrical release, not including earnings from film rentals or sales, or the entire profit made by a film.

Grotesque: A term originally coined by Federico Fellini to describe the bizarre-looking or deformed background characters in his films; a grotesque is a live-action caricature with exaggerated features, but not necessarily to be viewed as frightening or sinister

Guerrilla film: A low-budget film usually shot without seeking location permits, using non-SAG (Screen Actors Guild) actors, etc.

Guillotine splicer: A device used for butt splicing film with splicing film.

Guillotine: A type of tape splicer which uses unperforated splicing tape.

Guilty pleasure films: An escapist film that engenders low expectations (usually an awful B-movie or a critically-lambasted film) that the public enjoys despite or, more likely, because of its flaws; these are often quite personal film choices that are sometimes embarrassing to admit. Universally-loved 'guilty pleasure' films become cult films.

H

Hairstylist: Person responsible for maintaining actors' hairstyles during filming.

Halation: Halation is the effect that occurs when the bright areas of an image appear to softly bleed around the edges of dark areas. This is caused by light going through the emulsion layer, bouncing off the base of the film and exposing the adjacent emulsion. Some film is manufactured with a black anti-halation coating on the base side.

Halogen: This is the gas contained in the lamp of a Quartz Light, which prolongs the life of the tungsten filament. Quartz Lights are sometimes called Halogen Lights for this reason.

Hand-held camera: A filming technique in which the camera is not placed on a tripod, dolly, crane, or other carrying device or platform, but is, rather, held by the operator during a take. Prior to the invention of cameras which afforded through-the-lens viewing, the technique was used largely for newsreel or other actuality purposes.

Handheld shot: A shot taken with a handheld camera or deliberately made to appear unstable, shaky or wobbly; often used to suggest either documentary footage, 'realism,' news reporting, cinema verite, or amateur cinematography; contrast with Steadicam Frequently exaggerated and currently overused, such as in The Blair Witch Project (1999); also in the heroin overdose scene in Pulp Fiction (1994).

Handheld: Shooting without a tripod, but with the camera held by the cameraperson.

Hand-in-hand rule: In many Hollywood action pictures, the woman characters are incapable of fleeing from danger unless dragged by a strong man, who takes the woman's hand and pulls her along meekly behind him. This convention is so strong it appears even in films where it makes no sense, such as SHEENA, in which a jungle-woman who has ruled the savage beasts since infancy is pulled along by a TV anchorman fresh off the plane.

Handle: An extra number of frames attached to the head and tail of an optical print as a safety precaution.

Hard disk: A data storage and retrieval device consisting of a disk drive and one or more permanently installed disks. Increasingly common for storing sound effects and archiving for future use.

Hardtop: Slang for a normal indoor theatre.

Harmonic distortion: Acoustic distortion characterized by unwanted changes between input and output at a given frequency.

Hay wagon: Rural version of "Fruit cart!" (q.v.). At the beginning of chase scenes through colorful ethnic locales, knowledgeable film buffs anticipate the inevitable scene in which the speeding sports car will get stuck on a narrow country lane behind a wagon overloaded with hay.

Hays production code: In the 1920s, the American public became alarmed at the increasingly frequent portrayal of violence, sex, and lawlessness on movie screens. Wishing to avoid government regulation, the Motion Picture Producers and Distributors of America created their own regulatory body and appointed Postmaster General Will H. Hays as head. His influence became so great that this body became known as the "Hays Office". The Hays Production Code for Motion Pictures was introduced in 1934, and by today's standards was extremely strict. It was mainly concerned with violence and sex, but had references to crime in general. After WWII, the growing popularity of television provided the public with more viewing choice. The Hays Office came under increasing fire for restricting the creativity of filmmakers, as it had defined specific requirements for depicting certain events.

For example, under the Hays Code a filmmaker could not present revenge in modern times as being justified, nor could they depict details of how crimes were committed, or show a criminal profiting from crime. Following the Supreme Court's Miracle decision in the 1950s, films were recognized as protected under the First Amendment, and as such the Hays Office's demands were not legally enforceable. Films such as Who's Afraid of Virginia Woolf? and Blowup inspired MPAA president Jack Valenti to abolish the Hays Code as his first step in overhauling the certificates system in 1967.

Hazeltine: A machine which a color time at a lab or optical house uses to determine how to 'time' a film print for the proper amounts of red, blue, and green light. Also called a color analyzer.

Head room: The space between the top of a subject's head and the top of the frame. Headroom must be carefully apportioned so that there is not too much or too little, especially if shooting for transfer to video or for blowup, where the frame will be cropped in a little on the top and sides.

Head: **1.** The beginning of a shot or a roll is called the head. **2.** A small round clamp, usually used in conjunction with an arm on a C-Stand. 3. The Tripod Head

Head-on shot: A shot in which the action moves or comes directly toward or at the camera, to enhance the audience's feelings of participation; works well with 3-D films; also may refer to a head shot.

Helm: Terms used to refer to the director of a film.

Hero/heroine: Refers to the major male and female protagonists in a film with whom the audience identifies and sympathizes. Character traits often include being young, virtuous, handsome, pretty, etc.; contrast with the antagonist or heavy.

Hertz (Hz): Unit for measuring frequency of d signal; formerly called "cycles per second."

Hey! Cody! Rule: Bad guy has drop on good guy. Can pull trigger and kill him. Inevitably shouts "Hey! Cody!" (fill in name of good guy), after which good guy whirls, sees him, and shoots him first.

Hi Hat: This is a square of plywood with a bracket attached, to which a tripod head may be added (or is sometimes permanently affixed) used for filming with the camera very low to the ground. Its name is a bit of a contradiction, to its use nowadays, but it used to be that a Hi Hat was for shooting from very high up, with the plywood board being mounted up high somewhere.

Hi-Con: Generally a high contrast film print which provides the maximum contrast between the light and dark elements.

High concept: Describes a film that includes and/or exploits certain elements (e.g. fast action, big-name stars) in order to attract a large audience.

High-angle shot: A shot in which the subject is filmed from above and the camera points down on the action, often to make the subject small, weak and vulnerable; contrast to low-angle shot.

Highboy: A heavy-duty rolling stand, usually with a combo head, that has a junior receiver and a large grip head. Also called Overhead Stands.

High-concept: Refers to the saleable or marketable elements of a film; a high concept (actually low-concept in practice) refers to a film's main premise expressed as a simple formula in just a few words (as a one-liner) that can be easily understood by all; this idea portrays a shallow, condescending attitude toward undiscriminating film audiences by Hollywood's marketers and often results in having film content controlled by what appeals to the lowest common denominator type market.

High-definition: An on screen television image that will appear in a ratio of 16:9 compared to today's analog signal ratio of 4:3; the image will be 'high-def' due to increased lines of resolution (e.g., 1080 lines rather than the 525 of analog).

Highkey: An overall brightly lit scene with realtively few shadows.

Highlighting: The use of thin beams of light to illuminate selected or limited parts of the subject.

High-pass filter: An electronic filter used in various audio circuits to attenuate all frequencies below a chosen frequency.

Hike: Slang term for the following verbs, meaning "to increase", "to raise" or "to promote".

Hiss: Asperity Noise. Noise caused by minute imperfections in the recording medium (tape).

Hitting a mark: An actor's term for moving to the correct, predetermined position during rehearsals and during camera takes so that the camera can smoothly record the action; 'mark' refers to pieces of crossed tape on the floor to signify positions.

HMI: This is a type of light. HMI stands for Halogen Metal Incandescence. HMIs are very bright, power efficient lights. They are balanced for the Color Temperature of Daylight, making them handy in mixed lighting situations. However, they are rather expensive, costing something in the few thousands of dollars, and are not very portable due to the large and heavy ballast that is attached. Also, and this is vitally important to keep in mind, they must be used with a Crystal Sync camera, otherwise they will flicker and throb.

HOD: An abbreviation for "Head of Department". Sometimes known in US as coordinators.

Hold over: The term used by a director for an actor used for an extra day

Hold: A word used on a continuity report to indicate that a particular take should be kept, but not developed.

Hollywood box: A stage plug-type box without fuses.

Hollywood car: Looks like a normal automobile, but backfires after being purchased from used car lot by movie heroine who is starting out again in life and is on her own this time.

Hollywood cop car: Driven by the slovenly member of the team in all police versions of the Opposites in Collision plot (q.v.) Always unspeakably filthy, dented, rusty, and containing all of the cop's possessions in the back seat, as well as several weeks' worth of fast-food wrappers. Usually, but not necessarily, some kind of distinctive make or model.

Hollywood grocery bags: Whenever a scared, cynical woman who never wants to fall in love again is pursued by an ardent suitor who wants to tear her wall of loneliness, she will go grocery shopping. The bags will always break to (1)

symbolize the mess her life is in, or (2) so that the suitor can help her pick up the pieces of her life and her oranges.

Hollywood hospital: Where people go to die. Victim checks in, doesn't check out, because screen time is too valuable for characters to go into the hospital only to recover a few scenes later. Dialogue clue: When any seemingly able-bodied character uses the word "doctor," especially in a telephone conversation not intended to be overheard, he/she will be dead before the end of the film.

Homage: Usually a respectful tribute to someone or something; this often occurs within one movie when a reference is made to another film's scene, image, etc.

Home market: The Home Market refers to revenue derived from people viewing movies at home. It is broken down into three sections: rentals, sales and TV rights. Combined these bring in more than double the domestic box office and can turn a film that was a mid-level hit to a monster hit, or lift a film that struggled at the box office to one that shows a considerable profit. And to think, just a couple of decades ago studios were suing VCR manufacturers and Video Rental stores claiming they would kill the industry! Of course now DVD is king, representing more than 80% of rentals and nearly all of the sales.

Honeywagon: Usually a trailer, or truck and trailer combination outfitted for and used as the dressing room for actors when on location shoots away from permanent soundstages.

Hoofer: A slang term denoting a dancer Examples: 'hoofers' in Busby Berkeley's dance production numbers.

Horny teen-ager movie: Any film primarily concerned with teen-age sexual hungers, usually male. Replaced, to a degree, by Dead Teen-ager Movies (q.v.), but always popular with middle-aged movie executives, who like to explain to their seventeen-year-old starlets why the logic of the dramatic situation and the teachings of Strasberg require them to remove their brassieres.

Horror (films): A popular film genre designed to frighten and thrill with familiar elements (monsters, killers, vampires, zombies, aliens, mad scientists, the devil or demons, etc.), gothic qualities or settings (e.g., castles), psychological terror, etc.; initially influenced by German expressionism; subgenre types include slasher films, occult films, and gore-fests; often combined with the sci-fi genre.

Horse opera: General slang for a western film, not for a "singing cowboy" film; also known as an oater (for the food that horses eat).

Horse: A support for one or more rolls of film used on a cutting table.

Host wraps: The short segments of TV show where the host of the program talks or discusses topics; common in reality TV, where a host summarizes what has happened before the show returns to the action.

Hot set: A set where set dressers and prop persons have finalized placing funiture and props for filming a scene and on which a scene is in the process of being shot; labeled thus to indicate that it should not be changed or disturbed.

Hot splicer: A Cement splicer with an electric heater inside. The heat improves the bonding of the cement splice. Hot splicers are really not dangerously hot, just warm.

Hot splicer: A film splicing machine of precision construction in which portions of a film are overlapped, cemented, then warmed and dried by a heating unit.

House lights: You can request "House Lights" for a print and the lab will not time your film, but print it without any exposure or color correction. House lights are typically at the middle of the printing scale: 25 - 25 -25.

House sync: An internal timing reference used to synchronize all transports within a facility.

Hybrid (film): A film or production that combines or intersects two or more distinct genre types, and cannot be categorized by a single genre type.

Hype: The abbreviation for hyperbole; refers to manufactured promotional buzz and excessive advertising/marketing for a film or project, including celebrity appearances, radio and TV spots or interviews, and other ploys; a similar word - hypo - means to increase or boost.

Hyperfocal Distance: The hyperfocal distance is a distance set on the focusing ring of the lens that will most efficiently use the Depth of Field present. A depth of field chart will list possible distances and graph out the area of focus at different f-stops. There does not necessarily have to be a subject to focus on at that distance.

I

I.S.O.: The equivalent of A.S.A. and I.E., just with another name, it is another way of saying the same thing. This is the least frequently used of the three, but is sometimes found on the light meter. Treat it just as if it was A.S.A. I.S.O. stands for International Standards Organization.

Iconography (or icon): The use of a well-known symbol or icon; a means to analyze the themes and various styles in a film.

Idiot plot: Any plot containing problems which would be solved instantly if all of the characters were not idiots.

Image: Generally refers to the picture that is the result of the photographic process.

IMAX: A specialized, big-screen film format about ten times larger than the traditional cinema format (35mm) and three times larger than the standard 70 mm widescreen format; IMAX films are shot and projected on 15 perforation/70mm gauge film - "15/70", the largest film format in existence, which produces incredible high-definition sharpness in films projected on up to eight-story high screens (often dome-shaped) in theatres equipped with advanced digital surround-sound systems.

Impregnable Fortress Impregnated: Indispensable scene in all JAMES BOND movies and many other action pictures, especially war films. The IFI sequence begins early in the picture, with long shots of a faraway fortress and Wagnerian music on the sound track. Eventually the hero gains entry to the fortress, which is inevitably manned by technological clones in designer uniforms. Sequence ends with destruction of fortress, as clones futilely attempt to save their marvelous machines.

In the can: A term for an entire film or a subset of shots that are all finished shooting; also denotes when a director has the take that he wanted.

In-camera editing: Refers to filming in the exact order required for the final product, thereby eliminating the post-production editing stage; a fast, albeit unprofessional way to produce a film, often employed by student or amateur film-makers; requires advanced planning to tell the desired story in order.

Incident light reading: An incident light reading measures the amount of light hitting the subject. You take an incident reading with a light meter equipped with a white half-sphere which acts as a stand-in for the subject. The sphere is pointed at the camera, so that the same light hitting the subject is hitting the sphere. The other type of light reading is a Reflective Light Reading.

Incoming scene: The second scene to appear in a dissolve or wipe effect.

Independent film: A movie not produced by a major studio.

Independents (indie and independent films): Small independent, low-budget companies, mini-majors, or entities for financing, producing, and distributing films (i.e., Miramax, New Line Cinema, Polygram) working outside of the system or a major Hollywood studio; however, an indie may lose its independent status when its grows large and powerful; also refers to a movie, director, distributor or producer (sometimes unconventional) not associated with or produced by a major Hollywood film studio; often with groundbreaking subject matter designed for sophisticated audiences, and not necessarily produced with commercial success as the goal, unlike mainstream films.

Inductance: The resistance of a coil of wire to rapidly fluctuating currents which increases with frequency.

Industry, the: Another name for the film or entertainment industry; also referred to as the biz, show business, show-biz, Hollywood, or the town.

Inevitable sister: In any movie where the heroine catches her boyfriend dancing in public with another woman, and makes a big scene, the other woman invariably turns out to be the boyfriend's sister.

Infinity: The furthest distance on the focusing ring of a lens.

Ingenue: A young, teenaged female actress often in an important or lead role in a film; usually portrays an innocent, sometimes naive, and attractive character; also refers to an actress sometimes known as a starlet; the male counterpart is known as a juvenile.

Ink: Verb: to sign a contract. Noun: press coverage.

Inkie: A small (250 watt) fresnel type light.

Inning: A period of time.

Insert editing: Used in videotape or digital audio editing to describe the process of replacing a segment located between two specific and previously dubbed segments.

Insert shot: A shot that occurs in the middle of a larger scene or shot, usually a close-up of some detail or object, that draws audience attention, provides specific information, or simply breaks up the film sequence (e.g., a quivering hand above a gun holster in a Western, a wristwatch face, a letter, a doorbell button, a newspaper headline, a calendar, a clock face); an insert shot is filmed from a different angle and/or focal length from the master shot and is different from a cutaway shot (that includes action not covered in the master shot); also known as cut-in.

Insert: A close-up shot of an object, often produced by the second unit. The term probably came about to reflect the fact that this shot will be "inserted" into the final version of the movie during editing.

Inside joke: In a film, an obscure, show-biz related joke that is understood (or realized) only by those who know the reference (outside the context of the film).

Intelligence: In most movies, "all that separates us from the apes." In SHEENA, Queen of the Jungle, what we have in common with them.

Intercutting: An editing method whereby related shots are inserted into a series of other shots for the purpose of contrast or for some other effect.

Interior: Not only the obvious diametric opposite of "Exterior", interior designates an indoor setting. It is much more commonplace to film interiors on sound stages than it is exteriors.

Interlock projector: A projector used to reproduce the picture while synchronized sound is played back on an accompanying machine or other linked sound device.

Interlock: A term that generically refers to two or more machines running in sychronization; often shortened to "locked."

Interlocked: Two or more devices (most commonly dubbers in a mixing facility) with motors that run in sync are interlocked. It is not quite correct to say that a sync sound camera and tape recorder are interlocked, regardless of whether they use crystal of cable sync, since the tape recorder is recording pilottone and not really running with its motor interlocked with the camera motor.

Interlude: A brief, intervening film scene or sequence, not specifically tied to the plot, that appears within a film.

Intermediates: A general term for color masters or duplicates.

Intermodulation Distortion: An amplitude change in which sum and difference tones (harmonics) are present in the recorded signal.

Internal multiplier: A film's weekend box office divided by its Friday number. It's basically a measure of the film's word-of-mouth, with 3.0 being the best most films can get these day while 2.3 is generally the bottom rung. Certain films have an inherent advantage (like those aimed kids), while the Fanboy Effect can shrink the number as the hardcore fans flock to the movie on Friday.

International box office: Total box office from all nations outside United States and Canada.

Internegative: A color negative duplicate made from a color positive. Internegatives are used for release printing in order to protect the original negative from damage.

Interpositive: An intermediate copy of a film, made on a very fine-grained stock, usually required as an intermediate step to making an internegative.

Intertextuality: The rich propensity of film texts to quote other film texts, conventions, genres, and/or components thereof. Intertextuality has significant implications for audience expectation and the definition of genre. Brian De Palma's 1987 film "The Untouchables" provides an excellent example

Intervalometer: A device that attaches to the camera for filming single exposures, much like an animation motor, exept that an intervalometer is capable of exposing single frames automatically, as in the technique of Time Lapse photography.

Invisible cut: A cut made during the movement of a performer which is achieved by overlapping the action or by using two cameras, then matching the action during editing.

Invisible protective shield: Protects characters during fight scenes. They get hit by fists, chairs, bottles, etc. and thrown through walls, doors, glass, but wear only a small bandage in next scene, and later have no marks, although they should be black and blue for the rest of the movie.

IP/IN: The process of making a new negative of a film by striking an interpositive and then, from that, striking a new negative (internegative).

Iris wipe: A wipe effect in the form of an expanding or diminishing circle.

Iris: An earlier cinematographic technique or wipe effect, in the form of an expanding or diminishing circle, in which a part of the screen is blacked out so that only a portion of the image can be seen by the viewer; usually the lens aperture is circular or oval shaped and is often expanded or contracted as the film rolls, often from one scene to the next; known also as diaphragm. The camera movment is often termed iris wipe, circle-in/circle-out, or iris-in/iris-out; also refers to the adjustable opening in the lens that allows light to pass through - the measurement for the iris opening is f-stop.

It list: Refers to the tendency in show business to prioritize individuals as 'hot' or 'watchable' - highlighting those who have suddenly 'burst onto the scene' and are either notable and bankable; those who had some transient success or 'brush with greatness, but then were demoted from the list are called forgotten, has-beens, shooting stars, or flashes in the pan.

J

Jam sync: A process of locking a time code generator to an existing coded tape in order to extend or replace the code, used when code is of poor quality.

Japanese lantern: A paper-covered wire frame globe into which a socket and bulb may be placed.

Jib arm: A mechanical are which is supported on a dolly, tripod, or other device, which is counterweighted to hold a camera for an increased range of motion.

Jib: The arm of a mechanical crane.

J-lar: A transparent tape which is used to splice jels together.

Joel silver rule: All women in action-adventure flicks are extraneous to the plot unless naked or dead.

Judder: An instability introduced when images sampled at one frame rate are converted to a different frame rate for viewing. This effect is most noticeable when frames are repeated or deleted in order to obtain slow motion or fast motion.

Juicer: An electrician.

Jukebox musical: A filmed musical (drama, or animation, etc.) that uses pre-existing popular songs (usually from a variety of artistic sources) as its song score; the songs are often re-imagined with different song styles.

Jump cut: An abrupt, disorienting transitional device in the middle of a continuous shot in which the action is noticeably advanced in time and/or cut between two similar scenes, either done accidentally (a technical flaw or the result of bad editing) or purposefully (to create discontinuity for artistic effect); also contrast with an ellipsis and match cut.

Junior: A 2K fresnel light unit. It may also mean any 1 1/8 inch spud or mounting pin or any 1 1/8 inch female receiver.

Juvenile: The role of a young, teenaged male character; the female counterpart is known as an ingenue.

K

K: "K" has two different meanings, and both apply to movie lights, so one should be careful to differentiate one from the other. **1.** An abbreviation for Kilowatts. There are 1,000 Watts in 1 Kilowatt. It is used when talking about quartz lights or HMIs, as a way to measure their brightness based on their power consumption. A "1K" is a 1,000 Watt light, a "2K" a 2,000 Watt light, etc. **2.** An abbreviation for Kelvin, such as 3,200K for tungsten balance, 5,400K for daylight, etc.

Kelvin: This is the Color Temperature scale that takes its name from the scientist Lord Kelvin.

KEM: A brand name for a common 'flatbed' film editing machine.

Key grip: The chief grip who works directly with the gaffer in creating shadow effects for set lighting and who supervises camera cranes, dollies and other platforms or supporting structures according to the requirements of the director of photography.

Key light: The main or primary light on a subject, often angled and off-center (or from above) that selectively illuminates various prominent features of the image to produce depth, shadows, etc.; high-key lighting (with everything evenly and brightly lit, with a minimum of shadows) is termed realistic, while low-key lighting is termed expressionistic (and often used in film noir); three-point lighting uses: (1) a fill (or filler) light - an auxiliary light to soften shadows and areas not covered by the key light, (2) a back light behind to add depth to a subject, and (3) a bright key light.

Key numbers: Numbers placed on the edge of the film stock by the manufacturer as a unique identification point (35mm - every 16 frames: 16mm - every 20 frames).

Kick: An object with a shine or reflection on it from another object.

Kick-off: A term denoting the start of production or principal photography.

Kinetic energy amplification phenomenon: In scenes involving gunplay, the kinetic energy of the bullets will be enormously amplified as they strike the victim, enabling him to be hurled great distances and through objects. This phenomenon is particularly common around windows and balconies, especially in high-rise buildings.

Kinetic energy distortion phenomenon: When someone is shot while standing near a window, balcony or ledge, the kinetic energy will always be distorted so as to throw him outward, regardless of the direction the bullets came from. This enables victims to be hurled out a window and into a spectacular plunge even if the shots came from outside to begin with.

Klieglight: A type of powerful carbon-arc lamp that produces an intense light, often used in film-making; also used for promotional purposes at film premieres.

Kookalora: A specialty flag, sometimes called simply a "cookie"; the kookalora has irregular openings so that light going past it simulates sunlight through leaves or other equally irregular patterns.

Kookalouris: Name for a large sheet of cardboard or plywood with holes in it, which is moved back and forth in front of a light to illuminate a character's face with moving light patterns. Popular in the 1930s; back in style again with the movies of Steven Spielberg, who uses a kookalouris with underlighting to show faces that seem to be illuminated by reflections from pots of gold, buckets of diamonds, pools of fire, pirate maps, and radioactive kidneys.

L

L.F.O.A.: This stands for Last Frame of Action, and basically it is just what it sounds like: the last frame of image and sound on a reel. It is important to the people who mix your film (it should be written on the cue sheet), especially if you need to do Pull Ups.

Lab roll: A large roll (usually up to 1,000 feet) made up of camera rolls joined together by the lab for printing.

Lamp: A reference to the bulb inside a lighting unit, but may sometimes be used to refer to the entire lighting unit.

Land boom rule: In any movie where there is a cocktail party featuring a chart, map, or model of a new real estate development, a wealthy property developer will be found dead inside an expensive automobile.

Landmark film: A revolutionary film, due to either its technical or performance artistry; those films recognized by the National Film Registry.

Latent edge numbers: Precisely, the edge numbers, and not inked-on code numbers.

Latent image: The invisible image which is recorded on film through the exposure of light but before the process of development which renders the image visible.

Latitude: The degree to which a certain film stock can tolerate under- or overexposure. Reversal film, for all practical purposes, has a very little latitude. Color negative has a higher latitude, and particular of its latitude it is tolerant of much more overexposure than underexposure.

Lavalier (microphone): A miniature type of microphone, usually omni-directional and wireless, and small enough to be taped or clipped to an actor, to record dialogue; aka lav, lapel or lap microphones.

Lavalier mic: A small microphone that can be easily hidden on a piece of clothing so as not to be seen by the camera.

Law of canine/Feline superperception: Household pets can unerringly detect and react to the presence of ghosts, aliens or other nonhuman entities. Their warnings are invariably ignored.

Law of economy of characters: Movie budgets make it impossible for any film to contain unnecessary characters. Therefore, all characters in a movie are necessary to the story—even those who do not seem to be. Sophisticated viewers can use this Law to deduce the identity of a person being kept secret by the movie's plot: This "mystery" person is always the only character in the movie who seems otherwise extraneous.

Law of inevitable immersion: Whenever characters are near a body of water, the chances are great that one of them will jump, fall or be pushed into it. If this does occur, it is inevitable that the other character(s) will also jump, fall or be pushed in.

Law of movie brand loyalty: Thanks to product placement, all characters in a movie, no matter how heterogeneous or geographically dispersed, drink one brand of beer, use one brand of sporting equipment, drive cars produced by one company, etc.

Law of take-out chinese food: Take-out Chinese food is eaten in one of only two situations: Communally by a large, multi-ethnic group enthusiastically working on a common project, or in bed by two post-coital lovers. In the former case, the meal predicts success; in the latter, that the couple will break up.

Law of video box caricature, The: If you're trying to pick out a video and the actors on the box are cartooned caricatures which are not recognizable, pick another movie.

Lawyer with one case scenario, The: In nearly all legal dramas, the lawyers involved have only one case—the case that the movie is about. They are never distracted by other cases, clients or causes.

Layback: Transfer of the finished audio mix back onto the video edit master.

Layoff: Transfer of audio and time code from the video edit master to an audio tape.

Layouts: A person responsible for working out the action before filming begins, including where the characters should be, and the camera angles.

Layover: Transfer of audio onto multitrack tape or hard disk. Also referred to as "layup."

L-C-R-S (Left, Center, Right, Surround): The four playback channels used in 35mm motion pictures, now available on home hi-fi systems. L, C and R speakers are located behind the screen. The S channel surrounds the audience and may be mono or encoded stereo.

Lead character technical director: Oversees the work of a team of character technical directors, partners closely with the Lead Artist to address all issues related the creation of animated film and/or game characters. Responsible for setting and maintaining the aesthetic and technical quality bar for the character creation team.

Lead role: Refers to the most important, main character in a film, often distinguished by gender; usually there is at least one male and female lead role; also usually known as protagonist; contrasted to supporting roles or characters.

Leader: An extra amount of film which is at the start and end of the roll to protect the exposed film and to enable it to be laced into the projector.

Leadman: Member of the art department who is in charge of swing gangs and/or set dressers and reports to the set decorator.

Legs: A film that has 'legs' has strong and profitable box-office, stamina and audience drawing power far beyond the opening weekend; the term usually applies to films that last many months.

Leitmotif: An intentionally-repeated, recurring element or theme associated with a particular person, idea, milieu, or action; the element presents itself as a repeated sound, shot, bit of dialogue, piece of music, etc., that helps unify a film by reminding the viewer of its earlier appearance; sometimes presented along with a film's tag line on a film poster.

Leko: An ellipsoidal reflector spot light. Usually used for theatrical purposes.

Lenny Rule: Named for the gentle giant in Steinbeck's Of Mice and Men, this rule dictates that if a film character is of less than normal intelligence or ability, he or she will inadvertently get into serious trouble during the film.

Lens aperture: The opening in a camera lens created by the diaphragm, which opening determines the quantity of light which the lens projects onto the film. Lens aperture is measured on a scale which uses units known as f-stops. The relationship between the lens aperture, the time of exposure, and the desired depth of field must be carefully calculated as each of these elements significantly affects, and is affected by, the others.

Lens filters: Optical glass which is either tinted or otherwise treated so as to prevent certain frequencies of light from penetrating through the lens to the film. These devices are usually placed in front of the camera lens, but in any event between the light source and the film plane.

Lens flare. It is caused when light strikes the lens and either causes the entire image to be fogged in appearance, or for a little row of polygons (the silhouette of the iris) to appear from the light hitting the surfaces of the many elements in the lens. It is solved by flagging the lens.

Lens: A piece of glass in a camera through which light passes before hitting the film stock inside; various types include wide-angle lens, telephoto lens, normal, etc.; to lense means to film a motion picture.

Letterboxing: As the aspect ratio of movies are rarely the same as the aspect ratio of a television screen, when showing movies on TV it is necessary to make sacrifices. "Letterboxing" is a video mastering process whereby a film source with an aspect ratio greater than that of the video master (4:3 for NTSC/PAL and 16:9 for HDTV) is transferred to the video master in such a way that no film image is cut off to the left or the right, requiring the addition of (usually) black bars at the top and at the bottom of the image so that it entirely fills the screen—in other words, the technique of shrinking the image just enough so that its entire width appears on screen, with black areas above and below the image. The advantage of this technique is that the film images are shown as originally intended by the film's creators, not interfering with their shot composition and artistic intentions. The disadvantage is that the entire image must be shrunk, which makes viewing on smaller TVs more difficult. Contrast with pan and scan (for DVD, also anamorphic widescreen).

Level: The ratio of an acoustic quantity to a reference quantity. A measurement of amplitude in decibels.

Lexan: A plastic sheeting material, available in varying widths, that is optically clear and used to protect camera personnel from explosions or the results of other action.

Library shot: Stock footage shot or other footage which is germane to a given visual presentation but which was not generated for that specific film or television presentation.

Light value: A reference to a fast acting, variable opening shutter to control the light intensity in printing film.

Lighting board operator: A member of the electrical department who runs a console that controls the level or intensity of the lights, creating a look for the show. This can be simple or complex, involving intensity matching for shot continuity, on-screen effects, moving light control and synchronized work with other departments, like special effects and visual effects.

Lighting crew: A group of technicians who install, operate, and maintain lighting.

Lighting department: The section of a production's crew responsible for lighting and other electrical matters during filming. Individual positions within in this department include: Gaffer, Best Boy, Lighting Board Operator, Lamp Operator, Rigging Gaffer, Riggers and genny operator.

Lighting instrument: The actual lamp which generates light with which to light a scene. There are many sizes and uses.

Lighting technician: A member of the electrical department that is responsible for operating lights and lighting equipment on

Lighting: The placing of controlled illumination upon a scene or object to be filmed and thus the ultimate tool of the cinematographer. Light sources may be natural or artificial or both. If natural, the light may be directed onto the scene by reflecting devices. If artificial, it is of course aimed at the specific target area designated by the director of photography, and channeled through the use of such devices as cookies, flags, and doors. The light may also be diffused either by the lens of the lighting instrument or by butterflies, or it may be sharply focused. If, as is accurately said, cinematography is painting with light, lighting is the palette which the painter employs. Though methods for lighting a scene are highly varied, the one most commonly used in conventional practice is known as the "Three-point System." The intensity and sharpness of light and corresponding shadow (or lack of same) which illuminates a scene is described as being either high or low key. This is true irrespective of whether the film is monochromatic or color.

Lightleak: Stray light that penetrates into a camera giving the film little patches of fog. Also the term for the access point itself. Typically light leaks occur around the camera door or where the magazine is joined to the camera body. Often they can be easily prevented with camera tape around the door.

Light-struck leader: Film which was fully exposed to light which is then used as leader.

Line producer: A producer who is responsible for managing every person and issue during the making of a film. Line producers only work on one film at a time.

Lined script: A copy of the shooting script which is prepared by the script supervisor during production to indicate, via notations and vertical lines drawn directly onto the script pages, exactly what coverage has been shot. A given vertical line indicates, via the line's start and end point, what script material is covered in a particular shot, and whether given dialog or action is on-screen or off-screen in the shot, indicated by the line changing between straight and wavy respectively. Different coloured lines usually represent certain types of shots: close-up, insert, steadicam, etc. Each vertical line is also notated with the slate of the shot (e.g.

"3C"), the printed takes (e.g. "1, 3, and 4"), and a brief shot description (e.g. "M2S Rolf & Liza"). The lined script also frequently incorporates the script supervisor's script notes on the facing pages for a given scene. The lined script is used by the film editor as a reference to what coverage was shot and to changes made to the script during production. Lined scripts give editors a quick view of all available coverage at a glance, so that he or she can make quick editing decisions without having to sort through all the footage repeatedly.

Lines: Refers to the spoken dialogue belonging to a single performer; also refers to the full complement of spoken words in a film or stage script; also known simply as dialogue.

Lip-sync: The relationship of sound ad picture that exists when the movements of speech are perceived to coincide with the sounds of speech.

Liquid gate: A printing system in which the original is immersed in a liquid at the moment of exposure. This is done in order to reduce the adverse effects of surface scratches and abrasions.

Live area: A camera's viewfinder actually shows (and records on film stock) a greater area of the scene than will appear in the final product. Markings are etched in the viewfinder to indicate to the camera operator the extents of the "viewable" film (called the live area). An area beyond that (called the safe area) is also marked; it is in this area that the camera operator might direct the boom operator to place the boom microphone.

Loading booth: A small darkroom sometimes found on a sound stage for loading film into magazines as a roomier alternative to a Changing Bag.

Location (or on location): The properties or places (interior or exterior) used for filming away from the studio, set, or (back)lot, often to increase the authenticity and realism of the film's appearance; exteriors are abbreviated as ext., and interiors as int.

Location filming: Filming which occurs at a place not constructed specifically for the production. Typically this is either outdoors, a well-known location, or a real place which suffices.

Location manager: A person who manages various aspects of filming a movie on location, such as arranging with authorities for permission to shoot in specific places. The Location Manager is not based on set and therefore has an Assistant Location Manager who represents the department and manages the department's interests on set where the Location Manager's permission is not required or where elements of the Location Managers job has been delegated the Assistant Location Manager to oversee.

Location mixer: A sound mixer responsible for mixing sounds recorded on location.

Location scout: A person who looks for suitable locations for filming.

Location sound: This is the sync sound, or any other sort of wild track or room tone that was recorded at the shoot. Same as Production Sound.

Lock it down: A direction given by the assistant director for everyone on the set to be quiet, move out of frame, and to secure the set against anything or one interrupting the shot as it is happening. It is called just prior to speed. The phrase can also be used to securing a location for filming.

Locked cut: The so-called final cut of a film when there are to be no more changes to picture.

Locked down shot: A shot taken with the pan and tilt releases on the tripod tightened so that the camera will not move. Often done for certain effects where camera movement would ruin the illusion, such as a cut that causes a character to magically disappear from a scene.

Logline: A short, introductory summary of a film, usually found on the first page of the screenplay, to be read by executives, judges, agents, producers and script-readers; all screenwriters use loglines to sell their scripts; also known as premise.

Long (clip: 476 K) from"Henry V" (Branagh): Lens having a focal length trom 100 to 150mm are generally considered long. They not only amplify the subject considerably even when compared to tight lenses, but they also create a marked distortion in perspective which in which succeeding planes of action in the frame appear to get squashed together, the exact opposite, in other words, of the effect of wide-angle lenses upon perspective relationships.

Long lens: A lens with a focal length greater than 25mm in 16mm, or 50mm in 35mm, which, like binoculars, will provide a view that magnifies a small area.

Long take: Not to be confused with "long shot", a long take is measured in temporal rather than spatial terms. What this means is, simply, that long takes comprise shot where the camera is left running for a long period of time. As in all other aspects of life, time in film is relative: a shot which lasts 90 seconds may well be designated as a long take, though some film-makers (Renoir, Welles, Altman and others), have filmed takes of considerably greater length.

Long-haired woman seen from behind: When approached by hero, inevitably turns out to be a man.

Long-shot (LS): A camera view of an object or character from a considerable distance so that it appears relatively small in the frame, e.g., a person standing in a crowd of people or a horse in a vast landscape; variations are the medium long-shot (or mid-shot) (MS) and the extreme long-shot (ELS or XLS); also called a wide shot; a long shot often serves as an establishing shot; contrast to close-up (CU); a full-shot is a type of long shot that includes a subject's entire body (head to feet).

Look development lead: A person who works in a Digital/CG department and is responsible for wrangling the information from departments upstream like Modeling, Textures, Concept Art, Shaders and Effects and coming up with the final visual design on the look of characters, props, fx and sets that will eventually be used by lighters downstream on final shots. Usually referred to as lookdev.

Loop: **1.** Slack film above and below the gate to allow a transition from the constant motion of the supply and take up rollers to the intermittent motion that takes place at the gate. 2. A small magnifier useful in the editing room.

Looping: Refers to the process in which dialogue is re-recorded by actors in the studio during post-production, matching the actor's voice to lip movements on screen; aka ADR (Automated Dialogue Replacement); contrast with dubbing; loop refers to a length of film joined from beginning to end for repeated continuous running.

Low con print: A low contrast print specifically for transfer to video, which favors less contrast in the transfer process.

Low contrast original: An original reversal film which is designed to yield prints having good projection contrast.

Low-angle shot: A shot in which the subject is filmed directly from below and the camera points up at the action or character, to make the subject appear larger than life, more formidable and menacing, or perhaps tall and regal; contrast to a high-angle shot.

Lowboy: A heavy duty rolling stand, usually with a combo head, but without the height of a 'highboy'.

Lowkey: A high contrast lighting style with lost of shadows and large areas of darkness.

Lowpass filter: A filter that attenuates frequencies above a specified frequency and allows those below that point to pass.

M

M&E: M&E stands for Music and Effects. After a mix a big production will have an M&E track made, which is used when the film is dubbed into other languages so that all the Music and Effects do not also have to be redone. An M&E track is only essential if you plan on dubbing your film into a different language.

M.O.S.: A shot, a sequence, or a film that is shot without sound, which is added later. M.O.S. stands for "Mit Out Sound," and derives from an old Hollywood story about a German director asking for a shot to be filmed "mit out sound," and the camera assistant complying with this request by writing "M.O.S." on the slate.

Ma bell rule: Whenever a telephone is seen in a movie, the telephone will eventually ring.

Macguffin: A term used by Alfred Hitchcock to refer to an item, event, or piece of knowledge that the characters in a film consider extremely important, but which the audience either doesn't know of or doesn't care about. Examples: the engine plans in The 39 Steps, the statue with the microfilms in North by Northwest, and the contents of the briefcase in Pulp Fiction.

Machine leader: Strong leader threaded through a film processing machine which is used to pull film through the machine during its operation.

Macro lens: A lens that can be used for extremely close to the subject. The focusing ring will keep going past the lowest setting (on the Switar lens a red ring will appear to let you know) all the way around again. When in macro the distances on the focusing ring no longer apply.

Mad slasher movies: Movies starring a mad-dog killer who runs amok, slashing all of the other characters. The killer is frequently masked, not because a serious actor would be ashamed to be seen in the role, but because then no actor at all is required; the only skills necessary are the ability to wear a mask and wield a machete.

Made-fors: Short for movies filmed or made-for-television, often mid-way in style between a short drama and a cinematic release.

Mag stock, Mag track or **Magnetic film:** Mag track is a piece of film that is coated with an emulsion of magnetic oxide instead of silver halides. Basically, it is sound recording tape that is the same size as film, complete with perforations. For editing, all the sound, location sound and additional sound, is transferred to mag stock, where it is run on an editing machine in tandem with picture, one frame of picture equaling one frame of sound.

Mag: 1. Short for Magazine. 2. Short for Mag Track.

Magazine: An attachment to a camera with one or two light-proof chambers that hold 400 or 1,000 feet of film. One camera will typically have two or three magazines which can be loaded ahead of time.

Magenta: A red-purple color which is the complementary color of green.

Magic hour: The minutes just around sunset and sunrise, where light levels change drastically and quickly, lending a warm orange glow to earlier shots, and a clearer blue in later minutes that allows a crew to shoot night scenes while light still remains.

Magnetic film (mag film): Film which is coated with an iron oxide compound on which sound is recorded and from which sound is reproduced.

Magnetic soundtrack: A composite print in which the soundtrack is recorded on the attached strip of magnetic tape. Largely obsolete due to high cost and maintenance difficulties.

Mainstream: A Hollywood-made film with major stars, big budgets, and big hype; compare to independents; its extreme opposite is termed counter-cinema (forms of alternative cinema, such as avant-garde, art films, Third World cinema, etc.)

Maintenance engineer: A person responsible for general maintenance and repair.

Majors: Refers to the major Hollywood motion picture producer/distributor studios at the present time (i.e., DreamWorks SKG, MGM/UA, Paramount Pictures, 20th Century Fox, Sony (Columbia/TriStar), Warner Bros, Universal, and Disney); contrast to the smaller, mini-major production-distribution companies (i.e., Miramax, New Line Cinema, and Polygram) that compete directly with the bigger studios.

Makeup: Refers to the materials that are used to prepare the performer for his/her respective role(s) before the camera, anywhere from facial pancake to elaborate costuming, latex masks, and other ghastly transformations; the makeup department is headed by a makeup artist.

Making of... : A specialized documentary that focuses on the production of a specific film; most "making of..." documentaries are extended promotional advertisements before the release of the film, and almost all of them are shot while the film is in production; some specialized documentaries of classic films (called retrospectives), made years after the film was released, gather interviews and behind the scenes clips, etc.

Marathon Hero, The: A hero in pursuit of a purse-snatcher or getaway car can run for many blocks, even up the hills of San Francisco, without getting winded.

Mark: On a film set, actors must be very exact as to where they place themselves before, during, and after a movement, because different areas seen by the camera are lit for precisely those exact locations. Marks of various kinds are placed where the camera can't see them, (for example, a piece of tape on the floor of the set) and, once they have been pointed out to the actors, it is then their responsibility to hit that mark precisely, even if, as is the case with the actor in the clip, they have to fall to the mark.

Mark it! : What to say to the person with the slate to get them to clap the sticks together.

Marquee value: The projected value of a film before its released. Gauged according to the reputations of the major stars and creative personnel.

Martial-arts: A film which features hand to hand combat, usually using various Asian combat systems like Karate and the Chinese fighting styles popularly known in the west as Kung Fu. "Chop-socky" is a slang and scornful term for martial-arts movies.

Martini shot: The last shot of the day's shoot... because the next "shot" is in a Martini glass.

Masking: A phenomenon whereby one or more sound "trick" the ear into not hearing other, weaker, sound that are also present.

Master (print master): A positive print made specifically for duplicating purposes.

Master shot: A continuous shot or long take that shows the main action or setting of an entire scene (most scenes are shot with one or two master angles and then broken up into a series of smaller or tighter angles (such as one-shots, two-shots, and reaction shots); a master refers to a positive print made especially for duplication purposes.

Match cut: A transitional technique, in which there's a cut between two shots (outgoing and incoming) that are joined, matched, or linked by visual, aural, or metaphorical parallelism or similarities; there can be audio matches, segues, and visual match-cuts of various kinds.

Match dissolve: A dissolve linking images which have similar content.

Matched cut: A cut joining two shots whose compositional elements match, helping to establish strong continuity of action.

Match-image cut: A cut from one shot to another shot having an image of the same general shape as the one in the prior shot.

Matching action: The process of aligning or overlapping the shots of a film sequence in order to achieve a smooth transition from the action in one shot to the action of the succeeding shot.

Matching: Arranging for the impedances presented by a load to be equal to the internal impedance of the generator. This is essential to avoid loss of power. In microphones, the loss results in poorer signal-to-noise ratio. Matching is done by means of a transformer.

Mater: A small adjustable clamp with a baby stud which can be interchanged with a variety of accessories.

Matte artist: A person who creates artwork (usually for the background of a shot) which is included in the movie either via a matte shot or optical printing.

Matte box: A square shade that goes in front of the lens, usually supported by a pair of rods that attach to the camera. A matte box often has filter holders for square glass filters.

Matte shot: The optical process of combining (or compositing) separately-photographed shots (usually actors in the foreground and the setting in the background) onto one print through a double exposure that does not meld two images on top of each other, but masks off (or makes opaque and blank) part of the frame area for one exposure and the opposite area for another exposure; the second image is printed in the masked-off area; it is a photographic technique whereby a painting or artwork from a matte artist - usually painted on glass - is combined with live action footage to provide a convincing setting for the action; also sometimes known as split-screen.

Maxi-brute: A 9 light unit with (9) 1000 watt PAR 64 lights.

MB: The acronym for megabytes which is a measure of computer storage capability; the equivalent of 1,000 bytes.

McGuffin (or MacGuffin): Alfred Hitchcock's term for the device or plot element (an item, object, goal, event, or piece of knowledge) that catches the viewer's attention or drives the logic or action of the plot and appears extremely important to the film characters, but often turns out to be insignificant or is to be ignored after it has served its purpose; its derivation is Scottish, meaning a "lion trap" for trapping lions in the lion-less Scottish Highlands (i.e., a trap that means nothing, since it is for an animal where there is no such animal).

ME track: This refers to the music and effects tracks which are combined into one (or a stereo pair) for use with foreign language re recording of a film or video program.

Meat axe: An grip arm-like accessory which is designed to clamp onto the hand rail of a studio overhead catwalk, or other suitable surface, and has a gobo head at the end of the arm.

Medium Close Shot (MCS): An arbitrary mid-point between a close shot and medium shot.

Medium Long Shot (MLS): An arbitrary mid-point between a medium shot and a long shot. Sometimes known as an American shot.

Medium shot: Refers to a conventional camera shot filmed from a medium distance; although it is difficult to precisely define, it usually refers to a human figure from the waist (or knees) up; between a close shot and a long shot; abbreviated as m.s.

Megaplex (multiplex): Both refer to movie chains (i.e., Loews, AMC Theatres) with movie theatres that screen more than one film at a time, as opposed to single-screen theatres. A multiplex has from 2 up to 16 screens, a megaplex has 16 or more screens; plex is the abbreviation for a multiplex theatre.

Melodrama: Originally referred to "a drama accompanied by music"; a film characterized by expressive plots with strong and intensified emotion, often with elements of pathos, illness and hardship; called 'women's films' or 'weepies' (tearjerkers) during the 1940s; aka meller; sometimes used disparagingly to describe films that are manipulative and crudely appeal to emotions.

Mercer clip: A trade name for a small plastic clip which is used to hold film ends together during film assembly.

Merchandising: Non-filmic goods which are released under the film's theme, such as toys, T-shirts and posters.

Metaphor: A filmic device in which a scene, character, object, and/or action may be associated, identified, or interpreted as an implied representation of something else (that is unrelated).

Method acting: A style of acting formalized by Konstantin Stanislavsky which is believed by some to create more realistic performances. Essentially, the theory requires actors to draw experiences from their own personal lives that correlate to the character they are playing - an extremely demanding process emotionally. In some cases, "method" actors take the theory even further by arranging events in their private lives to resemble the lives of their characters. See the trivia entries for Down and Out in Beverly Hills and One Flew Over the Cuckoo's Nest for examples, and the trivia entry for Marathon Man for an amusing anecdote.

Mickey: An open faced 1K lighting unit. Also known as a 'Redhead'.

Microphone impedance: The nominal load impedance for a microphone indicates the optimum matching load which utilizes the mike's characteristics to the fullest extent. Impedance is a combination of dc resistance, inductance and capacitance, which act as resistances in ac circuits. An inductive impedance increases with frequency; a capacitative impedance decreases with frequency. Either type introduces change in phase.

Microphone: A device which converts sound into electrical impulses, usually for recording or amplification.

MIDI: Musical Instrument Digital Interface. A machine protocol that allows synthesizers, computers, drum machines and other processors to communicate with and/or control one another. (Sound)

Midnight movies: Offbeat, often independent (non-Hollywood) counter-cultural cult films exhibited at theatres for late-night shows - sometimes involving audience participation; appealed to various small segments of niche audiences with different tastes; these films (originally sexual thrillers, slasher flicks, etc.) were often box-office bombs upon initial release, but then gained a faithful following; the phenomenon began in the early 70s, then mostly disappeared in the 80s, but has recently been revived.

Mid-wife crisis: Any character whose wife and/or kids are introduced more than an hour into the movie and who hugs and kisses any or all of them will be dead within the next 20 minutes. e.g., "Goose" in TOP GUN.

Mime (or pantomime): Acting without words, emphasizing facial expressions, body movements, and gestures; common during the silent film era.

Miniatures: Small-scale models photographed to give the illusion that they are full-scale objects; also known as model or miniature shots.

Mini-majors: Studios which are large but not as large as the majors: Embassy, Gramercy, etc.

Mini-series: A television series with a set number of episodes which tell a complete story, usually filmed at the same time. Contrast with serial.

Miracle of available parking space: When a character needs a parking space, even on the busiest streets in the busiest cities, one is quickly found.

Mirror gimmick: Tired old cinemagraphic trick in which we think we are seeing a character, but then the camera pans and we realize we were only looking in a mirror.

Miscast: Refers to an actor/actress who is completely wrong, untalented, or unbelievable for the role he or she has been cast in.

Mise en scène: A French term for "staging," or "putting into the scene or shot"; in film theory, it refers to staging action that 'covers' or records an entire uninterrupted scene within the frame of the film, and the arrangement, composition and content of the visual elements before the camera (usually in a long-shot) - the content includes settings, decor, props, actors, costumes, lighting, performances, and character movements and positioning; the scene plays out in front of a continually-running camera in real-time, without cutting, but instead by using techniques such as blocking, zoom, and camera movement; includes both technical and non-technical elements that make up a scene's look and feel; the term connotes that there is a psychological unity that exists from one frame to the next; it can be contrasted to montage (a French word that simply means 'editing', or many cuts or separate images of a dramatic scene put together in rapid succession to create a composite picture), preferred by director Sergei Eisenstein

Mise-en-scene: Literally translated from the original French, the phrase means "to put upon the stage"; otherwise, staging. In film practice, however, the term has come to designate the totality of how the director designs and actuates a given scene. All films use essentially the same techniques and processes. However, each individual film assembles and/or employs all of the variable elements provided by the technology and the imponderables of production in it's own distinct way. The elements generally used to define and/or analyze mise-en-scéne are: Setting Actor Placement Actor Movement Actor interpretation (ideally but not always a collaboration between director and actor) Camera movement Costumes Make-up

Mix (mixing): The electrical combination of different sounds, dialogue, music, and sound effects from microphones, tape, and other sources onto the film's master soundtrack during post-production; dubbing (or re-recording) refers to the mixing of all soundtracks into a single composite track; the soundtrack is blended by a mixer (chief sound recording technician)

Mix cue sheet (cue sheet): A sheet having several columns for notations of footage, fades. volume levels, and equalizations which are used in mixing sound tracks where each column usually represents one track.

Mix master: This is a copy of your sound mix on mag stock, or on DAT, which you sometimes have to request in addition to the optical track. It is always a good idea to get a copy of the mix on tape, which will be of much better quality than the optical track for transfer to video, or to save some mixing time in the event you have to remix.

Mixer: **1.** A device for blending together sounds from multple sources with a volume control for each. **2.** The person who sits at the mixing console during the mix, who decides initially on how the sounds are to be combined (you are the one with final say), and operates the faders and other audio controls.

Mixing house: A sound studio specifically for mixing sound for film.

Mockumentary: A fictional, farcical film that has the style, 'look and feel' of a documentary, with irreverent humor, parody, or slapstick, that is deliberately designed to 'mock' the documentary or subject that it features; related to docudrama (a film that depicts real people and actual events in their lives).

Modern (or modern-day) classic: A popular, critically-acclaimed film in recent years destined (possibly?) to ultimately become an all-time classic.

Mogul: Refers to a domineering, autocratic head of a major film studio; most commonly used when the studio system dominated film-making; now popularly called a studio chief.

Money shot: Aka payoff shot; a term originally borrowed from the pornographic film industry; referring to a scene, image, revelation, or climactic moment that gives the audience "their money's worth," may have cost the most money to produce - and may be the key to the movie's success.

Monitor: Refers to a small television screen hooked up to the camera and/or recording device that allows crew other than the camera operator to check the quality of a scene as it is being shot or to check and see if it needs to be reshot

Monologue: A scene or a portion of a script in which an actor gives a lengthy, unbroken speech without interruption by another character.

Montage theory: Basically a theory which develops the proposition that it is through editing that film finds its greatest—and most unique—powers of expression. This premise is based on the dialectical relationship between two shots, "A" and "B",in a cut. By putting shot "A" in juxtaposition (and in opposition) to shot "B" the result is not a sum of the two, but a new idea which might be called "C". Obviously, there has to be significant involvement on the part of the audience to make the dialectical relationship effective. Thus simply put, this brief definition does not convey either the theoretical and artistic force nor the profound influence which the theory had on subsequent film making. Clearly, though, these theories, and the practice in film making to which they gave rise and through which they were developed and refined, stand at the diametric opposite from continuity editing. Some history: following Lenin's admonition that "Film is the most important of the arts", the first film school in the world, the USSR State School on Cinema Art, was founded following the Soviet victory in 1917. In charge was a young film maker by the name of Lev Kuleshov. Under his tutelage, a workshop for the development of Soviet Film makers was organized at the school. This workshop operated under the most severe material handicaps, principal amongst which was the almost total shortage of raw film stock, which prevented them from shooting their own footage with which to experiment. As a result, in order to both develop their various theories and begin to work with film in spite of these shortages, the members of the workshop began tc reedit whatever existing footage they were able to forage. The subsequent experiments with this "found footage" led them to discoveries about the nature and effect of film editing which subsequently developed not only into whole theoretical constructs, but which theories also formed the basis of the films they subsequently went on to make. Among others of Kuleshov's other pupils were Sergei Eisenstein, and V.I. Pudovkin, both of whom became profound influences on the evolution of the motion picture and its techniques. For a sampling of some practical results which derived from the theory, a number of clips are set out below from the works of Eisenstein. Though image quality is deteriorated lost as a result of necessary video compression, a viewer can nevertheless perceive the dynamic and compositional relationship of one shot to the next in the sequences illustrated by the clips. It is suggested that once the clips are downloaded, they be viewed through once or twice, then reviewed by manipulating the control bar as slowly as possible so that the relationship of one shot to the next can be carefully observed.

Montage: Literally, "putting together" or "assembling shots"; refers to a filming technique, editing style, or form of movie collage consisting of a series of successive short shots or images (often disconnected in time or place) that are rapidly juxtaposed into a coherent sequence to suggest meaning or a larger idea; usually a montage is not accompanied with dialogue; dissolves, cuts, fades, super-impositions, and wipes are often used to link the images in a montage sequence; an accelerated montage is composed of shots of increasingly-shorter lengths.

Moppet: The term for a child, or pre-teen child actor.

Morality tale (or play): A literary term mostly, but used also to refer to a film (often heavy-handed and obvious in tone) that presents a judgment on the goodness/badness of human behavior and character, and emphasizes the struggle between good and evil.

Morph: The transformation of one digital image into another with computer animation.

Mos: The designation for filming a scene (or scenes) without simultaneously recording sound. Legend has it that the acronym was created by the Middle-European accents of the many film directors and technicians who came to the US before the Second World War. Apparently (if the legend is to be believed) they wanted scenes shot, as they allegedly pronounced the phrase, "mittout sound", hence MOS.

Motif : Refers to a recurrent thematic element in a film that is repeated in a significant way or pattern.

Motion artifact: The visual interference patterns between a shot's frame rate and a filmed object's periodic motion or change. If a shot is filmed with a frame rate R, any images of periodic events of a frequency greater than R/2 (the "Nyquist Limit") will be misrepresented on film. A commonly-occuring example of this artifact is the illusion of spoked wheels appearing to turn in the wrong direction or at the wrong rate. Incorrect frame rates and synchronization can also cause strobing during shots of projected movies or of television screens.

Motion blur: Shots of objects that quickly move in the camera's, frame, and/or shots with a slow shutter speed are likely to produce a "smearing" effect, since the object is in a range of positions during a single exposure.

Motion capture: An animation technique in which the actions of an animated object are derived automatically from the motion of a real-world actor or object.

Motion control: A camera setup which records the motion of a camera during a shot so that visual effects can be easily synchronized with the photographed scene.

Motion Picture Association of America: The Motion Picture Association of America and its international counterpart, the Motion Picture Association serve as the voice and advocate of the American motion picture, home video and television industries, domestically through the MPAA and internationally through the MPA. Through the Classifications and Ratings Administration (CARA), the MPAA issues certificates.

Motion Picture Association: The Motion Picture Association of America and its international counterpart, the Motion Picture Association serve as the voice and advocate of the American motion picture, home video and television industries, domestically through the MPAA and internationally through the MPA. Before 1994, the MPA was known as the Motion Picture Export Association of America.

Motion picture editors guild: A professional union for picture and sound editors, which now also includes re-recording mixers, projectionists, recordists, mic boom operators, engineers, and story analysts.

Motion pictures: A length of film (with or without sound) with a sequence of images that create an illusion of movement when projected; originally referred to the motion or movement (due to the principle of persistence of vision) perceived when a string of celluloid-recorded images were projected at a rate of 16 or more frames per second; an art form, and one of the most popular forms of entertainment, known archaically as a photoplay during the silent era.

Motivated and unmotivated lighting: Refers to lighting (or a light source) that is naturally existing in the real world, i.e., from a lamp post, table lamp, sunlight shining through a window, etc., that appears in a scene; for the lighting to appear natural in a film scene, it should seem to be coming from light sources that are visible or implied within the scene; the opposite effect is unmotivated lighting.

Motivated lighting: A lighting style in which the light sources imitate existing sources, such as lamps or windows.

Mouse (House): A slang term for the Walt Disney Co. or any division thereof — refers to the company's most famous animated character: Mickey Mouse.

Move brats: The younger generation of Hollywood directors who exploded onto the scene in the early 1970s; *e.g.* Spielderg, George Lucas, Brian de Palma, Michael Scorsese.

Movematch: The use of computer programs to combine and synthesize real footage with CGI effects.

Movie of the Week: A prime-time position for the screening of a movie on television.

Moviola: An Upright Moviola. Moviola is the company that makes this machine. They also make flatbeds, but when someone says "Moviola" the generally mean an upright.

Moviscop: Spelled Moviscop but pronounced "movie-scope." This is a small, 16mm table-top viewer, often used on an editing bench.

MPAA: Acronym-initials meaning 'Motion Picture Association of America' - an organization that represents the interests of the major motion picture studios.

M-S: (Mid-Side). A stereo microphone technique where two microphones are incorporated into a special configuration for recording.

Multichannel: In film, used to refer to a final mix that includes more than stereo information.

Multiplier: A film's total box office divided by its opening weekend box office. Another measure of the film's word-of-mouth but with a much wider range of possibilities. Films with below 2.0 are not unheard of, while 6.0 or more are a possibility. Just as a side note, not too long ago films with a multiplier of 10 or more were quite common, but the economics have changed and a big opening weekend is too important to the studios and the home market shortens a film's legs.

Multitrack: An audio tape recorder capable of handling more than two tracks of information separately.

Murphy's law: In movies made before 1985, any character named "Murphy" was a cop, a priest, a drunk, a tough guy, or all of the above. MURPHY'S ROMANCE was the first to break with this rule. Prior to TV's Murphy Brown, all Murphys were male. Any character named Murphy will sooner or later be shown in a saloon, or drinking heavily.

Musco lights: An array of permanently crane mounted HMI lights.

Music arranger: Someone who adapts a musical composition for voices, instruments, and/or performance styles other than those for which the music was originally written.

Music editor: A person who, in collaboration with the music supervisor and composer, performs editing on the score, live vocals, songs and source music of a movie.

Music preparation: Person who prepares printed parts from the composer's score for the musicians to play from at the score recording sessions.

Music supervisor: A person who coordinates the work of the composer, the editor, and sound mixers. Alternately, a person who researches, obtains rights to, and supplies songs for a production.

Musical (film): A major film genre category denoting a film that emphasizes segments of song and dance interspersed within the action and dialogue; known for its distinctive artists, stars, singers, and dancers; two major types are 'backstage' musicals and 'music-integrated' musicals.

Musical: A movie whose dramatic story structure includes unrealistic episodes of musical perfomance and/or dancing.

Myopia rule: Little girls who wear glasses in the movies always tell the truth. Little boys who wear glasses in the movies always lie.

Mysterious object antecedents myth: Whenever a movie involves time travel, there will always be an object that travels between the past and future without ever having actually come from anywhere.

Myth of the seemingly ordinary day: The day begins like any other, with a man getting up, having breakfast, reading the paper, leaving the house, etc. His activities are so uneventful they are boring. That is the tip-off. No genuine ordinary day can be allowed to be boring in a movie.

N

Nah reflex: Character sees someone but can't believe his eyes, so shakes his head and says "Nah." Inevitably it is the person it couldn't be.

Narration: The various means by which the events of the plot can be placed before the viewer. Also used of voice-over narration, a technique particularly associatedwith the fatalism of the film noir, like that of the mortally wounded hero in *Double Indemnity* (1944) or that of the dead man in *Sunset Boulevard* (1950).

Narrative film: A structured series of events, linked by cause and effect, that provide the plot of a film; a film that tells a chronological or linear story (with a beginning, middle, and end), as opposed to non-narrative films, such as poetic or abstract films.

Narrative: The structured series of events, linked by cause and effect, that provide the film's plots.

Naturalism: A stage, artistic, philosophical, or literary term as well as a film term, signifying an extreme form of realism in which life is depicted in a stoic, unbiased way.

Near miss kiss: The hero and heroine are about to kiss. Their lips are a quarter of an inch apart—but then they're interrupted.

Negative cost: The cost of a movie through the production of a finished negative, not including the costs of prints, advertising, or distribution.

Negative cutter: A person who matches the negative of a movie and conforms (matches) it to the final version of the film as decided by the filmmakers. From this negative the prints are made.

Negative pickup: An agreement where a distributor acquires a finished negative and agrees to pay P&A and distribution costs. As opposed to deals where the distributor is involved during production.

Negative print: A reverse light image capture.

Negative stock: In professional practice, the film which is exposed in the camera renders a negative image when developed (as in, reverse video or the negative of a snap shot). This type of film is called negative stock. The negative which results from the exposure of this type of film must then be printed onto another piece of film, which, logically enough, is then called the print.

Negative: The original film that is used in the camera, from which a positive print is made for editing. The negative is assembled to match the edited workprint, and an answer print, for projection of the completed film, is struck from the negative.

Neo-realism: An influential movement of the late 1940s and 1950s that originated in Italy; inaugurated by Jean Renoir, but associated with Italian post-war directors (Rossellini, Visconti, and De Sica); refers to films made outside the studio, with shooting on real locations, sometimes the absence of a script and/or non-professional casts and actors - all designed simultaneously to cut costs and increase the impression of spontaneity; neo-realistic films often deal with contemporary social and political issues.

Net profit: The amount of excess money available after exhibitors, distributors, cast, crew and financiers have taken their share.

Nets: A bobbinet on a frame used to cut lighting intensity by either a half stop or full stop.

Network sale: The sale of a film to a particular television network to gain that network exclusive rights to the film for a certain period.

Network TV: Originally referred to the "Big Three" (ABC, NBC and CBS), but now with additional competitors, including Fox Channel, often known as 'free-TV'.

Neutral Density (ND): Colorless filters that reduce the amount of light in controlled degrees.

New wave: Also known as Nouvelle Vague; originally referred to a group of individualistic, innovative, and non-traditional French filmmakers, directors and producers in the late 1950s and early 1960s, including Francois Truffaut, Jean-Luc Godard, Claude Chabrol, Eric Rohmer, and Alain Resnais, who began as critics on Cahiers du Cinema and espoused the principles of auteur theory; the New Wave film style was characterized by a cinema verite style with the use of the jump cut, the hand-held camera, non-linear storytelling, and loose, improvised direction; now used to generally refer to any new movement in a national cinema.

Newsreel: Refers to a filmed cinema news report.

Newton's laws repealed: In which action becomes mysteriously decoupled from reaction, usually in connection with a firearm. Typically, a bullet from the hero's handgun lifts the villain off his feet and hurls him backward (often through one of those ubiquitous plate glass windows that cars like to drive through) while the hero doesn't budge a millimeter.

NG: An abbreviation of the phrase "no good", which can be used to describe various aspects of filmmaking, i.e. "a ng take".

Nickelodeon: The term for a makeshift motion picture theater, often a converted store, which proliferated all over the US, mostly in working-class areas of metropolitan centers, during the first decade of the 20th century. The name was derived from the 5 cents/nickel charged to patrons.

Nihilistic (nihilism): A dark and brooding film that features a downbeat, depressing, dreary, cynical, gloomy or bleak tone; often doom-laden and concerned with the subjects of death, suffering, tragedy, unhappiness, and existential despair; the protagonist often meets with death or tragedy in a film's conclusion.

Nitrate film base: A highly-flammable kind of film base, composed of cellulose nitrate, used up until the late 1940s when it was then supplanted by acetate base.

Noble savage syndrome: Thrown into the company of a native tribe of any description, the protagonist discovers the true meaning of life and sees through the sham of modern civilization. Wisdom and sensitivity are inevitably possessed by any race, class, age group or ethnic or religious minority that has been misunderstood. Such movies seem well-intentioned at first glance, but replace one stereotype for another; the natives seem noble, but never real. They may be starving, but if they're noble and have a few good songs, why worry?

Noir: Usually refers to the classic black and white film noir style used in detective mysteries, typically employing hard lighting and dark, low key lighting.

Noise: In audio systems, noise is the electrical interference or other unwanted sound introduced into the system (i.e. hiss, hum, rumble, crosstalk, etc).

Non-linear editing: The computer-assisted editing of a movie without the need to assemble it in linear sequence. The visual equivalent of word processing.

Non-reflex: A camera that does not have a "through the lens" viewfinding system, but gives you an image in the viewfinder through a seperate lens. Older Bolexes and Bell & Howell cameras are non-reflex.

Non-speaking role: A small role in a film, usually a brief appearance on screen, that has no dialogue but where the individual is clearly identifiable and usually appears in the credits.

Non-sync (non-synchronized): Refers to a scene shot without synchronized sound - and sounds must be added later during the editing stage; sync sound is its opposite; also refers to a mis-matched soundtrack; aka asynchronous.

Non-traditional casting: A movement, now officially headed by the Non-Traditional Casting Project (NTCP) to "promote inclusive hiring practices and standards, diversity in leadership and balanced portrayals of persons of color and persons with disabilities"; not to be confused with cast against type or miscast.

Normal (clip: 680 K) from "Cabaret": The lenses most commonly used, they render perspective and relative dimensions more "realistically" (i.e., with less distortion—closer to the way in which the human eye interprets perspective) than their cousins at either extremity of focal length. In contemporary practice, lenses with focal lengths of 20-35mm are referred to as "normal".

Normal lens: In 16mm this is the 25mm lens. In 35mm it is the 50mm lens. It is the point between the widening of the image by the wide angle lens and the magnifiying of the image by the telephoto lens.

Nose grease: Just what it sounds like. Used in the old trick among camerapersons to lubricate the pressure plate by wiping it along the side of the nose.

Nose room: When a subject is in profile, nose room is the space between their face and the edge of the frame, similar to Head Room. In a profile shot, nose room is considered "good" when a little extra room in front of the person's face, rather than behind their head. The general rule is that the space around the subject should be apportioned to 2/3rds in front of the subject's head, and 1/3rd behind.

Nostalgia film: A film that wistfully looks back at an earlier past time, often depicting it as more innocent and uncomplicated than it actually was, historically; nostalgia films usually look back on the protagonist's or narrator's childhood.

Notch: A recess on the edge of a piece of film which automatically triggers a mechanism effecting some modification of the duplication process, commonly a change of exposure light intensity. (Film Editing)

Novelization; Refers to making a novel from a film or screenplay.

NTSC: An abbreviation, refers specifically to National Television System Committee that sets TV and video standards; also refers to the US and Japanese video systems that have 525 horizontal scan lines, 16 million different colors, and 30 frames per second (or 60 half-frames (interlaced) per second); competing systems in Europe and worldwide are PAL (Phase

Alternating Line) and SECAM (Sequential Color with Memory).

Nudie (or nudie flick): An old term for a pornographic movie, often used during the age of the Hayes Code when nudity was forbidden by censors in mainstream films on the silver screen; an era of nudie films was generated by filmmaker Russ Meyer in the late 50s.

Nut: In the movie-theatre business, refers to operating expenses associated with a film (the exhibitor's calculation of what it takes to lease his theater, to staff and run it. etc.).

O

O.C.N.: O.C.N. stands for Original Color Negative. It is simply your developed negative.

Obie: An eyelight mounted on the camera.

Obligatory scene : A cliched and expected scene for a particular genre, e.g., a love scene in a romance or dramatic film, a shoot-out in a Western, the solving of a crime in a mystery, a rescue in an action film, etc.

Octave: The interval between two sounds having a basic frequency ratio of 2 to 1.

Odd couple formula: Seemingly incompatible characters are linked to each other in a plot which depends on their differences for its comic and dramatic interest. Essential that one member of each team be a slob, as revealed by presence of fast-food wrappers in back seat of his Hollywood Cop Car (q.v.).

Odds on edge rule: The odds that a car in real life will be able to travel any appreciable distance balanced on two wheels: 1 in 7 million. The odds that this will happen during a chase scene in a movie: 1 in 43.

Off book: When an actor has completely memorized their lines and cues, they are described as being off-book.

Off-line editing: Editing which involves the transfer of tape to and from multiple sources.

Off-line editor: A person who performs the off-line work, completing preliminary editing done in a lower-cost editing facility, to prepare a list of edits for the final, or on-line editor.

Offline: The videotape editing process whereby the final edit list is compiled, usually in a more inexpensive edit room, in preparation for the on-line edit.

Off-scale: Outside the range of the standard light values of a printer.

On the visible stage, or within the boundaries of the camera's field of vision: One-liner a term for a short, one-line joke (that contains its own punchline); also the term may refer to the 'high concept' description of a film - a few words used to describe a script, storyline or a film's premise that a person can easily understand with a simple one-liner.

One light: The alternative to a Timed Print, a one light is a print that has not been corrected shot by shot, but shows what all the shots look like with the same printing lights in contrast to each other. Sometimes this can be helpful to know the range of fluctuation in exposure and color. (But it is curiously common for a lab to do some timing, even on a one light print, at the change of locations, at the change of rolls, or if one shot is so drastically off from the rest and it would be practically unseeable otherwise.)

One man (or woman) show: A scripted or filmed narrative (or an avant-garde or experimental film) featuring a solo performance piece with only one actor or actress who sometimes plays multiple roles or characters; often presented by a stand-up comedian; contrast with concert film.

One-at-a-time attack rule: In any situation where the hero is alone, surrounded by dozens of bad guys, they will always obligingly attack one at a time.

One-light print: A print made with a single printer light setting for all shots in the film being printed. A common method to produce a 'daily' color print.

One-reeler: Refers to a film 10-12 minutes long.

One-sheet: Refers to the typical size of a movie poster.

On-line editing: The final editing process in which the final video cut is merged with titles, sound effects and other special effects.

On-line editor: A person who performs the on-line work, who completes the final editing and preparation for distribution of film, with edits often from a list of changes created by the off-line editor.

On-line: The process of final editing and preparation for distribution of film, with edits often from a list of changes created during off-line.

Opacity: The ratio of the amount of light falling on a surface to the amount of light which is transmitted.

Opaque leader: Any strip of flexible, optically opaque material used to space picture in A/B roll film cutting and editing.

Opaquer: An artist who colours in the individual cells of an animated film.

Open: The time at which a movie is first released in theatres. Movies will often open at different times in different countries/regions.

Opening credits or title (sequence): The presentation of the 'opening credits' (as an introduction to the audience about the film and including selected important members of the production) is known as the opening credits sequence; sometimes it is superimposed on the action, but often exists as static letters on a solid background; since the closing or end credits usually list the entire cast and production crew, the opening credits sequence is usually positioned to set the mood of the film, and sometimes even lacks any credits except the film's title

Opening weekend: When a movie is first released in each country, its success is often measured in terms of its gross for the first weekend it opened. A disproportionate number of people usually see a movie on its opening weekend so box-office numbers are a good guide as to whether the movie will be a hit or not.

Optical effects: A laboratory or print procedure in which shots are modified by use of an optical printer. These are most commonly seen as fades and dissolves, however, it can include a wide range of special effects procedures.

Optical printer: A laboratory machine for combining the images of one or more reels of film through photographic techniques. Contrast with digital compositing.

Optical printing: Basically, rephotographying film frame by frame. this is a way to make a copy of a film with many more possibilities than contact printing, but, at least with 16mm, resulting in a little added contrast and a little loss of clarity.

Optical sound: Optical Sound is the system used by a projector to play back sound from a film print. The sound is exposed onto the film as a clear modulating line against black. It corresponds to the moduations of the sound. The projector reads the track by passing it between the exciter lamp a light-sensitive photo-electric cell which generates a voltage that is amplified and fed into a speaker.

Optical soundtrack: A composite print in which the soundtrack is recorded via the varying width of a transparent track which runs beside the sequence of frames on a print.

Optical stereo: A film recording system replayed by scanning the stereo tracks by means of a photo cell lamp.

Optical track: An intermediate step from going from your mix master to your final print is to have an optical track struck. An optical track is photographed onto a blank piece of special high contract stock by the facility where the mix is done, or by the lab. The optical track is a separate roll of film from the original negative and is combined with picture when a print is struck.

Opticals: In film-making, refers to a visual device, e.g., a fade, wipe, dissolve, superimposition, freeze-frame, split-screen, composite (a train reflection in a car window), or another effect, some of which can be created in the camera, and others that have to be achieved in post-production by mixers or other specialized techniques.

Option: To buy the exclusive rights to a script, within a specified time at a set price, effectively guaranteeing that during the indicated time period, the writer will not share the idea with anyone else.

Orange stick: An orange stick is found at the drug store for cleaning your nails. It is the preferable way to clean the gate.

Orchestral arrangements: An adaptation of the score for all instruments in an orchestra.

Orchestrator: A person who writes orchestral arrangements.

Orientation: Within the film frame, compositions can be either oriented properly (usually this is the case), or disoriented - to intentionally create a dramatic effect.

Original: Any film, negative or reversal, that was shot by a camera, as opposed to a print or intermediate copy. The term original can be used interchangeably with negative, but is as especially handy term when taking about reversal film, where it is the clearest way indicating whether something is a dupe or the original.

Oscar bait: Often used in a derogatory way to describe studio-invented pre-release PR buzz that a film (usually an epic or serious biopic released late in the year) is worthy, meaningful, and deserving of Oscar awards; the term was reportedly first used by Hedda Hopper in a "Looking at Hollywood" column on June 1, 1948; the term either refers to (1) a self-proclaimed, "important", often over-produced film, undercut by its attempt to appeal to all demographics, or (2) a showy acting performance designed to draw attention to itself; these kinds of films and performances were the sort that used to guarantee an Oscar from Academy voters during the film industry's adolescent years of the 1950's and early 1960's, but are now considered either pretentious and/or cheesy in the modern age, and ironically often hurt the film's or actor's chances at winning an Oscar, though some films still succeed.

Oscars: The name given to the awards of AMPAS (the Academy of Motion Picture Arts and Sciences) given each year to various performers and others in the film industry; officially known as the "Academy Award of Merit"

Outdated stock: Film is perishable. When it starts getting stale the dyes will shift color and the grain will build up, giving you a generally fogged, muddy and desaturated effect. It is only after about 2 or 3 years that this will start to happen, provided the film is refrigerated. Faster films tend to become outdated slightly faster than slow films. Likewise, color film will become outdated a little sooner than black and white. The flip-side is that outdated stock can be gotten quite cheaply, and often for free.

Outgoing scene: The first scene of a dissolve or wipe effect which changes into the second, or incoming scene.

Outline: An expanded synopsis of the story created by the writer. Usually just a few pages in length, it details the main plot, sub-plots and the relationships between the main characters.

Out-takes: Refers to camera shots that are not included in the final cut or print of a film, often retrieved from the cutting room floor, and shown during the closing credits.

Overacting: Poor, overly-broad, or 'over-the-top' acting by a 'ham' actor; aka "hamming it up" or 'chewing up the scenery'; sometimes considered in a positive light as 'campy'; contrast with underacting.

Overcrank: To run the camera faster, producing slow motion. The term has survived from the time when you would crank a camera.

Overexposure: Filming a scene with more light than the emulsion of the film can easily tollerate. The image will be too light and there will be less depth of field than if the lens had been set correctly. If compensated for in printing, the image will appear contrasty.

Overlap: The carry-over of dialogue, sounds, or music from one scene to another; occurs when the cut in the soundtrack is not at the same time as the cut in the image; aka overlap sound.

Overlapping and matching action: Repeating part of the action in one shot at the beginning of the next shot, or covering the action with two or more cameras, then matching the overlaps on the editing table for the purpose of making a smooth cut on action.

Over-the-shoulder (OTS) shot: A commonly-used camera angle or view in films, mostly in shot/reverse-shot editing, in which the camera records the action from behind the shoulder and/or head of one of the characters, thus framing the image; the two characters are thus linked or connected to each other, and their positions are established.

Overture: In film terms, a pre-credits or opening credits musical selection that sets the mood and theme for the upcoming film.

Ozoner: Slang term for a drive-in movie theater; aka passion pit.

P

P & A: The marketting and launch costs of a film. It is the amount of money spent of Prints and Advertising.

P.O.V. shot (or point-of-view shot): A subjective shot made from the perspective of one of the characters to show the audience the scene as it would look through the character's eyes; usually coupled (before and/or after) with a reaction shot (or a three-shot sequence called a shot reverse shot) to establish the POV; also known as first-person point-of-view shot or subjective camera.

Pace: The speed/tempo of the dramatic action, which is usually enhanced by the soundtrack and the speed of the dialogue, the type of editing, etc.

Package: The marketing elements of a film project, such as script, signed film stars, director, locations, 'high-concept' hook, etc.

Packaging: Similar to the Marquee Value of a film, it is the combination of the reputations of the major stars and creative personnel. This is used to gain investment dollars and pre-sales to distributors.

PAL (Phase Alternating Line): The European color television standard that specifies a 25Hz frame rate and 625 lines per frame.

Pan (or panning shot): Abbreviation for panorama shot; refers to the horizontal scan, movement, rotation or turning of the camera in one direction (to the right or left) around a fixed axis while filming; a variation is the swish pan (also known as flash pan, flick pan, zip pan, blur pan, or whip pan), in which the camera is purposely panned in either direction at a very fast pace, creating the impression of a fast-moving horizontal blurring of images across the screen; often confused with a dolly or tracking shot.

Pan and scan: A technique that avoids the 'letterboxing' of a widescreen film for a full-framed 4x3 home video or TV picture, by focusing on the elements of the picture that are most important to the plot and by adjusting or cropping the image; when an important part of the image drops out of the visible screen, the picture is mechanically panned to the side (left or right in a ping-pong effect) to show the missing part - hence, the term pan-and-scan; approximately 43% of the visuals are sacrificed or cropped out in the pan-and-scan version, affecting the director's original intent and aesthetic sense.

Pan: A horizontal camera move on an axis, from right to left or left to right. In a pan the camera is turning on an axis rather than across space, as in a dolly shot. Not to be confused with Tilt, technically it is not correct to say "pan up" or "pan down," when you really mean tilt.

Paper tape: A skinny roll of tape used to tape down the ends of film when editing, called paper tape to distinguish it from splicing tape.

Parallel editing: The technique of intercutting between two simultaneous stories or scenes.

Parallel: Editing that cuts between two sequences taking place at different locations and possibly different times; parallel action refers to a narrative device in which two scenes are observed in parallel by cross-cutting; parallel sound refers to sound that matches the accompanying image; aka cross-cutting, inter-cutting.

Parallels: Temporary Scaffolding, used as a platform for the camera, lighting, or other rigging.

Parody: A comedy that imitates or makes fun of an existing work(s) in an absurd, non-sensical way, and exaggerates its characteristics.

Pass bypass principle: Any theater that accepts passes will invariably exclude their use for any movie worth seeing.

Pay or play: A contract provision which commits the production company to compensate a cast or crew member for a project whether or not that project ever goes into production.

Payoff: A dramatic scene that justifies everything that preceded it; the necessary result of a complication for which the audience has been prepared; contrast to punchline and money shot.

Payola: Refers to bribery or under-the-table payments.

Pen: To write, especially a script.

Perf: Perforations. The sprocket holes in a piece of film.

Persona: Literally, Latin for "mask"; related to the on-screen image or personality associated with a star.

PG: A certificate issued by the MPAA indicating that a film's content is suitable for viewing by children, but recommends parental guidance.

PG-13: A certificate introduced by the MPAA on July 1, 1984 to indicate that a movie's content is rated as slightly stronger than a PG certificate.

Phantom power: A method of remotely powering the preamplifier or impedance converter which is buitlt into many microphones by sending a voltage along the audio cable.

Phase distortion: This is a shifting of output voltage relative to input by an amount which is disproportional to frequency. This will not detectable until it an amplifier.

Phase shift: The displacement of a waveform in time. Some electrical components introduce phase shift into a signal. When various frequencies are displaced differently, distortion occurs. Electrical cancellation may occur when two equal signals are out of phase by 1~3()¡. However, this may also be used are a encoding method where the shift is removed on playback (similar to the method in which a Dolby Surround sound track is encoded and played back.

Phase: The timing relationship between two signals.

Photo flood: A photo flood is a high power screw-in light bulb that is often used in with a clamp light fixture. Photo floods are usually anywhere from 250 watts to 500 watts.

Pic(s) (also pix): Slang terms for motion picture(s).

Pick-up shot: Reshooting a portion of a scene, the rest of which was acceptably filmed in a previous take.

Pick-up: The re-shooting or sound recording of a scene without using the entire crew, just those involved in the aspect which needs to be perfected.

Pickups: Movies made by one studio that have been acquired by another. Alternately, any footage shot after production wraps.

Picture car: A vehicle shown in a movie.

Picture within a picture: A particular story-telling approach, literally, to have one film within another; in some cases, the characters are aware of the 'film-within-a-film,' and break the fourth wall and enter into or interact with it; aka subset film or film within a film.

Picture: The workprint, to distinguish it from the mag tracks.

Pigeon: This is a heavy round disc with a lighting stud, used to position a light on the floor, much lower than a stand will go. Basically, it is a Hi Hat for lights.

Pilot tone: A sine wave signal, recorded by various field audio recorders at a known frequency, which is used to resolve the tape speed on playback to retain sync with film camera footage.

Pilottone: A 60 Hz reference signal recorded onto the audio tape to allow transfer to mag precisely at sound speed, used for Sync Sound filming. (In Europe in it is 50Hz.)

Pin: A component of a camera or printer mechanism which engages with a perforation hole to move and locate film for exposure.

Pink noise: A sound signal that has an equal amount of energy per octave or fraction of an octave. (Sound)

Pin-up girl: Refers to the most sexually-attractive star-actresses of an era, who would be popularized in seductive poses usually semi-clad - in pictures, calendars, or mass-produced posters that were usually literally "pinned-up", usually with thumbtacks, on bedroom walls, the insides of lockers, and so forth; this practice started especially amongst GI servicemen away from home during military combat who pined for the 'girl-back-home'; related terms are cover girl (for magazine covers), model or cheesecake.

Pipeline: A schedule of movie projects in production.

Pitch(es): Orally or written (sales) proposals for film projects usually made by screenwriters (to sell a screenplay idea), or independent producers for studio producers or executives to obtain financial backing; anything from a one-line description to a two- to three-page treatment of an idea (before becoming a script); also refers to short phrases that capture or succinctly sum up the script.

Pivotal character: Refers to the character that launches the action between the protagonist and the antagonist; or the character who sets the main events of the plot in motion; films with a classic "love triangle" involve a woman who serves as the 'pivotal character' between two rival suitors

Pix: An abbreviation for Picture used on the leader.

Pixelation: Visual squarelike digital break up that appears on the monitor when playing back a video from a digital medium such as a miniDV or a Digibeta resulting from some sort of corruption of the video. Also, A variant of stop-motion animation where actors are the objects being filmed. The key example is Neighbours.

Pixillation: An animation technique in which the illusion of continuous, real movement of three-dimensional objects, often people, is broken and/or made to move unevenly or jerky through the use of stop-action cinematography (single frame animation) or by printing only selected frames from the continuously-exposed negative.

Plastic leader: This is leader for putting at the head and tail of a print. It is, as one would guess, made out of plastic, and is more durable than Emulsion Leader and much less expensive, and so it is the better choice for a print. However, it cannot be Cement Spliced, so it should not used for your negative.

Plate: A background for any type of process shot.

Play back: The playing of music or special sound effects during the shooting of the scene. The sound will be re-recorded later in the editing suites. This technique is often used to keep dancers and singers in time with the music while they are acting.

Plot and plot point: Refers to a series of dramatic events or actions that make up a film's narrative; a plot point is a key turning point or moment in a film's story that significantly advances the action; plot points either set the story further into motion, or disrupt and complicate the plot; also known as beat or A story; contrast to a subplot (aka B story or C story) - a secondary plot in a film; a plot plant is the technique of 'planting' an apparently trivial piece of infoımation early in a story - that becomes more important later on.

Point of view (POV): The perspective from which the film story is told; also refers to a shot that depicts the outlook or position of a character.

Point of view shot: Is a shot where the action is seen through the eyes of a particular character, the shot generally preceded or followed by a shot of the character looking. Hitchcock's *Rear Window* (1954) structures its whole action around this principle and Robert Montgomery's *The Lady in the Lake* (1948) also experimented with a subjective camera by showing us only what the leading character himself saw and only showing the character himself in the mirror.

Polyester base: Polyester base is a very durable type of film, that is virtually unrippable. Some people claim that it is harder to splice, but that is more a matter of getting used to the technique. Significantly, it cannot be Cement Spliced, making it impractical as original material (also, its durability could spell disaster for the delicate mechanism of a camera in the event of a jam). However, its durability makes it very advantageous for release prints.

Pops principle, the: In movies with teenage characters, there is usually a character named Pops who runs the local hang-out or dance club.

Porn (porno): Refers to a film that exploits sex.

Pornographic film: A film in which sex is graphically depicted to a large degree.

Positive print: An original light image captured on film.

Positive scratch: The black image on a print of a scratch on the positive from which the print was made.

Post-credits sequence: Either a throwaway scene or an epilogue that happens during or after the end credits; sometimes used as a bonus for theatergoers who remain to watch the credits, and partly to generate 'buzz' about the extra scene.

Post-modern: Refers to a return to tradition, in reaction to more 'modernist' styles.

Post-production co-ordinator: A person who works many facets of the post-production process, including ensuring the smooth operation of the editorial department, coordinating the production and delivery of final delivery elements, scheduling and coordinating ADR sessions, managing the administration of the department including post-production accounting and final delivery paperwork, organizing final post-production related documents, and coordinating the final wrap and proper storage of final video and audio masters and offline editorial materials.

Post-production supervisor: A person overseeing the entire post-production of a project. They report directly to the producer and/or the studio in charge of the feature. Working side by side with the director and editor, the supervisor has the responsibility of finishing the film on time and on budget while satisfying the wants of the director. Post-production supervisors have authority over post-production co-ordinators. Typical duties include: Controlling all activities with vendors such as optical houses, sound facilities, inserts, ADR, reshooting, CGI, score, delivery requirements to domestic and international distributors, legal clearances, preview screenings, color timing, video mastering and budgeting the movie through the completion and delivery.

Post-production: The final stage in a film's production after principal photography, involving editing, the addition of sound/visual effects, musical scoring, mixing, dubbing, distribution, etc.; post-synchronization refers to recording the sound after the film has been shot; aka post; contrast to pre-production.

Potboiler: A literary reference to the hard-edged, American detective/crime thrillers (also often called 'pulp fiction' or 'dime novels') rapidly written and filled with violence, crime, and sex - to literally 'boil the pot'; also known as hard-boiled.

Practical: A practical is any photo flood-type of bulb, used within the shot, in a household lamp or otherwise visible. The term practical is sometimes used interchangeably with photo flood, even though it specifically refers to a light used in the shot.

Preamplifier: An electronic device that boosts extremely weak signal voltages, such as those from microphones or mag heads, to a level that is usable by power amplifiers.

Pre-blacked: A video tape which has already had a control track, usually with SMPTE encoded time code, but without any picture or sound. This is done to facilitate the video editing or assembly process.

Pre-code: Refers to the four-five years (1930-1934) before the enforcement of the Hays Production Code in Hollywood, to rigidly sanitize and censor films. In film plots from mid-1935 and lasting about the next 30 years, adultery and promiscuity were prohibited (unless they ended in a miserable downfall), and all crimes (and their criminals) had to be punished.

Pre-light: Setting up the lights and any scaffolding required prior to shooting. Just a time saving exercise.

Premiere: The first official public screening of a movie, marking the kick-off, opening or opening night; a 'red carpet' premiere is one with greater publicity and hoopla (sensational promotion), ballyhoo, or hype; aka a bow, debut, or preem.

Premise: The main idea of a movie, usually explainable in a few sentences.

Pre-production: The planning stage in a film's production after the project is finally greenlighted, and before principal photography or actual shooting commences, involving script treatment and editing/rewriting, scheduling, set design and construction, casting, budgeting and financial planning, and scouting/selection of locations; contrast to post-production.

Prequel: The second or third film in a series of films that presents characters and/or events that are chronologically set before the time frame of the original movie; contrast to sequel.

Preroll: Preroll is extra time at the beginning of a sound take to accommodate the slow lock-up time of some post production time code devices.

Prescoring: Recording of music or other sound prior to the shooting of the picture which is to accompany it. The most common usage is in animated film.

Pre-screen: To view/watch/see a movie before it is released for the public (at the premiere).

Presenter: A presenter is person (often famous or well respected) who introduces a movie or show on screen or via voice-over. Some films include a credit "Presented by", or "presents", which indicates the person is an executive producer as opposed to someone who appears in the film.

Pressure plate: Part of the internal workings of a camera, the pressure plate is located on the other side of the film from the gate. It is a smooth, spring-loaded plate that holds the film on the film plane and acts as a brake, helping to hold the film steady while it is exposed.

Preview: A short film, usually with excerpts from a future film, intended as an advertisement; a sneak preview refers to an unadvertised, often surprise showing of an entire film before its general release or announced premiere, often to gauge audience reaction; aka trailer.

Previsualization artist: An designer who uses low resolution proxy models, quick OpenGL hardware renderings, and other 3D FX systems to completely conceptualize a sequence that requires either visual FX or character animation with the goal of to producing usable data that will help streamline the production process.

Prime lens: A prime lens is one with a single focal length, wide, normal or telephoto, as opposed to a Zoom Lens, which has a variable focal length. They often come in a set of different focal lengths. Prime lenses tend to be sharper, faster and will often focus closer than zoom lenses.

Principal photography: Refers to the filming of major and significant portions of a film production that involves the main/lead actors/actresses; contrast to second-unit photography.

Principals: Refers to the main characters in a play or film (usually those that have dialogue); contrasted to protagonists or antagonists, or extras.

Principle of evil marksmanship: The bad guys are always lousy shots in the movies. Three villains with Uzzis will go after the hero, spraying thousands of rounds which miss him, after which he picks them off with a handgun.

Principle of pedestrian pathology: Whenever a character on foot is being pursued by one in a car, the pedestrian inevitably makes the mistake of running down the middle of the street, instead of ducking down a narrow alley, into a building, behind a telephone pole, etc. All that saves such pedestrians is the fact that in such scenes the character on foot can always outrun the car.

Principle of selective lethality: The lethality of a weapon varies, depending on the situation. A single arrow will drop a stampeding bison in its tracks, but it takes five or six to kill an important character. A single bullet will always kill an extra on the spot, but it takes dozens to bring down the hero.

Print stock: Film used by the lab for making copies (prints). It is usually of a longer pitch than camera stock so as to be smoothly sandwiched against the camera stock on the printing machine. It is also much slower (with an A.S.A. of about 12) than camera stock, as light is less of a problem in printing than it is when it is being focused through a lens in a camera.

Print: A projectable version of a movie, usually consisting of one or more reels. When refering to a particular take on a continuity report, "print" indicates that the take should be developed.

Printer's sync: This is the offsetting of sound 26 frames earlier than picture, corresponding to the distance between the sound reader and the gate of the projector. To be in sync on a projector all prints are lined up in printer's sync. Usually the lab lines up the sound and picture in printer's sync, putting the beep on the track 26 frames earlier than the "2" in the Academy Leader. This is known as pulling up the sound. If there was some reason for you to line up the sound yourself, it is very important to label the sync mark "printer's sync" so that the sound is not accidentally pulled up twice.

Printing sync: The relation between the picture and sound components in which they are printed to give the necessary displacement for projection as a composite print.

Prints and Advertising (P&A) budget: Prints are the actual physical film that are shown in theaters and are quite expensive to make and distribute, costing about $2,000 per print. Each theater needs at least one print and possibly more depending on how many screens the film is playing on. The advertising part of the budget is the amount spent on just that, advertising. Most of the money is spent on TV, but radio, newspapers and magazines, the Internet and in theater advertising are also very important. The average film spends $34.4 million on P&A, while some films have spent more than $100 million.

Prism shutter: A device used on many film viewers, editing machines, and some high-speed cameras, consisting of a rotating prism of four or more sides through which the viewer light passes as film is pulled continuously through it.

Prison film: A very popular sub-genre with the film's plot usually set within the walls of an institutional prison; themes involve imprisonment and/or escape, the effects on the characters involved and interactions between officers and inmates, and issues of justice/injustice; the prison flick sub-genre can be found in any major genre (animated, drama, comedy, musical, science fiction, sexploitation, etc.).

Process (projection or shot): A technique that shoots live action in front of a screen on which the background view is projected; a process shot refers to a shot of live action in front of a process projection.

Process shot: A shot that will be composited from two other shots. The background part of this process is called a 'plate'.

Producer (film): The chief of a movie production in all logistical matters (i.e., scheduling, budgeting) save the creative efforts of the director; raises funding and financing, acquires or develops a story, finalizes the script, hires key personnel, and arranges for distributors of the film to theaters; serves as the liaison between the financiers and the film-makers, while managing the production from start to finish.

Product placement: A business arrangement whereby the filmmakers agree to show the products or logo of a particular company, usually in return for payment or other consideration.

Production (value): Production refers to an entire movie project; pre-production refers to the stage at which a film is prepared to go into production; post-production refers to the stage at which editing, scoring and effects are executed on a motion picture; production value refers to the overall quality of a film, based not on the script, acting, or director, but on criteria such as costumes, sets, design, etc.

Production accountant: The person responsible for managing finances during the production.

Production assistant: A person responsible for various odd jobs, which could include such disseparate tasks as running errands, stopping traffic, acting as couriers, fetching items from craft service, etc. Tasks and levels of responsibility can vary greatly, depending on the film, the needs of the rest of the team, and the skills of the individuals PA themselves. Production Assistants are often attached to individual actors or filmmakers.

Production budget: The amount of money it cost make the movie including pre-production, film and post-production, but excluding distribution costs. The average cost of a wide release is about $65 million, with the most expensive films topping $200 million.

Production buyer: A person who purchases supplies, equipment, and property necessary for a production.

Production company: A general term for a company that is associated with the making of a movie.

Production coordinator: The person responsible for overseeing practical matters such as ordering equipment, getting near-location accommodations for the cast and crew, etc.

Production design: Refers to a film's overall design, continuity, visual look and composition (colors, sets, costumes, scenery, props, locations, etc.) that are the responsibility of the production designer; the art department refers to the people in various roles (e.g., matte painters, set designers and decorators, illustrators, title designers, scenic artists, and storyboard artists) who work under the production designer's supervision; the art director is responsible for the film's physical settings (specifically refers to the interiors, landscapes, buildings, etc.)

Production designer: An artist responsible for designing the overall visual appearance of a movie.

Production dupe: A duplicate negative prepared in the final form for release printing.

Production illustrator: A person responsible for drawing the storyboards and anything else that needs to be drawn during the production of the movie.

Production manager: Reporting to the film's producer, this person supervises the budget, hires the crew, approves purchase orders & time cards, and generally makes sure all departments are doing their respective jobs within the parameters of the budget.

Production report: A daily report of actual progress versus the production schedule. Includes dope sheets, continuity reports, and call sheets, as well as extensive notes regarding on-set happenings, activities of the cast and crew, and explanations of unexpected events.

Production schedule: A detailed plan of the timing of activities associated with the making of a movie, of particular interest to production managers.

Production secretary: Secretary to the production manager.

Production sound mixer: The head of the sound department on the set. They are responsible for the process of recording all sync dialog and sync sound effects in a scene. The Production Sound Mixer has a number of duties: selection and operation of the microphones, and recording equipment used on the set, directing the boom operator, combining the sound of multiple microphones used to capture dialog and effects on a set, recording sound ambiance and room tone for all scenes, and wild track that will aid the editor and sound mixer in matching the different sound takes in a scene for smooth sound transitions.

Production sound: Recording and/or mixing sound on location during the film or video shoot. Typically this has been recorded to an analog Nagra reel-to-reel machine, though DAT recorders and other digital formats are now making significant inroads.

Production: The general process of putting a film together, including casting, set construction, costuming, rehearsals, and shooting; also refers to the middle stage of production which is preceded by pre-production and followed by post-production.

Projection leader: A short length of film having standard markings on it, used to enable projectionists to make instant changeovers from one projector to another.

Projection-contrast original: An original reversal film which is designed to have normal contrast when projected.

Projectionist: A studio or cinema employee that operates a projector.

Projector: The machine that rapidly puts ('projects') a succession of motion picture images (individual frames) up onto a screen, using the principle of illusion of motion.

Prologue: A speech, preface, introduction, or brief scene preceding the the main action or plot of a film; contrast to epilogue.

Promo: Slang term for sales promotion.

Prompter: A person who supplies actors with the correct lines from the script if they forget.

Prop: Anything an actor touches or uses on the set; e.g. phones, guns, cutlery, etc. Movie animals and all food styling (food seen or eaten on set/screen) also fall into this domain.

Property assistant: Responsible for the placement and maintenance of props on a set.

Property master: The person responsible for buying, acquiring, and/or manufacturing any props needed for a production. The property master is responsible for all aspects of prop use on the set and, in conjunction with the script supervisor, for maintaining set continuity. Contrast with set dresser.

Props (or property): Abbreviation for properties - refers to the furnishings, fixtures, hand-held objects, decorations, or any other moveable items that are seen or used on a film (or stage) set but that are not a structural part of the set; usually the responsibility of the prop man or property master.

Prosthetic appliances: Makeup that requires gluing additions (prosthetic appliances) made of a material such as latex or gelatin to an actors skin. May be applied by someone other than the designer.

Protagonist: The lead or main character in a film; also known as hero/heroine; contrast to antagonist.

Publicity department: The section of a production's crew responsible for promoting a movie. Individual positions within in this department include: unit publicist, publicity assistant, and stills photographer.

Publicity director: Person employed by a studio to conceive and oversee the publicity campaign that opens a movie. In many cases, this person never even appears on the set — especially if the movie is a pickup and didn't have a releasing studio at the time it was produced. In other cases, this person is frequently on the set and directly supervises the efforts of the unit publicist.

Pull down: A transfer of sound slowed down from film speed, 24 film frames per second, to video speed, 29.97 video frames per second, which is the equivalent of 23.98 film frames per second. This must be done to line it up with a video transfer of picture when transferring sync sound to video.

Pull processing: Pull processing is a special type of processing where the film is developed for a shorter time than normal, usually to make up for intended overexposure.

Pull up: This term can be a little confusing since it has three meanings that both apply to sound. **1.** The process of offsetting the sound 26 frames ahead of picture when making a print. **2.** Pull Ups, as a noun, are transfers of the first 26 frames of sound from a reel that are spliced onto the outgoing sound of the previous reel so that sound is not lost when the film is printed with the sound pulled up, since 26 frames of sound are cut off when reels are joined. **3.** A transfer of the sound from a video, sped up from video speed, 29.97 video frames per second, which is the equivalent of 23.98 film frames per second, to film speed, 24 film frames per second. This must be done when the optical track is made after having mixed in video.

Pulldown claw: The pulldown claw is part of the camera movement, which advances the film from the exposed frame to the next unexposed frame while the camera's shutter is closed.

Punch: A device for punching a hole in film leader to locate a starting point for editorial or printing synchronization. Also refers to specular light.

Punchline: A funny, witty line that culminates a story, joke or scene; contrast with payoff and one-liner.

Puppeteer: Someone who operates puppets; these may be either physically controlled (e.g., worn), cable operated, or radio controlled. This may also refer to remote-controlled portions of a costume.

Push processing: Push processing is a special type of processing where the film is developed for a longer time than normal, usually to make up for intended underexposure. It should be noted that only entire rolls can be pushed, not individual scenes. Pushing film will add some contrast and graininess.

Pyrotechnician: A member of the crew with expertise in fire or explosions.

Q

Q rating: Refers to an ad research rating that gauges how easily a celebrity is recognized — and how well the celebrity is liked.

Quarter inch: A reference to the standard width magnetic audio tape which is used to record film production sound.

Quarter: A quarter of a year; three months. Used by production accountants and publicity departments for financial issues.

Quartz light: Can also be called halogen light or tungsten light. A quartz light is a very bright type of light that uses a tungsten filament that is contained in a quartz envelope. The color temperature will be a fairly consistent 3,200K. They can get very hot when in use. It is also very important never to touch the bulb with your bare hands at any time. Oil from your hands will cause the bulb to blister and explode.

Quartz: Tungsten-Halogen lights or lighting units. The name is derived from the material which encloses the lighting element.

Quick recovery syndrome: Any person critical to the movie's sequel (such as the hero's buddy) can be on the edge of death throughout the film, but by the end of the movie recovers fully.

Quick release shoe: The part of the quick release that attaches to the camera is called the quick release shoe, and is inevitably worth double-checking, as they frequently stray away the tripod when left behind on the camera.

Quick release: A latching device for quickly mounting and removing the camera from the tripod.

Quid: Slang for a pound sterling (UK).

Quota quickies: Low budget, short subjects made in the UK in the 1930s. The Cinematographic Films Bill, passed in April 1927 stipulated that all UK cinemas would have to include a proportion of British films in their programmes. The percentage varied, rising to 20% at one time. The "Quota Quickies" were generally of a quite low quality but there are some gems hidden in their midst, notably those by Michael Powell.

R

R: A certificate issued by the MPAA indicating that persons under the age of 16 would only be admitted when accompanied by an adult. The age was later raised to under 17 years old, and varies in some jurisdictions.

Rack focus: A shot where focus is changed while shooting. Unlike a Follow Focus shot, a rack focus shot is usually done not from the necessity of keeping someone in focus but to shift attention from one thing to another.

Rack focusing: Refers to a film technique that requires a shallow depth-of-field - an on-screen focus change from an object in the foreground to an object in the background or vice versa, to direct, shift, and steer the attention of the viewer forcibly from one subject to another; also known as selective focusing or pull focus.

Rack: A frame carrying film in a processing machine. Ofter used to refer to frame edit alignment in which the projected film remains properly framed on the screen (in rack).

Railroad consultant: A person who advises a production on railroad history, architecture, business practices, economics, equipment, locations, and strategies to attain maximum on-screen production/artistic values.

Railroad coordinator: A person who advises a production on railroad history, architecture, business practices, economics, equipment, locations, and strategies to attain maximum on-screen production/artistic values, and then locates/scouts/evaluates railroad equipment and locations; coordinates railroad equipment assembly/dispersal at a filming location; plans and executes for camera railroad operations; exercises overall set safety management (in accordance with US Federal Railroad, Transport Canada, and Ferrocarill de Mexico regulations); is responsible for equipment and railroad operations budget development and management.

Rank: A respectable and commonly used brand of Telecine machines. The word is sometimes used interchangeably with telecine in much the same way as "Steenbeck" is used in place of "flatbed."

Rating system(s) or ratings: Also known as the MPAA (Motion Picture Association of America) film rating system, first officially instituted in late 1968; it refers to the ever-evolving classification system for films usually based upon age-appropriateness, and the judgment of a film's suitability for various audiences, in terms of sexual content, offensiveness, or violence.

Raw stock: Unexposed film.

Reaction shot: **1.** A shot of someone looking off screen. Used either to lead into a P.O.V. Shot (and let the viewer know that it is a P.O.V. shot), or to show a reaction right after a P.O.V. shot. **2.:** A reaction shot can also be a shot of someone in a conversation where they are not given a line of dialogue but are just listening to the other person speak.

Real time: Actual time it would take for an event to occur in reality, as contrasted to filmic time (time can be sped up or slowed down). Real and filmic time often coincide for long sequences within a film.

Realism: Filming so that the reality outside the camera is shown in a neutral style with as little distortion and interference as possible; realism is attained by long, uninterrupted takes, deep focus shots, and other filmic techniques; contrast to expressionism; similar to the 'reality' of docudramas.

Rear (screen) projection: A special effects technique to create backgrounds, in which actors are filmed in front of a screen on which a background scene is projected; commonly used in early films to produce the effect of motion in a vehicle.

Recans: Leftover film that was loaded into a magazine but (unlike a Shortend) not even partially shot, and then loaded back in the film can. Basically, it is a roll a film that has been opened, but not used.

Red carpet: Literally, to "roll out" a welcoming 'red carpet', laid down for major ceremonies (film premieres, awards ceremonies) to signify an important, honorary event with dignitaries and esteemed guests attending; often the locale for live interviews and photo opportunities.

Red herring: An instance of foreshadowing that is deliberately planted to make viewers suspect an outcome—but the audience is to be deceived - the opposite happens and the false clue 'plant' is irrelevant; often done for humor, irony, or for other thematic reasons.

Redhead: An open faced 1K lighting unit. Also known as a 'Mickey'.

Redlighted: Refers to a film project that was in production, but lost its financial backing - resulting in a premature abandonment by the studio; aka a film in turnaround.

Reduction print: An optical reduction of a film from one gauge to another, such as 35mm to 16mm.

Reduction printing: The production of a copy of a film which is of a smaller size or gauge than the original (i.e. 35mm to 16mm). This is done of an optical printer.

Reel: Refers to a plastic or metal spool for winding film; also, earlier films were measured in reels (one reel = about 10 minutes of running time).

Re-enactment: A film production that re-creates an actual event as closely as possible.

Reference: Refers to how one film in its storyline (through dialogue, images) alludes to, recalls, or refers to another film; similar to homage.

Reflective light reading: A reflective light reading measures the amount of light bouncing off the subject. You take a reflective reading with a light meter equipped with a honey-comb or lensed grid. The meter is pointed at the subject, so as to read only the light bouncing off the subject. The other type of light reading is an Incident Light Reading.

Reflex: A viewfinding system in a camera where the image you see in the viewfinder is viewed through the same lens that is used to photograph the image on film.

Registration pin: A registration pin is found in the movement certain cameras, such as the Arriflex and the Eclair, and acts to steady the image during exposure.

Registration: The degree to which one frame lines up with the next is registration. A camera with poor registration will create an image that will gently bobble when projected. Projectors too can have good or poor registration (sometimes making it difficult to tell if it was the camera). Good registration is most important for certain types of special effects shots where images are layered and will call attention to themselves if they are gently bobbling out of sync with each other.

Reissue: Refers to a studio releasing a work subsequent to the original or initial release; similar to re-release.

Relational editing: Editing of shots for the purposes of comparison or for the contrast of content.

Release negative: A duplicate negative from which release prints are made.

Release print: This is a print made after the answer print has been approved. It is not retimed, but struck using the same timing as the final answer print. Because it is not retimed it is generally much cheaper than an answer print. On a big production, these are the prints released to movie theaters, hence the name.

Release: When a movie is shipped to exhibitors by the distributor, it is deemed to have been released for public viewing - there are no longer any studio restrictions on who can see the movie.

Remake: Refers to a later production (of a previous film), with different credits, script, and cast; a redone, second version of a film's narrative and subject matter; remakes have been common throughout all of film history.

Rentals: Refers to that portion of film grosses that goes to film distributors; also refers to videocassette (or DVD) rentals.

Re-recording mixer: A member of the sound crew responsible for mixing the final sound elements (dialogue, music, sound effects and foley). In most feature films and some television shows there is a crew of three re-recording mixers (one for dialog, one for sound effects and foley and one for music.) Sometimes in television the music mixer mixes the foley for expediency. There are also two-person crews in which the dialog mixer (generally considered the lead mixer) mixes music as well, with the other person mixing sound effects and foley.

Re-recording: The process of mixing all edited music, effects and dialog tracks of a film or video production to mono, stereo, multichannel or whatever audio format is desired for the final print master.

Re-release: The revival or rebroadcast of a work by the original distributor, studio, releaser, or broadcaster.

Reshoot contingency: Refers to the funds kept or saved by a producer in case supplementary shootings (reshoots) are required - often occurring after test screenings or decisions made by studio executives.

Resolution: The outcome, or the "untying" of tension in the scenes after the climax of a film; refers to how things turned out for all of the characters; some films abruptly end without a scene following the climax.

Resolver: A device that governs the speed of a tape recorder during the transfer to mag, insuring the sound will be in sync with picture. The resolver uses the pilottone as a reference for adjusting the playback speed, hence something can only be resolved if it has been recorded with a properly equipped tape recorder. The Nagra IV has a built-in resolver.

Resolving: The process of regulating tape speed by comparing a reference signal on the tape with an external reference and adjusting the speed so that they match.

Retrospective: Usually a tribute, exhibition, or 'looking back' at a film star's, artist's or director's work over a span of years with a comprehensive compilation or montage of film clips or excerpts; also known as a retro; also, in terms of a screenplay, a film in which nearly the entire story is looking back in time at events that have already taken place, usually accomplished by flashback.

Reverberation: The presence or persistence of sound due to repeated reflections.

Reversal film: A film that is manufactured and processed in such a way as to produce a positive image after exposure.

Reversal intermediate: A second generation duplicate which is reversed to make it the same type, negative or positive, as the original. It is used for printing in order to protect the original.

Reversal original: A reversal film designed to be exposed in a camera.

Reversal: A type of film and method of processing that yields a positive original. This is the movie-film equivalent of slide film and processing, in still photography.

Reverse action: An optical effect in which the action appears backwards from its chronological sequence.

Reverse angle shot: A basic camera angle composed of a shot photographed from the opposite side of a subject to provide a different perspective; in a dialogue scene between characters, a shot of the second participant is commonly composed as an over-the-shoulder shot; sometimes known as an 180 degree angle shot or change in perspective; the alternating pattern between two characters' points of view is known as shot/reverse shot; a reverse motion (or reverse action) shot is created by running film backwards in the camera or during optical printing.

Reverse angle: A shot that is turned approximately 180 degrees in relation to the preceding shot.

Reverse shot: A shot from the other side of the previous shot, such as cutting between two characters talking, a person exiting and entering though a doorway, a reaction shot and P.O.V. shot, etc.

Revisionistic: Refers to films that present an apparent genre stereotype and then subvert, revise, or challenge it; aka deconstruction.

Revival house: Film or exhibition theatres that are dedicated to emphasizing or specializing in only one type of film - such as foreign films, older films, silent films, classics, rarely-screened films, etc.

Rewinds: A simple device for winding film, consisting of a crank and a spindle for mounting one or more reels, typically found mounted on either side of an editing bench.

Rigger: Workers responsible for the setting, hanging and focussing of lighting instruments and constructing scaffolding used in making film sets.

Rim: A hard backlight, is generally on the same level as the subject, that casts more light than the key light.

Riser: (1) A cylindrical metal device placed betwen the dolly head and the camera base to raise the camera. (2) A prebuilt platform used to raise the set, camera, or lights.

Rising sidewalk: No female character in an action film can flee more than 50 feet before falling flat on her face. Someone then has to go back and help her up, while the monster/villain/enemy gains ground.

Rivas: A type of tape splicer which uses perforated splicing tape. Two models exist: One for straight cuts used for picture, and one for slanted cuts used for sound.

RMS (root-mean-square): Effective sound pressure.

Roadshow: Refers to exploitation films (such as "sex-hygeine" films) with controversial content (disguised as educational medical information) that were heavily promoted and shown on the road, and would be packed up quickly in case of the authorities; also refers to films that were released early and shown in prestigious theatres.

Rock candy postulate: No hero is ever cut by glass while leaping through windows.

Roman a clef: A French term literally meaning 'novel with a key'; in film terms, refers to a film in which actual persons/events are disguised or masked as fictional characters - but with a 'key,' the true persons/events are revealed.

Room tone: A recording of the "silence" of a room or any location, to be used to fill in gaps when editing the sound. The silence of a location is really not very silent at all, and the room tone of one location is not a substitute for another, so a sync sound shoot will usually end with the sound recordist asking everyone to be quiet for the recording of 30 seconds of room tone.

Rotation: Refers to a camera rotation, causing the image to spin around and have a disorienting effect on the viewer.

Rotoscoping: An animation technique in which images of live action are traced, either manually or automatically.

Rough cut: An early edited (or 'cut') version of a film - with all the pieces of the film assembled in continuous, sequential order, but without any fancy editing; also sometimes known as first cut; one of the stages toward the final cut; often used in a focus group screening.

Rule of chronic tunnel vision: In a horror movie, the character being stalked has vision limited to the camera's field of view. Therefore, anyone coming at any angle not directly ahead will invariably scare the living daylights out of him or her.

Run of the picture: A cast member whose work may be required any of the days scheduled for principal photography without incurring liability for additional compensation.

Running time: A measure of the duration or length of a film, usually about two hours for a feature film.

Rush: The prints of takes (of the camera footage) from one day's shooting, usually without correction, for examination before the next day's shooting; aka daily-ies.

Rushes: The workprint, when it is just back from the lab, unedited, called the rushes because of the rush to see that everything came out alright. Also known as Dailies, in honor of the minority of labs that will have it later that day.

S

S.M.P.T.E. Leader: Another term for Academy Leader.

Sabre artist: A member of the production team utilizing a combination of software programs to create special effects.

Safe area: A camera's viewfinder actually shows (and records on film stock) a greater area of the scene than will appear in the final product. Markings are etched in the viewfinder to indicate to the camera operator the extents of the "viewable" film (called the live area). An area beyond that (called the safe area) is also marked; it is in this area that the production sound mixer might direct the boom operator to place the boom microphone.

Safety : An additional take, done after a successful one, as a backup.

Sandbag: A cloth bag with two chambers filled with sand, used as a weight on the legs of a light stand for additional stability.

Satire: A mocking, ridiculing commentary on an economic, political, religious or social institution, ideology or belief, person (or group), policy, or human vice.

Scenario: (1) the outline for a screenplay, or (2) a complete screenplay.

Scene chewing: An extreme, over-the-top performance that dominates the screen. "Chewing the scenery" suggests that actors are so engaged in their histrionic portrayals that furniture pieces and backdrops are left with big dental impressions.

Scene: Usually a shot (or series of shots) that together comprise a single, complete and unified dramatic event, action, unit, or element of film narration, or block (segment) of storytelling within a film, much like a scene in a play; the end of a scene is often indicated by a change in time, action and/or location.

Scenery: Refers to the outdoor background in a set (represented by either a backdrop or a natural view).

Scene-stealing: Usually refers to a character (or group of characters), usually subsidiary, whose appearance, actions and/or dialogue draws more attention than other actors in the same scene; similar to the term 'chewing up the scenery.'

Scenic artist: A member of the crew responsible for work which includes the preparation, painting and/or coloration of all textures, plastering, appliqueing on scenery, sets, and properties; the application of all decorative wall or surface coverings; all lettering and sign work (including signs and murals; miniature sets and/or models and properties and the painting and aging in the (construction) studio or on the set of costumes and costume accessories as specified by the cosume designer.

Score: The musical component of a movie's soundtrack, usually composed specifically for the film by a film composer; the background music in a film, usually specially composed for the film; may be orchestral, synthesized, or performed by a small group of musicians; also refers to the act of writing music for a film.

Scratch mix: A mix with little correction of the sound, that is usually done before the final mix in order to screen the film with all the sounds in place, to determine if there are any changes to be made. Typically this is not done on lower budget productions, as the added cost would be self-defeating.

Scratch test: A scratch test is done before shooting, by running either a foot or two of the beginning of a roll of film, or a dummy roll of film, and checking for scratches, to insure that neither the camera nor the magazines are scratching the film.

Scratch track: A sync recording made under conditions that make the sound useless, except for reference to the sound editor or to the actors for dubbing.

Scratch: Damage to a film in the form of a long gouge of either the emulsion or the base. A scratch on the emulsion is pretty much unfixable, since part of the image itself is missing. A scratch on the base can be alleviated with Wet Gate printing. Scratches on your workprint don't really matter at all, since you will go back to the pristine camera original for your final print.

Screen actors guild: An association with jurisdiction over some works that can be recorded by picture or by sound.

Screen direction: Refers to the direction a character or object is moving in a film's frame, either along a horizontal X-axis (left-to-right, or vice versa) within the frame, a vertical Y-axis (top-to-bottom, or vice versa) within the frame, or movement along a front-to-back Z-axis (from the foreground to the background, or vice versa).

Screen test: Refers to a filmed audition in which an actor performs a particular role for a film production; casting often depends upon the photogenic (the projection of an attractive camera image) quality of the star.

Screener: The term for a promotional DVD (or video) version of a film that is sent to voters (and film critics) by the movie studios for their convenience during the awards season, before the movie is officially available to the public through video rental chains.

Screening: The exhibition or display of a movie, typically at a cinema house/theatre; to screen (or unspool) a film means to show or project a film; types of screenings include a critical screening (a pre-release viewing for film critics), a pre-screening, or a focus-group screening (to test audience reactions to a film's rough cut); cinema is another term for a movie theatre.

Screenplay: A document text in a specific format which contains the dramatic elements of the film, as well as indications of other elements such as setting, light values, action, and, in general, everything which it is essential to see on the screen from the point of view of the whole narrative; in its relationship to the completed film, a screenplay is sometimes described as being analogous to a blue print of a structure. The analogy is true up to a point, but in fact there is no other kind of text which has the specific characteristics and constraints of a screenplay. And no other text which, when successful at attaining its goal—i.e., the finished film—effectively ceases to exist except as a historical and critical curiosity.

Screens & Screen count: The actual screen the movie is projected on. Most Theaters have multiple screens, with largest having two dozen screens or more. Screen Count is simply the number of screens a film is playing on, but this is rarely used domestically, but internationally it is used to measure how wide a release is.

Screenwriter: In spite of the unearned notoriety of people such as Joe Esterhaz, the screenwriter remains the much-maligned individual who is responsible for the creation of the screenplay, whether as an original work or as an adaptation of some other text.

Screwball comedy: A type of highly-verbal comedy prevalent in 1930's Hollywood, and typified by frenetic action, verbal wit and wisecracks (substituting or serving as a metaphoric euphemism for sex), a battle of the sexes with conflict that is ultimately resolved - all elements that serve as important plot points.

Scrim: A metal 'window screen' that can be placed in front of a lighting unit to decrease the lighting intensity by a predetermined amount.

Script department: The section of a production's crew responsible for the script of a movie. Consists of writers, script editors, and prompters.

Script editing: A process whereby a script is reviewed and changed, based on input from various sources such as the director or producer. Writers who specialize in script editing are called "script doctors", and are frequently uncredited.

Script supervisor: A person who tracks which parts have been filmed, how the filmed scenes deviated from the script; they also make continuity notes, creating a lined script.

Script: Refers to the written text of a film - a blueprint for producing a film detailing the story, setting, dialogue, movements and gestures of actors, and the shape and sequence of all events in the film; in various forms, such as a screenplay, shooting script, breakdown script (a very detailed, day-to-day listing of all requirements for shooting, used mostly by crew), lined script, continuity script, or a spec script (written to studio specifications); a screenplay writer is known as a screenwriter, scripter, scribbler, scribe or penner; a last-minute script re-writer is known as a script doctor; a scenario is a script that includes camera and set direction as well as dialogue and cast direction; a shooting script is a detailed version of the screenplay with the scenes arranged in proper sequence, and used by the cast.

Scrub wheel: A mechanical control for scrubbing film or magnetic tape.

Scrub: Moving a piece of tape or magnetic film back and forth over a sound head to locate a specific cue or word.

SDDS: Sony Dynamic Digital Sound System. A film sound format which encodes eight tracks of digital audio outside of the sprocket holes on both edges of a film print.

Seamstress: A person who makes the costumes.

SECAM: The standard for TV/video display in France, the Middle East, much of Eastern Europe, and some African countries. Delivers 625 lines (formerly 819 lines) of resolution at 50 half-frames per second.

Second assistant camera: An assistant to the assistant cameraman.

Second assistant director: An assistant to the assistant director. Duties include overseeing the movements of the cast, and preparing call sheets.

Second banana: In general terms, an actor who plays a subordinate or secondary role; aka second fiddle; in comedies, it refers to a performer who acts as a sidekick, foil or stooge (straight man) to a lead comedian.

Second second assistant director: An assistant to the second assistant director; responsible for (among other things) directing the movements of extras.

Second sticks! : If the clapper on the slate was not visible when the shot was being marked the camera person might call out "second sticks!" to tell the person with the slate to mark it a second time.

Second unit director: The director of the second unit.

Second unit: A photographic team that shoots scenes which do not involve the principal cast, such as stunts, car chases, or establishing shots.

Seeing-eye man: Function performed by most men in Hollywood feature films. Involves a series of shots in which

Segment (or seg): A section or episode of a film; a series of sequences that comprise a major section of the plot; segmentation of a film often helps to further analysis.

Selects: Sometimes it is useful to separate out all the shots you are going to use before beginning to edit. These are known as selects.

Sell-through: An industry term meaning prerecorded videocassettes or DVDs priced lower, to encourage their sale rather than rental.

Semi-obligatory lyrical interlude (Semi-OLI): Scene in which soft focus and slow motion are used while a would-be hit song is performed on the sound track and the lovers run through a pastoral setting. Common from the mid-1960s to the mid-1970s; replaced in 1980s with the Semi-Obligatory Music Video (q.v.).

Semi-obligatory music video: Three-minute sequence within otherwise ordinary narrative structure, in which a song is played at top volume while movie characters experience spasms of hyperkinetic behavior and stick their faces into the camera lens. If a band is seen, the Semi-OMV is inevitably distinguished by the director's inability to find a fresh cinematic approach to the challenge of filming a slack-jawed drummer.

Senior stand: A braced junior stand sufficiently rugged for large lights such as a 5K, 10K, or 'Big Eye'.

Senior: A 5K fresnel lighting unit.

Sensitivity: An indication of recording or playback efficiency as might be measure of a microphone or audio tape recorder.

Sepia tone: A black-and-white image that has been converted to a sepia tone or color (a brownish gray to a dark olive brown) in order to enhance the dramatic effect and/or create an "antique" appearance.

Sequel: A cinematic work that presents the continuation of characters, settings, and/or events of a story in a previously-made or preceding movie; contrast to a prequel, follow-up, serial, series, spin-off or remake.

Sequence shot: A long take that extends for an entire scene or sequence. It is composed of only one shot with no editing.

Sequence: A scene, or connected series of related scenes that are edited together and comprise a single, unified event, setting, or story within a film's narrative; also refers to scenes that structurally fit together in the plot; sequence usually refers to a longer segment of film than a scene; sequences are often grouped into acts (like a three-act play); a sequence shot refers to a long, normally complicated shot with complex camera movements and actions.

Sequencer: The hardware or software based brain of a MIDI studio. It receives, stores and plays back MIDI information in a desired sequence.

Serial: A multi-part, 'short-subject' film that was usually screened a chapter/episode per week at a film theatre; the predominant style of the serial was melodrama; often, each chapter or episode, continually presented in installments over several weeks, would conclude with an unresolved cliffhanger to ensure that audience would return the following week to discover the resolution; popular until the early 1950s; contrast with series and sequels.

Series: A sequence of films with continuing characters or themes, but with little other interdependence, especially with respect to plot or significant character development. Until the advent of television series, there were various film series such as The Thin Man and Blondie that were started with the intention of making more than one. In subsequent years, the term would apply to features such as Star Trek: The Motion Picture or Dr. No that made more than one sequel. In modern times, the term "franchise" has been used (perhaps cynically) to describe to the practise of creating a movie and product-marketing package which is contingent on commercial success. Batman and its sequels are typically used as an example of a franchise. Contrast with serial.

Set decorator: A person who has total charge of decorating the set with all furnishings, drapery, interior plants, and anything seen on indoor or outdoor sets. The set decorator has authority over a leadman.

Set designer: The person responsible for translating a production designer's vision of the movie's environment into a set which can be used for filming. The set designer reports to the art director.

Set dresser: A person who maintains the set per the Set Decorator's requirements, placing elements such as curtains and paintings, and moves and resets the set decoration to accomodate camera, grip and lighting setups. Contrast with set decorator, property master. Responsible for set continuity with script supervisor and property master.

Set dressing: Items of decoration which are not designated in the script or by the director as part of specific action.

Set medic: The set medic provides for the medical needs and emergency medical logistics of the entire cast and crew and is the safety liason between production/construction and various agencies. This person may be an emergency medical technician, paramedic, nurse, or physician. Most often the set medic is involved in the production from the beginning of preproduction or construction through filming or production through striking the set or post-production.

Set up: Each discrete position of the camera, excluding those in which a dolly or crane is used to move the camera during filming.

Set: The environment (an exterior or interior locale) where the action takes place in a film; when used in contrast to location, it refers to an artificially-constructed time/place (a backdrop painting or a dusty Western street with a facade of storefronts); supervised by the film's art director; strike refers to the act of taking apart a set once filming has ended.

Set-piece: Usually a self-contained, elaborate scene or sequence that stands on its own (i.e., a helicopter chase, a dance number, a memorable fight, etc.), and serves as a key moment in the film; in terms of production, it may also refer to a scene with a large set.

Setting: The time (time period) and place in which the film's story occurs, including all of the other additional factors, including climate (season), landscape, people, social structures and economic factors, customs, moral attitudes, and codes of behavior.

Set-up: The place or position where the director and the director of photography put the camera (and lighting) when shooting a scene; a scene is usually shot with multiple setups and with multiple takes from each setup.

Seven-minute rule: In the age of the seven-minute attention span (inspired by the average length between TV commercials), action movies aimed at teen-agers are constructed out of several seven-minute segments. At the end of each segment, another teen-ager is dead. When all the teen-agers are dead (or, if you arrived in the middle, when the same dead teen-ager turns up twice), the movie is over.

Sex comedy: A humorous, light-hearted film with an improbable plot about sexual relationships and extra-marital affairs, with various pairings between numerous characters, often characterized by slamming doors; aka sex farce or bedroom farce.

Sexploitation: Refers to non-pornographic, non-explicit, soft-core films that feature sexual themes or explicit sexual material and nudity often in an apparently crude, immature, leering way; these films exploited the concept of sex without violating long-standing cultural and legal taboos against showing it all on the screen; often with lurid titles; aka skin flick.

Sex-specific disintegrating outfit: When the male and female characters in a trashy action movie go to hell and back, only the woman's clothing begins to disintegrate.

Sharpie: A permanent felt-tipped marker useful for labeling the cans of exposed rolls out on a shoot and in the editing room for labeling your leader. Sharpie is a brand-name of the most common of these markers.

Shiny boards: A grip reflector used for reaiming sunlight to provide a key or fill light.

Shoot: The process of filming or photographing any aspect of a motion picture with a camera; the plan for a shoot is termed a shooting schedule.

Shooting ratio: The ratio of how much film shot compared to running time of the finished film. For instance a 5 minute film for which you shot 30 minutes of footage would have a shooting ratio of 6 to 1.

Shooting script: The script from which a movie is made. Usually contains numbered scenes and technical notes.

Short subject (shorts or short films): A film that is shorter than around 30 or 45 minutes; in the silent film era, most films were shorts, such as those shown in nickelodeons; then, during the early film era, the price of a movie ticket included not only the weekly feature but also "selected short subjects," as they were usually billed; contrast to features.

Shortends: The unexposed remainder of a roll of film in a magazine that is clipped and placed back into a can for use later. Unlike recans a shotend is something less than 400 feet.

Short-time syndrome: Applies to prison, war or police movies, where the hero only has a few more days until he is free, his tour is over, or he can retire with full pension. Whenever such a character makes the mistake of mentioning his remaining time ("Three days and I'm outta here!") he will die before the end of that time.

Shot composition: The arrangement of key elements within the frame.

Shot distance: The distance at which a viewer perceives that an object or person is located on the screen, in depth or in width or both. Conventionally, the human figure is used as a term of reference for the description of shot distance. This is a matter of convenience and interpretation rather than of exactitude since, among other things, the camera may not always frame the human figure. The individual references may be combined, as in "medium close shot."

Shot list: A list given to the film production crew which indicates the sequence of scenes being shot for the day. This list may include the scene number, the location of where the scene is being shot, a description of the scene, the length of a scene (listed by number of pages from the script), a list of actors who will be involved in the scene, and, special notes to all departments of what will be needed or required for a particular scene being shot.

Shot reverse shot cutting: Usually used for conversation scenes, this technique alternates between over-the-shoulder shots showing each character speaking.

Shot selection: The location of the camera, and what can be seen with it.

Shot, scene, and sequence: A shot, scene, and sequence together make up the larger dramatic narrative of film; scenes are composed of shots, sequences are composed of scenes, and films are composed of sequences.

Reverse Shot: A sequence of three shots: 1) a person's face; 2) what that person is looking at; and 3) the person again, giving the audience a chance to process the person's reaction to what (or who) s/he is seeing.

Shot: The basic building block or unit of film narrative; refers to a single, constant take made by a motion picture camera uninterrupted by editing, interruptions or cuts, in which a length of film is exposed by turning the camera on, recording, and then turning the camera off; it can also refer to a single film frame (such as a still image); a follow-shot is when the camera moves to follow the action; a pull-back shot refers to a tracking shot or zoom that moves back from the subject to reveal the context of the scene.

Shotgun mic: A highly directional microphone, usually with a long, tubular body; used by the production sound mixer on location or on the set for film and television productions.

Showcard: A white artists' cardboard which is used as a reflector or for making other special rigs. It is easily cut and formed.

Shutter speed: The length of time that a single frame is exposed for. Slower shutter speeds allow more light to enter the camera, but allow more motion blur.

Siamese: A splitter that divides a power line into two parts.

Sibilance: An exaggerated hissing in voice patterns.

Sider: A device which cuts the light from the side of a lighting unit, usually a flag or a cutter.

Sight line: An imaginary line that is drawn between a subject and the object that he/she is looking at.

Sign writer: The person in charge of writing and making signs shown in a production; possibly part of the set designer's team.

Signal to noise ratio: This is the ratio of the desired signal to the unwanted noise in an audio or video record/playback system.

Signal: The form of variation with time of a wave whereby information is conveyed in some form whether it is acoustic or electronic.

Silent camera: This term is often a little confusing because it does not mean a camera that is itself silent, and therefore usable for sync sound, but it means a noisy, unsilent camera, usable only for shooting silent, M.O.S. scenes.

Silent film (or silents): The term for motion pictures without sound (spoken dialogue or synchronized soundtrack), although they were often accompanied by live commentary, piano-music, sound effects, and/or orchestration; the period from about 1895 to 1927 (when "talkies" were introduced); contrast with talkies.

Silent speed: 18 frames per second. A slightly archaic notion left over from the time when 16mm was used exclusively for home movies. It is not always that easy to find a projector that will project at 18 frames per second and so films shot at silent speed will often be speeded up slightly, whether the filmmaker intended this of not.

Silk: A large section of translucent white cloth used to filter and soften a hard-light source.

Silver bullet: A solution that completely solves the complicated dramatic problem within a film; the term was derived from European folklore in which only a silver bullet could kill a werewolf.

Singer: A featured vocalist; often the person who sings a film's theme song.

Singing voice: Someone who performs an actor's vocal parts. Marni Nixon was the singing voice for Audrey Hepburn in My Fair Lady (1964); during post-production, Nixon's voice was dubbed over Hepburn's for the musical numbers.

Single perf: 16mm film with a row of perforations along one edge. On the film can this will be indicated by **1R** appearing on the label.

Single reel: In 35mm a reel is 1,000 feet of film (or usually a little less).

Single system: Single System refers to recording, editing or projecting sound and picture together on the same piece of film. Cameras used for tv news would record the sound on a magnetic stripe as well as photograph the picture. Also super-8 sound. Single system has some distinct editorial disadvantages, hence the more common use of Double System for shooting and editing.

Single: A shot with only one subject in the frame.

Single-stripe: Magnetic film that contains a single audio track, which is coated with oxide.

Situation comedy: A comedy in which humor is derived from people being placed in uncomfortable, embarrassing, or unfamiliar situations.

Size: Refers to a film element, used by the film-maker to indicate a character's or object's relative strength compared to other things or persons.

Sketch: An short scene that typically lasts less than 15 minutes that is typically shown as part of a TV series' content. It is typically used in comedies that feature these productions such as "Saturday Night Live" (1975) and "Monty Python's Flying Circus" (1969).

Skip frame: The optical printing effect of skipping or cutting out certain frames of the original scene to speed up the action.

Slapstick comedy: A broad form of comedy in which the humor comes from physical acts or pantomime, frequently harmless violence and pratfalls intended to produce laughter. The name was derived from a device called a slapstick, two boards that slapped together with a loud crack when used to strike something or someone; prevalent during the silent era and in early talkies, with its primary motif being pie-throwing.

Slasher film: Usually a cheaply-made sub-genre film (usually in the horror genre) designed for the teenage audience (teen movie), deliberately made to contain gory, blood-splattering, explicit deaths without any build-up, style or suspense, often committed by an unstoppable serial killer, with a sharp bladed weapon; most slasher films are created to generate sequels and repetitive boredom.

Slate board: Refers to the digital board held in front of the camera that identifies shot number, director, camera-person, studio and title; the slate has the clap sticks on top and the scene number, take and production name or title usually written on it, and the person operating the slate will say "mark" and clap the sticks for picture and sound sync purposes; originally the data was written with chalk on a slate board; the footage of the slate at the beginning of each shot or take is used in the laboratory and editing room to identify the shot.

Slate: The recorded identification of scene and take numbers, usually done with a clapboard. Most takes are identified at the beginning; a "tail slate" marks the end instead. Also used in an audition, to identify an actor's name, representation (if any), and the scene they will be performing in the audition.

Slave: An audio tape or videotape transport, projector or mag film dubber whose movements follow the movement of a single master transport. Accomplished electronically by using SMPTE time code numbers or mechanically by motor linkage of sprocketed machines.

Sleeper: A movie that is released with little publicity or pre-release buzz, often directed by and starring relatively unknown people, that eventually becomes popular (as a cult film) or financially successful beyond expectations, usually due to positive word-of-mouth; the term is sometimes used incorrectly to describe unpopular movies that the critics love.

Slop print: An untimed black and white dupe print of your workprint, used for projection in a sound mix. A slop print is used because splices can jump and cause the film to go out of sync, and a slop print will have no splices.

Slow-motion (or slo-motion): Refers to an effect resulting from running film through a camera at faster-than-normal speed (shooting faster than 24 frames per second), and then projecting it at standard speed, in order to heighten the drama; if a camera runs at 60 frames per second, and captures a one second-long event, a 24-frame playback will slow that event to two and a half seconds long; overcrank(ing) means to speed up the camera, thereby making the action appear slower when projected - the term dates back to the old days of physically hand-cranking film through a camera; contrast to fast-motion (achieved by undercranking) or time compression.

Slug line: A header appearing in a script before each scene or shot detailing the location, date, and time that the following action is intended to occur in.

Slug: A strip of blank leader or image-bearing film used as leader.

Smash-cut: A cinematic term that refers to surprising the viewing audience with a sudden, unexpected change in the film's image (often accompanied by a change in sound too).

SMPTE time code: Also known as Longitudinal Time Code. A high frequency signal that allows the accurate "locking" of film audio and video equipment. Locator information is displayed as numbers.

SMPTE: Society of Motion Picture and Television Engineers.

Snake: A multi-channel audio cable intended for use with microphone level signals and/or line level signals.

Sneak preview: An unannounced screening of a movie before the premiere, often used to gauge audience reaction and feedback for final editing.

Snub: During nominations or awards proceedings, when a prominent, leading, or favored performer/director/crew member or film is inexplicably excluded or denied an award or nomination.

Society of motion picture and television engineers: An international technical society devoted to advancing the theory and application of motion-imaging technology including film, television, video, computer imaging, and telecommunications. The abbreviation also refers to various measurements and standards defined by the organization.

Society of operating cameramen: An honorary organization composed of several hundred men and women internationally, of outstanding and dedicated talent, who make their living operating film and/or video cameras in the cinematic media. Use of the abbreviation after a name indicates membership in the society.

Soft light: A type of light with a built-in surface to act as a bounce card, providing soft, indirect light on the subject.

Soft-focus: A cinematographic effect in which a filter, vaseline or gauze-like substance placed over the camera lens reduces the clarity or sharpness of focus, blurs the image, and produces a diffused, hazy light; often used to enhance romantic or dreamy scenes, or to remove wrinkle lines from an actor's face; common in the films of the 1930s.

Soliloquy: A dramatic monologue delivered by a single actor with no one else onstage; sometimes expressed as a 'thinking aloud' dialogue of inner reflections; delivered by a character to him or herself, or directly to the audience; contrast to an aside.

Sony dynamic digital sound: Sony has produced a noise reduction and sound enhancement process. Competitors include Dolby Digital and DTS.

Sorry I thought you were someone else rule: Whenever the hero wanders the city streets bemoaning his lost love, and sees a woman in the distance (usually from the rear) who looks exactly like his beloved, he will inevitably run up to her only to find a total stranger who will look at him as if he's demented.

Sound blanket: Basically just a quilted mover's blanket. Often it is thrown over the camera (and the camera operator) to cut down on camera noise, as a sort of improvised Barney.

Sound crew: The group of crewmembers directly involved with creating of a movie's soundtrack. Individual job titles include: sound designer, sound editor, sound effects, sound mixer, sound recordist, boom operator, re-recording mixer, music supervisor, and foley artist.

Sound designer: A film sound specialist responsible for the development and augmentation of all soundtrack material, or a significant portion thereof, and is ultimately in charge of the entire sound production. Occasionally, it is used to refer to a person who is responsible for creating unique sounds or sound elements which are incorporated into a sound track.

Sound editor: A member of the sound crew who performs editing on the soundtrack.

Sound effect: A recorded or electronically produced sound that matches the visual action taking place onscreen.

Sound effects editor: A sound editor who specialises in editing sound effects.

Sound effects: Sounds added during post-production by the sound crew. Also used as a job title.

Sound master positive: A sound print on made from the sound negative for producing duplicate negatives of the sound record track for release printing.

Sound mix: The process of recording the production sound on the set at the time of shooting.

Sound mixer: An audio engineer who works with a boom operator to record the production sound on the set at the time of shooting.

Sound negative: A negative sound image on film which is obtained by exposure through a positive sound image.

Sound print: Any positive sound track print which is obtained by printing from a sound negative, or direct positive recording. or by the reversal process from another negative.

Sound reader: A playback head for reading mag stock, mounted on a bracket that snaps onto a synchronizer. It is pugged into the squawk box.

Sound speed: 24 frames per second. The normal speed for filming and projecting.

Sound track: The audio equivalent of the picture, or, more accurately, the picture track, the sound track contains all the audio information which accompanies the film: dialogue, sound effects, music, and so on. In a composite print it is found on the edge of the film. It may be either optical or magnetic.

Sound: The audio portion of a film including dialogue, music, and effects; sound effects refers to all created sounds except dialogue or music.

Sound-on-sound: A method in which previously recorded sound on one track is rerecorded onto another track while new material is added.

Soundstage (or stage): A large, soundproof area/room in a studio used in film production, where elaborate sets are constructed, to allow film-makers greater control over climate, lighting, and sound, security, and spectators.

Soundtrack: Technically, this term refers to the audio component of a movie, including the dialogue, musical score, narration, and sound effects, that accompany the visual components. Popularly, it refers to a collection of songs heard during the movie, and often sold as an album.

Source music: Music that originates from a source (e.g. an orchestra, a band, a radio) within the film scene. If there's a scene where a character turns on the radio and listens to music, that's source music. Also known as 'Foreground music' (as opposed to 'background music', i.e. the film's score).

Spacer: A metal cylinder with a flat plate at one end and a hole through the center, used between reels on the spindle of a rewind to space out the reels the same distance as the gangs of a synchronizer. Although it is a little shorter, in a pinch you can use cores as spacers.

Spaghetti western: A western filmed in Italy, many times with American leading actors. This term appeared following the appearance of Clint Eastwood in a number of Sergio Leone movies.

Speaking role: A speaking role is one in which the character speaks scripted dialogue. A non-speaking role is a character specifically mentioned in the script but who doesn't have any lines of dialogue in the finished film. Speaking roles typically pay much more than non-speaking roles. While extras may or may not be heard to speak in a film, they are not included as either speaking or non-speaking roles.

Spec script: A script written before any agreement has been entered into ("on spec" or speculation), in hopes of selling the script to the highest bidder once it has been completed.

Special effects (or F/X, SFX, SPFX, or EFX): A broad, wide-ranging term used by the film industry meaning to create fantastic visual and audio illusions that cannot be accomplished by normal means, such as travel into space. Many visual (photographic) or mechanical (physical) filmic techniques or processes are used to produce special illusionary effects, such as optical and digital effects, CGI, in-camera effects, the use of miniatures/models, mattes, rear-camera projections, stop-motion animation, bluescreens, full-scale mockups, pyrotechnics, stunt men, animatronics (electronic puppets), rain/snow/wind machines, etc.; F/X are coordinated by the visual effects and the special effects supervisors; known negatively as trick photography.

Special effects supervisor: The chief of a production's special effects crew.

Special effects: An artificial effect used to create an illusion in a movie. Refers to effects produced on the set, as opposed to those created in post-production.

Special makeup effects: An artist who combines knowledge of makeup and hairwork, with technologies of mold- making and synthetic skin materials. Many have an art or sculpture background and familiarity with puppeteering, animatronics and CGI.

Specifics: In sound editing, these are any effects that directly relate to the picture, where we see a thing happen and hear it too. Backgrounds, ambiance and speech are not specifics.

Specular: A term used to describe highly directional, focused light. This is often perceived as a very 'hard' light.

Speed of sound: The velocity of sound in air is 770 mi/hr. This speed however, is influenced by temperature and air pressure.

Speed: An annoucement made by either the director of photography or camera operator indicating to the director that the camera is operating at the correct speed. Called just after lock it down, and just before action.

Spherical: An optical system in which the magnifications of the vertical and horizontal dimensions of the picture are the same.

Spider: Another, less commonly used, term for Spreader.

Spikes: Spikes are a term that comes from theater. They are little pieces of tape placed around the legs of furniture, or the tripod legs, before they are moved, making it easy to return things to their original position.

Spill: Light that is escaping from the sides of a lighting unit, or any light that is falling where it is not wanted. (Grip/ Lighting)

Spin-off: Refers to a derivative work (film or TV), either a sequel or a prequel which includes characters from the previous original product; contrast to a prequel, follow-up, serial, series, sequel or remake.

Splice: A method of joining two peices of film so they can be projected as one continuous piece. There are three methods: the Tape Splice (usually used for editing), the Cement Splice (used for original material), and the far less common Ultra-Sonic Splice (used for Polyester Base film).

Splicing tape: A special type of clear tape, not interchangeable with scotch tape, used to splice film. It comes in perforated (for use with a Rivas) and unperforated (for use with a Guillotine). Transparent splicing tape is used for picture and white splicing tape for sound.

Split reel: A very handy reel, the two halves of which may be unscrewed and film on a core placed between. Once screwed back together (but not too tight, or it will never open) your film on a core has quickly been converted into film on a reel.

Split-screen: The combination of two actions filmed separately by copying them onto the same negative and having them appear side-by-side within a single frame (without overlapping); a slight variation on split-screen is termed multiple image (different images are set alongside each other within a single frame); split-screen is usually intended to signify simultaneous action.

Spoiler: Information about the plot or ending of a film that may damage or impair the enjoyment of the film if known ahead of time; usually, critics or reviewers warn readers with a 'spoiler alert', or avoid revealing spoilers altogether.

Spoof: Usually a comedic film that pays tribute to an earlier film in a humorous way.

Spool down: Winding an unexposed 400 foot roll down onto four 100 foot daylight spools for use in a camera that will only take 100 feet of film. Spooling down can only be done in complete darkness. 42 turns on a rewind per daylight spool will divide a 400 foot roll pretty evenly. Also, it is vitally important that the film be wound all the way through once and then spooled down, otherwise the edge numbers will be on the wrong side, and not printed onto the workprint.

Spool: A flanged roll on which film is wound for general handling or projection.

Spot meter: A type of meter for taking a Reflective Light Reading with a short telescopic sight that enables you to take a very specific reflective reading of a small, well-defined area.

Spot: On a lensed light, the smallest beam spread. (Lighting)

Spotting: Used in scoring and sound effects editing to identify the specific scenes or points where music cues or effects cues will take place. Usually, this will include information on length and style.

Spreader: A piece of gear consisting of three arms on a central hub attached to the bottom of a tripod to keep the legs from collapsing outwards.

Spring lock: A round spring-loaded clamp that goes on the end of a rewind to allow several reels to turn together.

Sprocket holes: The same as Perf.

Sprockets: A series of tiny, square holes (sprocket holes) on both edges of a piece of film fit onto notches on wheels (sprockets) similar to gears within a film projector, used to pull the film through the projector from one reel to the other.

Spun: Spun glass diffusion material.

Squawk box: A small amplified speaker used on an editing bench and receiving sound from the Sound Reader.

Squib: A small explosive device, which - when detonated - will simulate the effect of a bullet/puncture wound or small explosion. When worn by actors, they typically include a container of blood which bursts upon detonation.

Stage box: A distribution box with six pockets for stage plug connectors.

Standby painter: A scenic artist available during filming for last minute changes.

Stand-in: A substitute person who is physically similar (in size and appearance) to an actor and who takes the actor's place during often lengthy preparation of a scene (the taking of light meter readings, camera setup, light adjustment, etc.) but not during filming. Not to be confused with a stunt double or a body double.

Standing waves: A deep sound in a small room or booth from low frequency caused by long waves with short reflection patterns.

Stanton-walsh rule: No movie featuring either Harry Dean Stanton or M. Emmet Walsh in a supporting role can be altogether bad. An exception was CHATTAHOOCHEE (1990), starring Walsh. Stanton's record is still intact.

Star system: Refers to the way in which studios "groomed" stars under contract, and sought star vehicles for them; studios served as protectorates for their stars.

Star vehicle: A film expressly made to show off the talents of a performer, with all other aspects almost secondary; compare with tour de force.

Star: The name given to famous, talented, and popular actors or celebrities, often in lead character roles, who can draw an audience to a film with their photogenic appearance, inspirational acting, or some other quality. Historically, a starlet (or ingenue) was an attractive actress promoted by a film studio in a small role as an up-and-coming star during the 40s and the 50s; also used in the term star quality and star system.

Static shot: An unmoving camera shot that is stationary, due to the use of a tripod.

Steadicam (shot): A hand-held camera technique, with a special, hydraulically-balanced camera apparatus (introduced in the late 70s), allowing the operator to take relatively smooth images and steady shots while moving along with the action (comparable to a tracking shot) or actor - without using a track.

Steadicam operator: A camera operator who operates a Steadicam.

Steadicam operators association: An organization which represents Steadicam operators around the world, providing referrals across the entire film and video industry. Additional services include oganizing and conducting workshops, and providing Steadicam equipment rentals.

Steady-cam: A camera platform in the form of an elaborate harness worn by the camera operator during a hand-held shot. The device steadies the camera by means of counter-weighed camera head fixations, which are further stabilized through the use of gyroscopes. The operator, who composes and frames the shot through a small video monitor which is part of the harness, has, via hand controls, the ability to execute compound movements such as tilts, pans, cranes, and so on, in addition to being able to follow the action irrespective of the direction of motion.

Stealing a scene (or scene-stealing): Usually refers to a supporting actor/actress attracting attention from the lead actor or actress to whom the center of interest legitimately belongs.

Steenbeck: A popular brand of flatbed. The word is sometimes used interchangeably with flatbed.

Step printer: A printer in which each frame of the negative and raw stock is stationary at the time of exposure.

Stereotyping: The act of portraying a particular character (or group) with a formulaic, conforming, exaggerated, and oversimplified representation, usually offensive and distorted.

Still out there somewhere: Obligatory phrase in Dead Teen-ager and Mad Slasher Movies, where it is triggered by the words, "The body was never found. They say he/she is..."

Still photographer: A person who photographs the action (often alongside the camera) to be used in publicizing the movie.

Still: Refers to a single, static image, either (1) a frame still from a finished film, (2) a production still taken from an unfinished film, or (3) a publicity shot.

Stinger: A single extension cord. Most often referred to a single 'hot' extension that is left lying around for occassional use.

Stock character: A minor character whose actions are completely predictable, stereotypical, or standard for his/her job or profession; similarly, a stock situation is a basic, recognizable plot situation (e.g., a lover hiding in the closet, twins mistaken for each other, etc.).

Stock footage (or stock/library shot): Previously-shot footage or film of common elements or scenes, such as canyons or deserts in the American West, or travelogue shots (e.g., skylines, airplane takeoffs/landings, famous places, etc.) that are kept in a film archive and used to fill in portions of a movie in different film productions, thereby saving the time of reshooting similar scenes over and over; a stock shot refers to an unimaginative or commonplace shot that looks like it could be stock footage.

Stock numbers: Edge numbers provided on film raw stock by the manufacturer.

Stock: A general term for motion picture film, particularly before it is exposed.

Stop frame: An optical printing effect in which a single frame image is repeated in order to appear stationary when it is projected. This may also refer to a camera technique in which only one frame at a time is exposed.

Stop motion photography: An in-camera special effects process, wherein the camera is stopped during a take, objects and/or characters are moved or removed or added, and the camera re-started. One of the earliest techniques which began to explore the cinematic potential of the motion picture.

Stop-motion (animation): A special-effects animation technique where objects, such as solid 3-D puppets, figures, or models are shot one frame at a time and moved or repositioned slightly between each frame, giving the illusion of lifelike motion. Stop-motion was one of the earliest special-effects techniques for science-fiction films, now replaced by CGI and animatronics; aka stop-frame motion.

Story producer: Nonstandardized reality television term for a writer/producer who may be involved (at any level of pre to post production) in producing/editing source footage to create and nuance story. Other duties may include writing host dialogue, VO and dialogue/action pickups. During the post-production process, most either work directly with editors or provide detailed paper edits for editors to work from.

Story: The events that appear in a film and what we can infer from these events; aka narrative or plot

Storyboard: A sequential series of illustrations, stills, rough sketches and/or captions (sometimes resembling a comic or cartoon strip) of events, as seen through the camera lens, that outline the various shots or provide a synopsis for a proposed film story (or for a complex scene) with its action and characters; the storyboards are displayed in sequence for the purpose of visually mapping out and crafting the various shot divisions and camera movements in an animated or live-action film; a blank storyboard is a piece of paper with rectangles drawn on it to represent the camera frame (for each successive shot); a sophisticated type of preview-storyboard (often shot and edited on video, with a soundtrack) is termed an animatic.

Storyliner: Commonly working on television series, storyliners create the plot twists for a given story line, keeping in mind the past storylines for a given character or pairing, and the work with the writers to bring those new plot elements to life.

Straight cut: An edit which is designed to maintain either temporal or spatial continuity, or both; the backbone of continuity editing.

Straight man: An actor/actress who serves as a stooge for a comedian (or funnyman), usually by adopting a serious stance or reaction to the comic partner; the straight man often feeds lines to the other irreverent comedian - who replies with witty comments; aka second banana or foil.

Stranger in a strange land principle: When a star of a movie shows up in a new town, that person will be famous in that town by the end of the movie.

Streamer: A grease pencil mark on the workprint indicating either a fade or a dissolve, called so because when projected it resembles a streamer trailing across the screen.

Striking: The breakdown process of a camera position, location, or set.

Stripe: 35mm mag stock that contains a stripe of magnetic tape rather than the complete coating found on Fullcoat. Stripe mag will also have a balance stripe to prevent warping.

Studio chief: The head or chairperson of a film studio who has the final authority for each film project (gives the green light - or authorization go-ahead), and oversees the many departments (financial, legal, marketing, advertising, distribution, etc.); also called the topper; in Hollywood's Golden Age, the chief was called a mogul.

Studio system: Refers to the all-powerful control the monopolistic film studios had over all aspects of filmmaking and film production until the 1950s, when chiefs - moguls (Mayer, Selznick and Zukor) ruled; tactics included the ownership of property, control of publicity and marketing, and iron-clad contracts with star-actors, directors, writers, and producers.

Studio(s): (1) the for-profit companies that specialize in developing, financing and distributing most American commercial films; (2) also refers to the actual site for a film production, with physical sets, stages, offices, backlots (located on the outdoor grounds of a film studio and used for filming exteriors), etc.

Stunt co-ordinator: A person who arranges and plans stunts.

Stunt double(s): A stunt performer(s) (aka stunts) that take the place of an actor when the scene calls for a dangerous or risky action (car crash, fight, window jump, etc.); doubles usually have the same build or appearance as the star; also called stunt performer, stuntman or stuntwoman; not to be confused with a stand-in or a body double; stunts are supervised, conducted and planned by a stunt coordinator.

Stunt performer: A specialist actor who performs stunts.

Stunt: A non-trivial and often dangerous piece of physical action. Often performed by a stunt performer.

Sturgeon's law: "90 percent of everything is crap." (First formulated in the 1950s by the science fiction author Theodore Sturgeon; quoted here because it so manifestly applies to motion pictures.)

Stylize(d): A term that refers to the artificial exaggeration or elimination of details in order to deliberately create an effect - in other words, to make (or interpret) a person, a face, a tree, a figure, or something as 'grotesque,' 'disturbing,' or 'overbright' as opposed to realistic or naturalistic.

Subjective or point-of-view (POV): A film in which the narrator has a limited point-of-view regarding the characters, events, action, places, thoughts, conversations, etc.; a subjective camera is a style of filming that allows the viewer to look at events from the POV of either a character or the author, when the camera position is close to the line of sight of the character; contrast to omniscient point-of-view.

Subplot: A secondary, subordinate, or auxiliary plotline, often complementary but independent from the main plot (the A story), and often involving supporting characters; not the same as multiple plotlines.

Subtext: The deeper and usually unexpressed "real" meanings of a character's spoken lines or actions - if the viewer can 'read between the lines'.

Subtitles: Words which are superimposed over a film which mirror the dialog that is heard at the time. Most often subtitles are in a different language than that which is being spoken, but this is not always the case: Trainspotting uses subtitles for humourous effect. Contrast with dubbing, intertitles, close-captioned.

Suicide: A term for a distribution wiring connector with male plugs at both ends, (Grip/Lighting)

Sundance: Short for the influential Sundance Film Festival, known for the exhibition and screening of the best of independent films each year in Utah.

Super 16: A format using single perf 16mm film on which a wider image is exposed than is the case with regular 16mm, using the area that would normally have the soundtrack. Super 16mm was conceived specifically for blow up to 35mm, and is typically rather inconvenient for anything else.

Super speed: Just a fancy way for Zeiss to describe a fast prime lens, typically with a T-stop of 1.3.

Superimposition: The appearance of more than one image on the screen at the same time where one is overlayed upon another without masking it; not to be confused with split-screen, where two distinct images co-exist on the screen along side one another.

Supervising sound editor: A chief sound editor.

Supporting Feature: A feature film which appears (typically in a double-bill) with a feature presentation.

Supporting role(s) (or players, characters): Characters seen less frequently than the lead role characters, but still in important, secondary roles; often termed a featured player or feature player; well-known guest stars often play brief supporting roles in a film; character actors are usually in supporting roles.

Surreal (surrealism): A term applied to a film, signifying a distorted or fantastic dream state, a nightmarish or hallucinogenic world, or a subconscious thought or death experience; often expressed by a random, non-sequential juxtaposition of images that go beyond realism.

Surround Sound: A sound system which creates the illusion of multi-directional sound through speaker placement and signal processing.

Suspenser: Another term for a suspense/thriller film.

Swashbuckler: Usually refers to adventure films with an heroic, athletic, sword-wielding character.

Sweeten/Sweetening: Enhancing the sound of a recording or a particular sound effect with equalization or some other signal processing device.

Swing gang: A group within the art department that construct and take down a set. The head of the swing gang is a leadman. Contrast with grips.

Swish Pan: In a swish pan the camera is purposely panned in either direction, right or left, at a very fast pace, creating the impression of a fast-moving horizontal blurring of images across the screen. Frequently, but not always, the actual panning shot is cut into the shots immediately preceding and/or following by means of a very short dissolve.

Sword and sandal epic: A colloquialism for an epic film with biblical or fantasy elements; named for the weapons and costumes that the characters typically wear.

Sword and sorcery: A term for the class of fantasy movies characterized by the presence of wizards and warriors, magic and sword fighting.

Symbol: An object in a film that stands for an idea, or that has a second level of meaning to it, e.g., a window or train=freedom, a rose=beauty, a cross-roads=a decision point, etc.; the more a symbol is repeated, the greater its significance.

Symmetry: Within a film when two or more distinct plotlines 'mirror' each other or develop variations on the film's theme or plot.

Sync beep (sync tone): In double system shooting with certain cameras, a tone feed into a magnetic tape recorder at the same time that a light in the camera exposes a few frames of film. The fogged section is later aligned with the beep tone to achieve synchronization of the sound to the picture.

Sync mark: **1.** The point at which the clapsticks come together at the beginning of a shot, and the accompanying sound on the sound track. **2.** An "X" mark on a single frame at the beginning of a reel of picture that lined up with a second sync mark on a roll of sound (May also be used anywhere where needed). Sync marks are also used at the beginning of A&B rolls.

Sync sound: Sync sound is sound recorded while shooting picture. Usually it involves footage of people speaking, and is thus sometimes called lip sync. It must be recorded with either crystal or cable sync to line up and not drift out of sync.

Sync: The degree to which sound and picture are lined up, in-sync being lined up exactly, and out-of-sync not so exactly. It can be applied to any specific sound and picture relationship, not just voices and not just sync-sound, but any type of specific effect too.

Synching dailies: Assembling, for synchronous interlock, the picture and sound workprints of a day's shooting.

Synchronizer: A very helpful tool of the editing room, a synchronzier is a device with a center axle and several sprocketed wheels attached to it. The wheels are called gangs. Film may be clamped into the gang, so that it can be measured with a footage counter on the front of the synchronizer. One revolution of the synchronizer equals one foot of film. Several elements, such as film and sound, A&B rolls, can be run in tandem can easily cut to the same length. It is used by the negative cutter for the assembly of A&B rolls, as well as for logging, measuring footage, syncing, and checking sync in the editing room.

Synchronous sound: Refers to sound whose source can be seen in the image's frame, or whose source can be understood from the context of the image.

Syncing: The actual lining up of sound and picture before editing a sync sound film. This also involves cutting the excess sound between takes, and adding filler, so that the picture and sound are now in sync for beginning to end.

Syndication: A package of off network programs sold or bartered to individual television stations in a local market, either strip (daily) or weekly episodic (series). A package of titles may require cash purchase, bartered or sponsored programming. Most packaged syndicated contracts offer exclusivity to a market for limited number of airings. Contracts are generally designed for one to two full season runs.

Synopsis: A summary of the major plot points and characters of a script, generally in a page or two. Contrast with treatment.

T

T stop: A true f/stop as opposed to one dereived mathe-matically. It is the actual light transmission of a lens as measured on an optical bench.

Tachometer: A gauge on a camera measuring the film speed when the camera is running.

Tag line: A clever phrase or short sentence to memorably characterize a film, and tease and attract potential viewers, or sell the movie; also creates a catchy 'soundbite' often repeated or presented in a trailer or on a film's poster, sometimes along with the film's leitmotif.

Tail leader: Leader used at the finish end of a strip of film.

Tail slate: Sometimes it is necessary to mark a shot at the end rather than at the beginning. When this is done it is called a tail slate. It is customary to call "Tail Slate!" just before clapping the slate, so that the person syncing the film does not get confused. To easily distinguish a tail slate, the slate is held upside down when marking the shot.

Tail: If in film terms "head" designates the beginning of a shot or a reel or a complete film, if follows logically that the tail describes the end of same.

Take Down: Reducing the light on an object by means of nets, scrims, dimmers or wasting light.

Take up reel: An empty reel, used on a projector to gather up the film after it has passed through the movement.

Take up spool: An empty spool in a camera used to gather up the film after it has passed through the movement.

Take: A single continuous recorded performance of a scene. A director typically orders takes to continue until he or she is satisfied that all of his or her requirements for the scene have been made, be they technical or artistic. For interesting exceptions, see the trivia entries for Stagecoach, The Gold Rush, Rope, Shi di chu ma, Some Like It Hot, and The Usual Suspects. A continuity report stores the status of each take. Of the ones that don't contain obvious errors, the director will order some to be printed.

Talent: A term applied to the actors, as a group, on a film set.

Talkie: An early term for a film with sound and especially recorded spoken dialogue. It is typically used today to make a distinction between silent and sound films made in the late 1920's and early 1930's when sound films establishing their marketplace dominance.

Talking head(s): A medium shot of people conversing; used as a criticism - denoting an uninteresting image.

Tap: A slang term, meaning to "pick", "select", "name", or "appoint".

Tape recorder operator: A member of the sound crew responsible for operating the audio recording equipment on a set.

Tape splice: A method of joining two pieces of film so they can be projected as one continuous piece. Tape splices are used in the editing stage. To cut the negative Cement Splices are used.

Tearjerker(s): An excessively-sentimental or emotional film, usually with suffering female protagonists, tragic circumstances, manipulative scenes, and dramatic musical scoring; aka melodramas or weepies; derogatively known as a 'woman's film' or 'chick flick'; contrast to feel-good film.

Teaser trailer: A short trailer that is generally released many months before a movie is actually released, to give a brief peek at what the movie will be like, and to build audience anticipation. Teaser trailers are usually much shorter than the final trailer, which reveals more of the storyline of the film.

Technical advisor: A person with expertise in a particular field who provides advice for the production.

Technicolor: The trade name for the best known color film process; 3-strip color is often used as a synonymous term; also used generically as a term for rich, bright, vibrant, sometimes garish colors; Technicolor films were described as highly saturated (with pure and vivid colors); Technicolor (a 3-color dye transfer system) was introduced in the Disney short cartoon, Flowers and Trees (1932).

Technopyromania: Affliction that compels filmmakers and special effects people to depict the malfunction of computers as being accompanied by smoke, flames, showers of pyrotechnic sparks, frenzied flashing lights, and wildly spinning tape drives spewing tape into the air.

Telecine: The process of transferring moving images from film to a video signal, including frame rate and color corrections. Also the equipment or facility used to do it.

Telefilm: Refers to a feature-length motion picture made for television; also known as telepic or telepix.

Telephoto lens: As their name implies, these lens are the "longest" of all. The same distortion of perspective which begins to be noticeable in the long lenses is much more evident in the telephoto lens, which have focal lengths of 200-1200mm. With telephoto lens, succeeding planes of the visual field will appear much closer to one another than they actually are, and perspective will appear as if crushed or compressed.

Teleplay: A script written to be produced for television.

Television movie: A feature-length movie funded by a TV network, intended to be premiered on television.

Television special: A television production of a singular event (such as an awards show or concert) as opposed to a regularly scheduled series. Contrast with series and television movie.

Telewriter: A writer who either adapts an existing work for production on television, or creates a new teleplay.

Temp dub: A preliminary mixing of dialogue, music, and sound effects, usually so that a first cut may be viewed with all of these elements incorporated.

Tenner: A standard studio 10K lighting unit, as opposed to a baby 10 or a Big Eye, which are also 10K lighting units.

Tentpole: An industry slang or trendy buzzword term, meaning a film that is expected to serve as a primary support for a studio, i.e., to be a top-grossing blockbuster, to compensate for a studio's other flops; usually the film is the start of, or an installment in, a franchise.

Terra-flite: A cross between a steadicam and a louma crane, used to steady images of running horses or cars driving over gravel.

Thanks, but no thanks: When two people have just had a heart-to-heart conversation, as person A starts to leave room, person B says (tentatively) "Bob?" A pauses, turns, and says "Yes?" B says, "Thanks."

The call: This is the sequence of directions that begin a take, typically: "Roll Sound!" "Roll Camera!" "Mark it!" "And... Action!"

The groundglass: A flat surface of etched glass in the viewfinding system of a camera that is the same distance from the lens as the film plane.

The hulk effect: Back in 2003 when Hulk came out, the studio bowed to incredible pressure from fans and released early footage of the special effects. The plan was to get the fans talking and build up the word-of-mouth. However, the special effects were in the early stages and were so bad that the buzz it generated killed any chance the film had. More recently the same happened to Catwoman with the early look at Halle Berry's outfit. Just goes to show you, sometimes there is such thing as bad publicity.

The movement: The parts of a camera or projector that move the film intermittently: the pulldown claw, the rollers before and after the loops, and the gears connecting these parts form the movement. If there is a registration pin, this is also part of the movement. Sometimes the shutter can also be considered part of the movement.

The sequel effect, a.k.a. sequelitis: Think of this as a sub-species of the Fanboy Effect specific to sequels. Such films have a built in audience due to the original movie.

The slate: A board with two hinged sticks attached. The slate is used to record a scene number and sync point (via the clapstick) at the beginning of a shot.

The sticks: **1.** The tripod or the tripod legs. **2.** The clapper on the slate.

The taking lens: On a turret, the lens that is actually in front of the gate, producing an image on the film.

Theaters & Theater count: A theater is any place a movie is showing from the smallest cinema on the art house circuit to the largest megaplex. A film's Theater Count is simply the number of theaters a film is playing in at a given time. Domestically Theater Count is used to measure how wide a release is.

Theatre - theater (film): The place for screening, presenting, or viewing a film or motion picture.

Theatrical: A slang term referring to a feature-length motion picture.

Theme (film): The central characteristic, idea, concern or motif in a film.

Theme music: The opening or closing music of a motion picture, often containing the film's 'signature' or leitmotif tune/ phrase that is associated with a character or situation within the film.

Third hand: Invisible appendage used by Rambo in RAMBO, in the scene where he hides from the enemy by completely plastering himself inside a mud bank. Since it is impossible to cover yourself with mud without at least one hand free to do the job, Rambo must have had a third, invisible, hand. This explains a lot about the movie.

Three-shot: Refers to a medium shot that contains three people; compare to two-shot.

THX: A theatrical film exhibition sound system which maintains a consistent sound standard from theatre to theatre. Generally, this system uses Dolby Stereo Surround as the basis of the exhibition standard, although a number of other systems have also now qualified.

Tic reversi: Nervous disorder that causes an actor to repeatedly pick up and put down an item upon each cut between reverse shots in a scene.

Tie in: A power feed obtained by temporarily clipping on to the main service of a location. This methodology is illegal in many areas. (Lighting)

Tie-in kit: A device for bypassing the fuse box and electrical wiring of a location by tapping power directly from the mains.

Tight: A tight lens is really just a variation of the normal lens, except that it will slightly amplify the subject, thus creating the impression of greater closeness. The focal lengths of tight lenses—50 to 75mm—are sometimes incorporated into the "Normal" category, which then would comprise lenses with focal lengths of 20-75mm.

Tight wind hub: A tight wind is useless without it. This is the hub that holds a core on the spindle of a rewind.

Tight wind: A handy attachment sometimes found on an editing bench on the right rewind, used to wind film onto a core and giving it a very smooth edge. It can be quicker than opening and tightening split reels if you are just rewinding an entire roll.

Tijuana: In modern Horny Teen-ager Movies, performs the same symbolic function as California did for the Beatniks, Marakeesh did for the hippies, and Paris did for the Lost Generation.

Tilt shot (or oblique angle): A camera tilted up or down on a diagonal along a vertical axis; a vertical camera movement from a fixed position often used to suggest an imbalance, or strangeness; also known as tilt pan, tilt up or tilt down (or reveal), or vertical pan, although not technically the same as "pan up" or "pan down", similar to a moving close-up; a dutch angle is filmed at an extreme diagonal tilt.

Tilt: A vertical camera move on an axis, up or down. Not to be used interchangeably with pan. It is not really correct to say "pan up" or "pan down," when you really mean tilt.

Time base signal: A signal recorded on the edge of film in a camera to match a signal recorded on a magnetic recording which is used as a fast means of synchronizing film and sound workprints.

Time code: Also known as Longitudinal Time Code. A high frequency signal that allows the accurate "locking" of film audio and video equipment.

Time lapse photography: A form of animation in which numerous single frames are filmed spaced at a given interval to show a process that would take a very long time to occur. i.e. a flower blooming, or the motion of the stars.

Time lapse: A method of filming where frames are shot much slower than their normal rate, allowing action to take place between frames, and giving the appearance of the action taking place much faster in the finished product; often done for nature filming (the blooming of a flower, the movement of clouds, etc.), allowing the viewer to witness the event compressed from real time (hours or days) into a few seconds; (one frame shot every 30 seconds over 24 hours of real time would equal two minutes of film time); opposite of slow-motion.

Timecode: Electronic guide track added to film, video or audio material to provide a time reference for editing, synchronization, etc.

Timer: The person at the lab who goes through your film, shot by shot and selects the printing lights.

Timing lights or printing lights: These are the lamps of the contact printer at the lab. Their brightness can be controlled, which is measured in a scale of 1 to 50, 1 being the darkest and 50 the brightest. In color there are three lights used together: Red: Green - Blue. When working with negative it is worth remembering that the values are reversed: the brighter the light, the darker the print will be.

Timing report: A list of the timing lights and corresponding footages the lab used in making your print. The timing report can be very helpful for analyzing the footage and judging the possibilities of further corrections. Any serious problems with the footage (out of focus, scratches, edge fog, etc.) are usually also noted on the timing report.

Timing: The lab's process of selecting printing lights to for the proper redition of exposure and color when making a print. The term is a little consuing, as it has nothing at all to do with "time" as in "running time" or such.

Tint: The use of color to physically tint film stock to achieve a desired mood, usually done selectively by hand; often used by silent black-and-white films before the widespread use of color film.

Title design: The manner in which title of a movie is displayed on screen is widely considered an art form. Saul Bass is considered a master title designer.

Title role: The lead part in a movie or other production for an actor or actress, that is named after the title of the film.

Titles: The words that appear on the film screen and convey information; categories of titles include: credit titles, main titles, end titles, insert titles, and subtitles; a creeper title, also known as a roll-up title, refers to a film title that appears to move solwly across the screen - vertically or horizontally; in silent film, "titles" (called title cards or intertitles) included the written commentary and full screens of textual dialogue spliced within the action; title design refers to the artistic manner in which the title of a film is displayed on screen; the working title is the name by which a film is known while it is being made, it was known as Production 9401.

Tone: 1. A 1,000 Hz sine wave used at the beginning of a tape to provide consistent volume when transferring sound. **2.** Room Tone.

Topline: To star in a motion picture; this can sometimes include the placement of a performer's name before the title on the credits and promotional items.

Track (dolly) back (or out): The camera dolly moves either away from the action (or character, or vehicle, or animal, or object) it is filming, or follows a character, (or vehicle, or animal, or what have you) moving backwards as the character moves forward.

Track (dolly) forward (or in): The exact opposite of track (or dolly) back: the camera dolly moves either forward upon the action it is filming, or follows a character as it/they move forward.

Track: A single component or channel of a soundtrack.

Tracking shot (or Dolly Shot): A shot wherein the entire camera is moved either forward (track or dolly "in") or backward (track or dolly "out"), or laterally, or in a circular or irregular pattern. The camera mechanism is placed on a movable device (the dolly) which moves either along pre-laid tracks or freely along a level surface. Tracking may also be accomplished with a hand-held camera or through the use of a steady-cam. In a tracking shot, the perspective relationships between the background and foreground planes of the visual field will change perceptibly, thus marking a significant difference between tracking shots and zoom shots in which these relationships remain constant as the target object is either magnified or reduced.

Trademark: Refers to a personal touch or embellishment of an actor, director, writer or producer within a film; aka signature, calling card.

Trades: Refers to the professional magazines and publications that report the daily or weekly entertainment news of the entertainment industry.

Trailer: A short publicity film, preview, or advertisement composed of short excerpts and scenes from a forthcoming film or coming attraction, usually two-three minutes in length; often presented at the showing of another film. Historically, these advertisements were placed at the end of a newsreel or supporting feature and so "trailed" them, hence the name; also commonly known as preview(s); also, another name for the tail - a length of blank leader (strip of film) at the end of a reel; a teaser is basically a very short trailer that only provides a few hints about the film.

Trainer: Someone who conditions animals to perform various behaviors on cue.

Transition (or transitional technique or device): One of several ways of moving from one shot or scene to the next, including such transitional effects or shots as a cut, fade, dissolve, and wipe; a transition focus between two scenes means the current scene goes out of focus and the next scene comes into focus.

Transitional device: There are essentially four editing devices which create a transition between two successive shots. These are: the cut, the dissolve, the fade and the wipe. Each of these transitional devices has implications for the construction of the narrative.

Transportation coordinator: The person responsible for managing drivers and co-ordinating the transporation of a production's cast, crew, and equipment from the various locations and sets used for filming.

Trash film: Refers to second-run, low-budget films that are deliberately over-the-top, infantile, amateurish, sometimes excessively gory or raunchy which are intended to shock, disgust, and repel mainstream audiences, and appeal to non-traditional audiences. Sometimes described as a sub-category of exploitation and cult films, or called a 'turkey' film.

Traveling matte: A process shot in which foreground action is superimposed on a separately photographed background by an optical printer.

Travelling matte shot: A shot in which foreground action is superimposed on a separately filmed background by optical printing or digital compositing.

Travelogue: A film made for the purpose of showing scenes from foreign, exotic places.

Treatment: A detailed literary summary or presentation of a film's story, with action and characters described in prose form, often used to market and/or sell a film project or script; a completed treatment is a late stage in the development of a screenplay after several story conferences have incorporated changes into the script; contrast to a synopsis.

Trilogy: A series of three movies that are closely connected by plot. Often, a storyline from the first film of a trilogy is altered, twisted or modified by the second or third part of the series.

Trim bin or editing bin or bin: A trim bin is a bin on wheels lined with a fabric bag and topped off with a frame with a row pins on which to hang film while editing. Oddly enough, a trim bin is not used for trims, which are small, but for selects and outtakes. Not to be confused with a waste basket!

Trims: Trims are outtakes of a few frames, usually a foot or less. To keep them from getting lost they are usually stored separately from longer outtakes, either in their own vault box or in a trim book.

Triple threat: Refers to an actor or actress who can sing, dance and act skillfully and equally well on a consistent basis; usually applicable to performers in the musicals genre; it also could refer to a person who can act, direct, and screenwrite!.

Tripod head: The part of the tripod with the pan and tilt mechanism to which the camera is attached.

Trombone: A tubular, extending device which is generally used for suspending lights from set walls.

T-stop: Similar to an F-Stop, some lenses, particularly zoom lenses, will have f-stops on one side of the aperture ring and t-stops on the other. To differentiate the two, the t-stops will be red and the f-stops white. T-stops are used in place of f-stops for setting exposure. Lenses with a lot of glass elements will often lose a little bit of light. The t-stops are calibrated to the actual amount of light that is hitting the film, rather than arrived at mathematically, as is the case with f-stops.

Tubthump: A term that denotes to promote or draw attention to; usually conducted by publicists, advertisers, and agents; from the ancient show business custom of actors wandering the streets banging on tubs and drums to draw an audience together.

Tuco's advice: Named for the character played by Eli Wallach in THE GOOD, THE BAD, AND THE UGLY. It comes in the scene where Tuco is taking a bath, and a guy bursts in the room, promising Tuco how he plans to have his revenge, only to have Tuco kill him. Tuco then advises the corpse, "If you have to shoot, shoot don't talk."

Tungsten: The color temperature of artificial light which is 3,200K on the color temperature scale. Quartz Lights use a tungsten filament, which burns at 3,200K, and gives us this term. Color film for indoor shooting is balanced for tungsten light, otherwise the image would appear orange in hue. If tungsten balanced film is used out-of-doors without a correction filter the image will have a washed-out blue hue.

Turnaround: A state of limbo that a movie enters after a studio decides to drop it. In turnaround, the producers have a chance to set the project up with another studio or with different talent. In union contracts, the time between when someone leaves work and when they start work the next day, or when someone is receiving compensation for not being given the contractual amount of time, it is sometimes said that they are in turnaround.

Turret: A rotating lens mount allowing for the mounting of three or sometimes four lenses on a camera, allowing for the quick change from one lens to another. Only one is in use at any given time, and this is known as the taking lens.

Turtle effect: Once a character is knocked down, they just lie there as if unable to get up.

Turtle: A flat, on the floor mount, for large lights with a junior receiver.

TV safe: The area of a filmed image which will normally appear on a home television set after a film has been transferred in a telecine and then transmitted.

TV series pilot: A TV series episode for a proposed television series which is produced for the benefit of the production company, TV network executives and/or syndication customers. The purpose behind is to show the prospective customers how a series' premise and characters would typically be presented to an audience.

Tweco: A device similar to a slip pin connector, which is used on a feeder cable, and which has a positive twist connection.

Twist ending: A film that is marketed as having a surprise ending that shouldn't be revealed (as a spoiler) to those who haven't seen the picture.

Two-fer: Slang for coupons that discount an film's admission price to "two for" the price of one.

Two-reeler: In the silent era, this referred to a film lasting a little over 20 minutes.

Two-shot: A medium or close-up camera shot of two people (often in dialogue with each other), framed from the chest up; often used to provide a contrast between the two characters; compare to three-shot.

Typecasting: When an actor or actress is commonly (but unfairly) identified, associated with, or 'stereotyped' by a particular character role; casting against type is the reverse of typecasting; typage refers to director Eisenstein's theory of casting that shunned professional actors in favor of 'types' or representative characters

U

Ultra-sonic cleaner: A sophisticated cleaning machine found at labs to clean negatives prior to printing or transfer to video. It uses sound waves to shake loose dust.

Ultra-sonic splicer: An expensive and sophisticated splicing machine used for splicing Polyester Base stock.

U-matic: Refers to 3/4 inch magnetic tape, originally a professional cassette tape format now being supplanted by new digital formats; a competing tape format was the inferior 1/2" VHS or beta.

Unbilled role: A 'supporting' role for a major (sometimes minor) star that is officially credited (usually in the end credits), but no mention (or billing) is made in the film's advertisements or the opening credits; contrast with cameo and uncredited role.

Uncredited role: A role that a major (or minor) star plays that is not credited in the credits or in the film's poster; contrast with cameo and unbilled role.

Undead dead: In horror movies, whenever the killer is killed, he is never dead. This rule is as old as the movies, but was given its modern shape in HALLOWEEN (1978) when the killer arose from apparent destruction to jump up behind Jamie Lee Curtis. Since then, all of the Dead Teen-ager Movies, most of the BOND pictures, and many other thrillers have used a false climax, in which the villain is killed—only to spring up for a final threat. In an ordinary thriller, the cliché of the Undead Dead is part of the game—but its use in FATAL ATTRACTION was unforgivable.

Underacting: Refers to an understated, neutral and muted acting performance; contrast with overacting.

Undercrank: To run the camera slower, producing fast motion. The term has survived from the time when you would crank a camera.

Undercranking: The process of slowing the frame rate of a camera down, so that when the captured pictures are played at the normal frame rate the action appears to be in fast motion. Historically, cameras were operated by turning a crank at a constant speed; hence "undercranking" refers to turning the crank too slowly.

Underexposure: Filming a scene with less light than the emulsion of the film needs for a correct exposure. The image will be too dark. If compensated for in printing, the image will appear grainy, and very muddy.

Underground film: A low-budget, non-commercial film, usually independently-made, without the traditional sources of funding or distribution.

Underscore: Music that provides emotional or atmospheric background to the primary dialog or narration onscreen.

Unions: Organizations that represent professionals in the motion picture industry (e.g., directors, actors, writers, etc.), and help those individuals negotiate contracts, receive recognition, pursue rights, protect interests, etc.; aka guilds.

Unit production manager: An executive who is responsible to a senior producer for the administration of a particular movie. Unit Production Managers only work on one film at a time. Only DGA members can be called Unit Production Managers.

Unit publicist: Member of the publicity department who works on location during the production of a movie. Duties includes working with the residents of the location where the film is being made, as well as setting up press visits and electronic press kit interviews. In addition, the unit publicist assembles the biographical materials and notes about the making of the movie that are later turned into the movie press kit. Unit publicists are itinerant — they move from production to production and are on the production payroll. They report to the filmmakers and, if the film has a releasing studio, they also report to the publicity directors. Once principal photography is over, the unit publicist moves on to another job.

Unmotivated close-up: A character is given a close-up in a scene where there seems to be no reason for it. This is an infallible tip-off that this character is more significant than at first appears, and is most likely the killer.

Unprofessional: An insult hurled at someone during a crisis when they have broken some unwritten rule of professional conduct. Commonly the term is used with the most frequency by people to whom it would just as easily apply.

Unsilenced revolver: Despite dozens of movies which think otherwise, a revolver cannot be silenced, because the sound escapes, not from the barrel where they fit the silencer, but from the gap between the frame and the cylinder. Only closed-breech weapons, like pistols with magazines in the grip, can be silenced—unless you wrap them in a pillow.

Unspool: A slang term meaning to screen or show a film.

Unsqueezed print: A print in which the distorted image of an anamorphic negative has been corrected for normal projection.

Upright moviola or upright: An editing machine with arms in back to hold the take up and supply reels. The film moves up and around to a screen on the front. Foot petals control motors for sound speed and variable speed viewing.

Utility person: The person responsible for various manual tasks, running errands, or performing whatever jobs other members of their crew assign them.

Utopia(n): Refers to an imaginary, ideal (or mythical), perfect state or place (especially in its laws, government, social and moral conditions), often with magical healing, restorative properties.

V

V: An IMDb notation to indicate that a particular title was originally released on video without a screening or being broadcast.

Vamp: A femme fatale or woman with a bad reputation, usually seductive and scheming in nature or behavior.

Vari speed: A motor or the control for a motor which will run a camera or an editing machine at speed faster or slower than sound speed.

Variable focus (or Zoom) (zoom-back clip:1.3M) from "Harold & Maude": First coming into general use in the early 1950's, variable focus lens have the ability to shorten or lengthen a visual field, from wide to long or vice-versa, without the need to change lenses or change the location of the camera. It thus became possible to create the impression, within the same shot and without the need for the camera to move, of the viewer moving closer to (or farther away from) the object being filmed. Note, however, that a zoom shot does not alter the perspective relationships between foreground and background, and in this it differs significantly from a tracking shot. Confusion frequently arises between these two types of shots. To distinguish between them, keep your eye on the foreground and background of the scene. If the relationship between them is altered, the shot is a tracking shot, if, on the contrary, there is no alteration and everything within the visual field is either magnified or reduced equally, it is a zoom shot. Look again at a zoom shot (zoom in this time) and look for this. Variable Focus (or Zoom) (zoom in clip: 1.5M) from "Billy Two Hats"

Variac: A simmer that reduces the voltage. It stands for VARIable AC.

Variety: A respected, oft-quoted show-biz periodical or trade paper (or one of the trades) that reports and provides coverage on the entertainment industry (including the film industry), and best known for its goofy, shorthand 'Varietyese' headlines, using made-up words, e.g. 'dee jay' (disc jockey), or 'B.O.' (box office or boffo).

Varispeed: Increasing or decreasing tape speed to match the musical pitch of tape playback.

Vaudeville: A stage variety entertainment show, featuring a series of short acts - songs, dancing, acrobatics, comedy skits, and animal acts; it was highly popular in America from the late 1880s to the 1920s, when it became overtaken by sound films and radio; most of the early film, radio and TV comedians found their start on the vaudeville circuit.

Vault Box: A white, flat, square cardboard box designed to hold 1,000 feet of 35mm or two 1,000 foot rolls of 16mm.

VCR: Literally, 'Video-Cassette Recorder'; aka VTR (video tape recorder); a consumer-level machine for home entertainment that plays-back and records images and sounds from TV on magnetized tape in a videotape cassette; VHS stands for 'Video Home System' or the 1/2 inch video cassette tape format.

Veeder counter: A trade name for a mechanical counter which is actuated using a rotary shaft movement which can be calibrated to any system of measurement such as feet or frames.

Vertigo effect: A camera technique created by Alfred Hitchcock during his film *Vertigo* that involves tracking backwards while simultaneously zooming in, making the person or object in the center of the image seem stationary while their surroundings change.

VG: An IMDb notation to indicate that a particular title is a video game.

Video assist: Motion picture cameras often include a video camera that allows instant review of a scene to monitor framing, focus, and performance. Both this system and the person operating it are referred to as video assist.

Video cassette recorder: A common household appliance for recording and/or playing prerecorded video tapes.

Video home system: Video Home System is a popular format for VCR systems worldwide.

Video: Literally, "to see," in other words, the visual or pictured image (either projected, taped, etc.), as opposed to the audio aspect of film; also refers to the visual component of television; digital video refers to a video signal represented by a series of binary numbers that are readable by computer - compare with analog video; aka vid (for short).

Vigilante film: Usually a type of action film in which the protagonist takes the law into his/her own hands as a self-appointed doer of justice, revenge, and payback.

Vignette: A scene in a film that can stand on its own; also refers to a masking device, often with soft edges.

Vinny rule: In every movie with Italian-American characters, one must be named Vinny

Virgin stock: Magnetic tape onto which nothing has yet been recorded.

Visual effects supervisor: The chief of a production's visual effects crew.

Visual effects: Considered a sub-category of special effects; refers to anything added to the final picture that was not in the original shot; visual effects can be accomplished in-camera (like stop motion, double exposures and rear/front projection) or via a number of different optical or digital post-production processes, usually with a computer.

VITC: Vertical Interval Time Code. A time code signal that is written in the vertical interval by the rotating video heads, allowing it to be read when the tape is not moving. Requires special equipment to read and write.

Voice-over (or v.o.): Refers to recorded dialogue, usually narration, that comes from an unseen, off-screen voice, character or narrator (abbreviated as o.s. meaning beyond camera range), that can be heard by the audience but not by the film characters themselves; narration is a type of voice-over; v.o. often conveys the character's thoughts, either as a 'voice' heard within one's head, or as other narrative information and commentary; often a technique in film noirs; the abbreviation is used as an annotation in a script.

Voice-over artist: The unseen person who does the speaking necessary to create a voice-over.

VU Meter: A meter designed to measure audio level in volume units which generally correspond to perceived loudness.

W

Wait right here scenario: The scene in a movie where one character, almost always a male character, tells another character, almost always a woman, "Now, you just wait right here in the car. Whatever you do, DO NOT follow me into that warehouse." Inevitably, the dumb and helpless woman goes into the warehouse, is captured by the villain and rescued by the hero.

Walk-on: A minor role consisting of a single, brief appearance on the screen, usually not appearing in the credits and without dialogue; contrast with extras, bit parts, and non-speaking roles.

Walk-through: The first rehearsal on the set, to figure out lighting, sound, camera positioning, etc.

Walla walla: Refers to the atmospheric, background sound effect for the indistinct murmurings and buzz of voices in a crowd; extras in crowd scenes, in older films (or in radio), would be asked to murmur a phrase ('walla walla.' 'rhubarb,' 'peas and carrots,' or 'watermelon,' etc.) to create the sound of the crowd and to pretend that they were talking.

Walla: Background conversation. Historically, when a script called for "crowd unrest" or "murmuring", the extras would be required to mumble the word "rhubarb", as this produced the required effect.

Wardrobe department: The section of a production's crew concerned with costumes. Individual job titles include: costume designer, costumer, and costume supervisor.

Wardrobe supervisor: The head of the wardrobe department.

Wardrobe: The general name for the costume department, or the costumes (and their accessories) themselves.

Waste: Shining a light on an object, then slowing turning the light away so that some of the light will miss or fall off the object.

Wave: A regular variation in electrical signal level or sound pressure level.

Weak-ankled female syndrome, The: Whenever a man and woman are on the run, the woman inevitably falls and sprains her ankle. As a result, the man must drag or carry her and their progress is slowed, stalled or halted.

Wedding cake rule: In any movie comedy involving a wedding, the cake will be destroyed.

Wedges: Wood wedges cut from 2x4 lumber which is used for leveling and stablizing.

Weenie: Refers to the object that motivates the main action in a serial.

We're alive! let's kiss! : Inevitable conclusion to any scene in which hero and heroine take cover from gunfire by diving side-by-side into a ditch, and find themselves in each other's arms, usually for the first time.

Western dolly: A plywood dolly, with four large soft tires, which is used as a camera dolly on smooth floors or on plywood. It is also used to transport other equipment.

Western: A movie set in the "Wild West" of the late 19th-century United States.

Wet gate: A contact printing method, made on a specially equipped printing machine, where the film is in a liquid that temporarily fills in any scratches on the base, preventing them from refracting light and showing up in the print. Commonly, answer prints are printed with a wet gate. Labs often charge a little extra for wet gate printing.

Wet road rule: Any road seen in a film, no matter how hot or dry the day has been, will be wet, slick, and reflecting headlights after nightfall. This is most commonly seen in deserts and draught-stricken cities like Los Angeles.

Whip pan: An extremely fast pan, incorporating much motion blur. The term refers to the "whipping" action that the camera operator uses to move the camera.

Whip: A section of feeder cable siamesed off the main line to a secondary location.

White (or color) balance: Refers to electronically setting or 'color-correcting' a camera's white balance - or the true color of white, since white doesn't appear 'white' with all lighting conditions.

White noise: A signal having an equal amount of energy per hertz.

Whodunit: Refers to a mystery/detective film.

Whoop-whoops: In sound effects, this refers to the extra noises added to a sound, e.g., bells, horns, or whistles to an explosion, to make it more interesting or exciting.

Wide angle (or Short) (clip: 408K) from "Brazil": Lenses having a focal length of 14-20mm. As the name implies, these lenses provide a wide field of vision. Short lenses create a distortion of perspective, making the field appear to be deeper than it actually is, though by several degrees "flatter" than fish-eye lenses.

Wide lens: A lens with a focal length smaller than 25mm in 16mm, or 50mm in 35mm, which, like looking into the wrong end of a pair of binoculars, provides an extended view of a large area.

Wide-angle shot: A shot (often abbreviated WS) taken with a lens that is able to take in a wider field of view (to capture more of the scene's elements or objects) than a regular or normal lens; a wide-angle shot exaggerates the distance or disparity between foreground and background planes, thereby creating greater depth-of-field and keeping all objects in focus; an extreme or ultra-wide-angle lens giving a 180 degree view is called a 'fish-eye' lens.

Widescreen: Refers to projection systems in which the aspect ratio is wider than the 1.33:1 ratio that dominated sound film before the 1950s; in the 1950s, many widescreen processes were introduced (to combat the growing popularity of television), such as CinemaScope (an anamorphic system), VistaVision (a non-anamorphic production technique in which the film is run horizontally through the camera instead of vertically), and Todd-AO and Super Panavision (that both used wider-gauge film); also known as letterboxing.

Wild line: A line of dialoge, recorded either on set or at a looping stage, without any picture running.

Wild sound: Scenes that are filmed without the sound being recorded at the same time. Dialog and/or sound effects may be dubbed in later.

Wild track: Audio elements that are not recorded synchronously with the picture.

Wild: Not sync. A wild motor is one that runs close to 24 frames per second, but not close enough for sync sound. Also applies in a few other cases, such as, if you are filming a rear screen projection scene and the projector and camera are not Interlocked they can be said to be running wild.

Wilhelm scream: Originally recorded as a sound effect for the film Distant Drums in 1951 and named after the character who yelped it out, this distinctive scream was archived in the Warner Brothers sound effects library, and was subsequently used in countless films, first simply as a generic stock scream, and later because sound supervisors and directors used it in their films as a sort of touchstone or homage to earlier films.

Wipe: A transitional technique or optical effect/device in which one shot appears to be "pushed off" or "wiped off" the screen by another shot replacing it and moving across the existing image; also called a push-over; a flip-over (or flip) wipe is when one scene rotates or flips-over to the new scene; wipes were very commonly used in the 30s.

Word-of-mouth: Moviegoers can't help warning their friends to avoid or not miss the movie they saw recently. After an opening weekend there's often enough feedback circulating from such warnings that it has a significant effect on how many more people go to see the movie. Negative word-of-mouth is often attributed to highly publicised movies doing poorly after the opening weekend, while positive word-of-mouth can provide a poor opener with legs.

Working title: The name by which a movie is known while it is being made. This is sometimes different from the title with which it is released.

Workprint: A positive copy of the original negative that is cut during the editing process. At the end of editing the original negative is then cut by the negative cutter to match the workprint shot for shot, and an answer print struck from the cut negative. A workprint can also be made from reversal original.

Workstation: This term generally refers to a disk-based audio recording and editing system.

Wow: Repetitive but slow variations in recording or playback tape speed.

Wow and Flutter: The deviation of frequency resulting from irregular motion in the recording or from deformation of the recording medium.

Wrangler: A person who is responsible for the care and control of entities used on a set that can't be spoken with. This person is typically a professional, certainly with expertise in handling the item, often with expertise in handling the item on a movie set.

Wrap: The span of the tape path along which the tape and head are in contact. (Audio/Video) More often, this refers to securing equipment at the end of the day or when work is completed at a particular set or location.

Writer: Refers to the individual who authors the content of the piece from pre-existing material or uses an entirely new idea; usually there are many writers involved with re-writes, adaptations, character development, etc.; aka screenwriter.

Wrong-headed commanding officer: In modern police movies, the commanding officer exists solely for the purpose of taking the hero off the case, calling him on the carpet, issuing dire warnings, asking him to hand over his badge and gun, etc.

Wunza movie: Any film using a plot which can be summarized by saying "One's a..." For example, "One's a cop. One's an actor." Or "One's a saint. One's a sinner."

X

Xenon: A very bright, daylight balanced projection lamp, or a projector with a xenon lamp. A xenon lamp is not interchangeable with a tungsten lamp or arch lamp, but requires a different lamp housing on the projector. Because xenon lamps are daylight balanced it is sometimes advisable with color film to have the lab make a print that is balanced for xenon. This is sometimes called a 5,400K print, the color temperature of daylight.

Xerography: The technique using an electrostatic process to copy or transfer an image, commonly found in office copiers and used in cartoon production.

XLR: One of several varieties of sound connectors having three or more conductors plus an outer shell which shields the connectors and locks the connectors into place.

X-Ray driver: In many thrillers, the hero crashes his car or truck through the window or wall of a building at the precise time and place to allow him to rescue a victim or kill the bad guys. How can he see through the walls to know exactly where his car will emerge? Why doesn't he ever drive into a load-bearing beam?

XXX: An informal voluntary certificate for a pornographic film, indicating large amounts of explicit sex. Contrast with NC-17.

X-Y pattern: A pair of cardioid microphones or elements aimed in crossed directions which feed two channels for stereo pickup.

Y

Y M C numbers: The 'timing lights' that the negative is printed at, representing the numerical value of the red, blue and green lights used in the printing process. These printing lights are referred to by their complements: yellow, magenta, and cyan.

Yarn: Slang for an apocryphal story.

Yawner: A slang term, meaning a boring film.

Youngblood Rule: No movie with a hero named "Youngblood" has ever been any good.

Z

Z: Pronounced "zed" in British movies, something most American audiences do not know.

Zero cut: A method of negative cutting specifically for blow up, where every shot is given Frame Handles so that the registration pin of the printer is never engaging with a splice, which can cause the image to wobble at the cut. It is most commonly used when you are blowing up from 16mm to 35mm. Zero cut should be done only if really necessary, because the lab can only print the film as an optical, which is far more expensive than a contact print. Zero cutting is a little more complicated than standard A&B rolls, so the negative cutter also charges more for it.

Z-film: Refers to a very low-budgeted, independently-made, non-union, less than B-film grade movie, usually with first-time director and actors; often quickly-made for the teenaged youth market and amateurish-looking, but with campy appeal; with exploitational subject matter that includes surfing films, motorcycle flicks, cheap horror films, etc.; Z-films become prime candidates for cult film status.

Zoom lens: A variable focal length lens. A zoom lens will have a third ring, besides ones controlling focus and iris, that will allow you to change the focal length within a range of wide to long.

Zoom shot: A shot in which the magnification of the objects by the camera's lenses is increased (zoom in) or decreased (zoom out/back). There is a subtle difference between the results of a zoom shot and a dolly shot. In a zoom, the relative positions and sizes of all objects in the frame remains the same, whereas in a dolly shot this will change as the camera moves. Alfred Hitchcock's much-imitated shot in Vertigo used a combination zoom in and dolly back, resulting in a dramatic change in perspective.

Zoom: An optical effect in which the image rapidly grows larger or smaller as though the camera is moving closer or away from its subject.

Zoopraxis: An early movie process developed by Eadweard Muybridge in the 1870's, which involves a disc that includes serial pictures being rotated in front of a light source, to create a sense that the objects projected were moving.

Zoptic special effects: A revolutionary special effects, 3-D process invented by cameraman Zorian Perisic, incorporating a camera system and a projector with synchronized zoom lenses.